DISPOSSESSED

DISPOSSESSED

Life in Our World's Urban Slums

MARK KRAMER

Royalties from the sale of this book go to support the ministry of Life in Abundance International, Addis Ababa, Ethiopia

ORBIS BOOKS

Maryknoll, New York 10545

Second Printing, November 2006

Founded in 1970, Orbis Books endeavors to publish works that enlighten the mind, nourish the spirit, and challenge the conscience. The publishing arm of the Maryknoll Fathers and Brothers, Orbis seeks to explore the global dimensions of the Christian faith and mission, to invite dialogue with diverse cultures and religious traditions, and to serve the cause of reconciliation and peace. The books published reflect the views of their authors and do not represent the official position of the Maryknoll Society. To learn more about Maryknoll and Orbis Books, please visit our website at www.maryknoll.org.

Library of Congress Cataloging-in-Publication Data

Kramer, Mark, 1974-
    Dispossessed : life in our world's urban slums / Mark Kramer.
      p. cm.
    Includes bibliographical references.
    ISBN-13: 978-1-57075-658-0 (pbk.)
    1. Squatter settlements—Developing countries—Case studies.
2. Squatters—Developing countries—Case studies. 3. Urban poor—Developing countries—Case studies. I. Title.
HD7287.96.D44K73 2005
307.3'364—dc22
                   2005023131

To Mom and Dad

*Thank you for teaching me
the meaning of compassion.*

Contents

Acknowledgments

The generosity and wisdom of numerous people made this book possible. I'm grateful to Scott Bessenecker, whose faith and vision for redemption in urban slums buoy my own faith and inspire me daily, and to Janine, his wife, and their family, Hannah, Philip, Laura, and Rosie for their spirited support. Barney Ford provided me with personal counsel at various points along the way, particularly during the formative stages of this book. Viv Grigg contributed the initial spark by challenging me to explore the subject of urban land rights, and Fred and Jeannie Everson provided me with space and encouragement to first formulate this project.

I depended heavily upon the hospitality and assistance of the following people as I conducted interviews and research: Daniel Melchor Caudillo, Danny Francisco, María Elena Martínez Garcia, Kirk and Marilyn Hanger, Steev and Teo Hardgrave, Clarice King, Sara Dominguez Maldonado, Imbumi Makuku, Nahum Alexis Licona Perez, Ronald Reyes, Elvira Lorenzo Roque and family, Humberto Sarmiento, Aaron and Emma Smith, and Nikki Toyama, among others. Though I met with dozens of organizations, AMEXTRA (Mexico City), Balic-Balic Christian Church (Manila), InterVarsity Christian Fellowship's Global Urban Trek (Madison, Wisconsin), and Servant Partners (Pasadena, California) played particularly pivotal roles. Vicky Birir, Kyle Stedman, and David Von Stroh, in Nairobi, Cairo, and Bangkok, respectively, helped conduct interviews, visit project sites, and gather information.

In addition to several of the above individuals, many people offered sensitive editorial input including Jenn Allen, Ash Barker,

Lisa Compton, Jeff Glaser, Eileen Hocker, Donna Lewein, Will Niewoehner, Rob Nixon, Julie Posselt, Tom Pratt, Travis Stiles, Derek Strohl, Jos Strengholt, Jack and Mary Anne Voelkel, Iman Wanis, and Heidi Williams, and, of course, Susan Perry, my editor at Orbis Books, and Catherine Costello, Orbis's production manager.

Lerline Beam, Gary Jepson, Todd Melicker, Chris and Melody Melville, Mike Moeller, Greg and Maren Rausch, and Dave and Mel Wilke contributed generous ongoing support and prayers. Fellowship funding from the School of Journalism and Mass Communications at the University of Wisconsin-Madison enabled me to finish this book. I also benefited from a Scott Kloeck-Jenson International Pre-Dissertation Travel Grant from the University of Wisconsin's Global Studies Program and a National Christian Foundation grant.

I thank Cynthia, my wife, for her steady eagerness to sacrifice alongside me in service to others, and the rest of my family for their loyal support, especially Cynthia's parents, Allan and Anita Eggleston, Mike Kramer, my brother and one of my most perceptive, intelligent readers, and George and Elaine Kramer, my parents, to whom I dedicate this book.

Finally, I'm grateful to the many men and women who welcomed me into their homes and willingly shared their stories with me. I mention some of them by name, but most of them remain anonymous. Thank you for trusting me, a foreigner, to tell others about you.

1

Introductions Are in Order

Meeting One Billion Squatters

EVERY STEP CLOSER TO GATE twenty-nine at the Mexico City International Benito Juarez Airport ushers me more into comfort. I begin my journey home from a hostel near the Monumento a la Revolución, just west of the city center. Lugging along my intrusive backpack and a handbag, I ride the metro for two pesos in the morning rush. The metro cars are packed. It's hot and I'm sweating. But the crowds disperse as I make my way to the city outskirts via several line changes, and I'm finally able to sit.

After more than an hour of riding, I exit the metro and walk a couple city blocks to the airport entrance and am glad to be among other travelers, glad to be less self-conscious about my luggage. I pass domestic departures, some arrival gates, money changers, and finally find the international concourse. The floors seem cleaner. There are more restaurants, a McDonald's, a Mexican cantina where a Coca-Cola costs several times more than it did in the city.

After checking in, passing through security, and trekking toward my gate on moving walkways, I feel air conditioning. I begin to see watches, cologne, perfume, leather, bottles of Tequila, and so much else that is "Duty and Tax Free." I sit down and am surrounded by more Caucasians, more English, and more cell phones than I have seen in almost a month. Across from me a man reads a J. R. R. Tolkien novel. I look around and see laptops and cups of coffee and American passports in white hands. I breathe clean air.

Just ninety minutes ago, while on one of my last metro legs, a boy of six or seven had approached me, had silently reached out his open hand. He had a deep scar, two inches long across his cheek, oil- and dirt-stained clothes spotted with holes.

I'd emptied my pockets of change, metro tickets, and candy and anything else I could find, a catharsis for me but hardly a noble act, as I only then knew that my ride was paid for, that my way was secure, that I had an airplane seat ready for me. Nobler would I have been had I made such a gesture days or weeks earlier in my stay in Mexico City. Instead I'd been anxious about my travel budget.

And just yesterday I sat with Ana in Lomas de San Isidro, a slum southeast of Mexico City. Built on an abandoned strip mine, the settlement lacks paved roads, piped water, and sewage systems. Squatter shanties cover several bare hillsides.

Just yesterday I sat on a homemade, wooden chair, which rested on a dirt floor, inside a home of plastic tarps, corrugated cardboard, and scrap wood, under the noonday sun, a one-room home for eleven of Ana's children and her husband. I'd breathed in dust. I'd wanted something more than the tortillas and peppers that Ana lovingly provided, the peppers dished up from a six-pound can that would, she said, along with the tortillas, be her family's only food for three days. She had little water, but Ana gladly poured me and my two companions glasses of lukewarm tea.

Ana was beautiful. She laughed and nervously nibbled on her pocketbook when I asked her about how she'd met Brijido, her husband, when I inquired about their first words to each other. She blushed and smiled and said that some things weren't to be spoken of, and everyone in the room laughed with her.

My ticket to Chicago likely cost the equivalent of two-months salary for Brijido. When I left Lomas de San Isidro yesterday, I had only fifty pesos to give to Ana.

This day of my departure from Mexico City summarizes my journey well, a vacillation between witnessing affluence and poverty, security and dispossession. It also encapsulates the disparity between life in urban slums in the global South and life as I know it in the United States.

A woman's voice from an overhead speaker tells me in English that it's time to board the airplane. As I stand in line and then lope through the gate, I wonder: Would Ana even know what to do with herself in an airport? As I board the plane, I deeply desire to share Ana's story.

A Squatter Nation, One Billion Strong

For the first time in history, more people live in cities than in the countryside. Our world is no longer simply going through the experience of urbanization. Our world has become urbanized. And a massive number of urban residents live like Ana and her family, in insecure, impoverished conditions. *One billion people—or one in every three urban residents—now live in an urban slum, the vast majority of them in developing nations.*

Illegal slum communities, populated by millions of people, have enveloped major cities in the global South that are unable to respond adequately to the burgeoning demands of urban growth. Many residents migrate as refugees or from the countryside to escape rural poverty, to seek relative progress amidst the seeming optimism of cosmopolitan opportunities. They come to work, they come to be with family, they come seeking health care and education. Out of necessity, these impoverished residents create their own homes and neighborhoods spontaneously, sometimes overnight, because of a void in affordable housing.

Such unplanned development leaves these communities without electricity, clean water, sewerage, garbage-collection systems, or, among other things, community organization. Residents devise their own jobs as vendors, restaurateurs, cleaners, garbage scavengers, nannies, day workers, and prostitutes. Yet they are insecure, disconnected, without a sense of place. They have little power.

Meanwhile, landowners, both private and public, unwittingly lose control of property. Legally registered businesses compete against enterprising informal workers who generally don't pay taxes or licensing fees or adhere to other regulations. City transportation systems lose prominence to informal drivers of vans, mopeds, and rickshaws.

Then, as disease, land disputes, political injustice, corruption, gender inequalities, inadequate legal codes, and war affect these urban settlements, urban poverty can seem hopeless and irrevocable, replete with risk and struggle. Yet for millions of people, such poverty is a daily reality.

My primary intention in this book is to introduce you, the reader, not just to cities or urban settlements, but to the people, the individuals living in them who struggle to raise their children, who enjoy friendships, seek employment, laugh, cry, and die in these settlements. For poverty and suffering are personal matters. Demographics, statistics, and myriad fields of research, as telling and important as they are, cannot fully capture the essence of life in urban slums. But by getting to know specific people while allowing related research to provide the context, we're able to personalize our understanding of urban poverty, put names and faces to issues that affect millions of residents.

Second, I intend to introduce you to some of the most pressing issues impacting these residents, including urbanization, land rights, the informal sector, colonial histories, and evictions and demolitions. While I highlight a few small development projects and agencies, this introduction to slums does not outline best practices for development, though some become evident through people's personal stories.

While I attempt to describe some fairly universal characteristics of urban settlements, I also omit information because of space limitations. I could have included more discussion on debt in the global South, the process of upgrading urban settlements, and some people's ability to organize and mobilize for social change in urban slums. Many settlements and cities are, of course, not represented in this book. About one-fifth of São Paulo, Brazil's 19.5 million people live in a slum, as do one-half of the 12 million people in Mumbai, India. Informal settlements exist in all regions of the world, in China, the Middle East, Latin America, Central Asia. The very vastness and diversity of our world's urban settlements demand consideration beyond anything this or any other single text can provide. Slums are not some easily summarized monolith of misery.

What "They" Know, What "We" Don't

I approached the writing of this book with an underlying conviction: Most of us in "developed" societies don't have a clue.

We certainly know a lot. We know about popular culture, professional sports, movies, television, and computers. We know what's cool; we know what's not. We're well versed in the ebb and flow of supply and demand, how to manage our money, and where to broker a good deal so we have change left over at the end of the day. We're creating better automobiles, dishwashers, palm pilots, stoves, guns, missiles, malls, highways, airplanes, air conditioners, satellites, telephones, and homes. And on and on and on and on.

Yet we truly know so little about much of the rest of our world, in particular the experiences of people living in economic want who know a language, social structure, and environment so unlike our own, the half of the world that lives on less than US$2.00 a day. Because we lack understanding of people in poverty, specifically people living in the global South, we lack real knowledge of our world. As one author puts it, ". . . the way the poor view the world is closer to the reality of the world than the way the rich view it. Their 'epistemology,' their way of knowing, is accurate to a degree that is impossible for those who see the world only from the vantage point of privileges they want to retain."[1]

Globalization demands that we seek common understanding in a world divided against itself. More and more we share common political, economic, and cultural interests with people thousands of miles from us. Every day our lifestyle choices influence others around the globe. Their choices affect us. Even beyond altruism and compassion, we must seek understanding because we have a common future with people in urban slums.

Still, I do write reluctantly.

Men, women, and children living in economic poverty don't need people gawking at them. They don't need photographs, videos, and television commercials showing us how atrophied their very thin famine-emaciated limbs have become. They don't need our pity. Besides, though some, in fact, do, most of "the poor" that get so globally lumped together do not match the overused images of abject need. Rather they labor hard at informal jobs or intermittently when work is available, barely making it but with clothes on their backs and, somehow amidst the struggle, smiles on their faces.

People living in economic poverty don't need another shadow of condescension cast upon them by a privileged Western writer who merely wishes to expose their wounds to cold scrutiny to summon that objectifying yet strangely consoling sense that "they" are simply "they," some "other" with whom we have no relationship. Such an exhibition exploits them and their stories merely for the sake of sentimentality, to tickle our nerves of analytical pleasure or to make us feel better that we're not in their situation. This is not my intention, though it is my ever-present dread. I write reluctantly for I fear falling into any of this. It's a frightening responsibility to take the stories of people's lives and convey them to others with authority and from a chosen angle. Storytelling is anything but exhaustive—accurate, I hope, but never the full story.

Nor is language exhaustive. The term "slum" generally refers to a once-attractive neighborhood that has deteriorated, but in the global South the word has come to describe illegal, spontaneous shantytowns lacking decent services and infrastructure. Yet slums around the world are complex and they change quickly. Local definitions of slums vary, though they generally include poor construction and illegality. Many definitions also include high population densities, a lack of basic services, low incomes, even the type of building materials residents use. People refer to them as *ciudades perdidas* (Spanish, "lost cities"), *barrios, favelas, aashwa'i* (Egyptian Arabic, "random"), informal settlements, squatter settlements, and peri-urban areas, among many other terms.

Meanwhile, "slum" can unnecessarily evoke stereotypes of dilapidation, crime, and foul living conditions that distance readers from individuals living in these neighborhoods. "Characterizing a community as a slum may identify it with chaos and squalor," writes one researcher. "It may also mark the people who reside there as dirty and chaotic, inappropriately confusing their disadvantaged status with an unshakeable feature of their identity—a mark of stigma and a source of shame."[2] Still, in some contexts the term lacks derogatory connotations and merely refers to low-income housing.

I generally prefer to use the term "informal settlements," by which I refer to illegal neighborhoods comprised of inadequate structures and services, both to mitigate the negative associations of "slum" and because "informal settlements" emphasizes the unauthorized nature of these communities. But because "slum" remains completely appropriate in some circumstances, I have chosen to use these terms somewhat interchangeably. Similarly, I prefer "global South" over "developing nations," a term that, even if unintentionally, could imply that some people are "underdeveloped." I use "developed" and "developing" foremost in economic discussions.

Many other terms concerning this book's subject matter are equally problematic. Even so, I recognize the irrationality of attempting to use completely neutral language, so I make these qualifications and then ask the reader for grace as I navigate the aesthetic and political complexities of language.

The People of Informal Settlements

Over a period of two years, I visited five cities to conduct research and interviews: Manila, Philippines; Nairobi, Kenya; Mexico City, Mexico; Bangkok, Thailand; and Cairo, Egypt. I chose these cities primarily because they are quickly urbanizing agglomerations in the global South and informal settlements comprise a large portion of their housing sectors. Second, I chose these cities because of personal contacts and convenient opportunities for research. I could have chosen a great many other cities, places like Rio de Janeiro, Lagos, Port-au-Prince, Johannesburg, Mumbai, or Istanbul to visit informal settlements. As our world becomes more urbanized and industrialized, there is no shortage of spontaneous settlements cropping up in and around our cities.

My sojourns lasted from about two to four weeks each. When possible, I lived in close quarters with residents. Otherwise, I lived in hostels or at the homes of people working to improve the living conditions of these settlements, churches and nongovernmental organizations (NGOs) for the most part. In three cities—Nairobi, Bangkok, and Cairo—I benefited from the assistance of fellow researchers, who helped gather facts and stories. We conducted interviews in English or through local translators. In Manila, my wife accompanied me as a photographer.

Each of the next five chapters focuses on a particular issue affecting urban settlements. I first describe urbanization in the global South during the last half of the twentieth century before turning my attention to the effects of historical and current colonialism. Then I consider urban land rights, the informal sector, and living conditions. I conclude by providing readers with suggestions for further learning and action. Throughout the book, I interweave various issue-oriented discussions, historical accounts, and economic data with people's stories to provide context and depth.

I change most residents' names for the sake of privacy and, in some instances, security, though the most prominent people in the book have granted me permission to use their real names. Profiles and quotes without citations draw from personal interviews and primary research.

Because statistics on cities in the global South, and on urban settlements in particular, can vary wildly, I seek to use consistent, conservative estimates and sources. For example, in the second chapter, United Nations' estimates on city populations are lower than many other sources, yet the agency's great pool of census statistics and authority as a leading organization in development make it as reliable a source as any for this data. Regardless, on-the-ground realities are dire and most of these statistical variances don't alter implications for policy and economic development.

I wish to romanticize the nobility of these people and places no more than I wish to inflate their poverty and helplessness. Either extreme is offensive. Yet, any honest exploration of urban poverty is a daunting endeavor, and so I first reflect on the genuine goodwill of my encounters.

In Mexico City, I stayed with Aline, a mother of two boys, Denzel and Gustavo. Aline welcomed me, helped me hone my Spanish, prepared the best tacos, *jamaica* (a hibiscus drink), and *frijoles negros* (black beans) I've yet tasted. Though I eventually overcame her protests, Aline refused to accept compensation to cover the costs of my stay.

In Cairo, I met Osama, a Coptic Christian who taught me hymns in Arabic. He and Maher, a friend, laughed good naturedly when I stumbled over my gutturals, sounds so necessary in Arabic yet so foreign to my first language. When I later attended a church service for thousands of people, during which his choir performed, Osama welcomed me enthusiastically and escorted me to a seat near the officiating priest, gave me a tour of the church, introduced me to friends.

Sunee, a mother of one in Bangkok, lovingly laughed her welcome to me as we shared meals on the floor of her home. She worries for her teenage daughter and about the influences of their community—drugs, drug dealers, violence. Sunee also struggles to love an abusive husband. Yet she hosted me warmly, surely to fulfill cultural protocol, but also to live out the generous nature of her own heart. She cried when my traveling companions and I left.

I have also met some of the most gracious people I've ever known: Imbumi, a Kenyan who has worked in Nairobi's squatter communities for more than twenty years developing churches and organizing residents; Yung, an elderly Thai woman whose faith I find humbling as she describes her fear of eviction, even while praying and singing and laughing with others in delight.

I don't discount the likelihood that my own power and place as an American influenced the welcome I received in these communities. Yet, I'm convinced that my hosts could not have mustered the kind of hospitality and warmth that I've enjoyed merely for self-serving purposes. I believe that, for the most part, this type of generosity seeks no reward, that it's simply characteristic of people living in economic poverty. This I've witnessed, time and again.

So while those of us in rich nations have much to offer Yung and Aline and the millions of other people living in urban settlements in the global South, they have much to offer us as well, their ideas and strategies, their charity and faith. I introduce these friends to you, the reader, and encourage you to listen closely to what they have to say, to embrace their troubles as your own, to let their stories change you.

2

Manila

Urbanization in the Global South

The Esguerra Family

*F*ORTY-FIVE YEARS AGO, Tess Esguerra, then four years old, moved with her family to Balic-Balic in the Sampaloc district of Manila, Philippines. Her family squatted on then-unoccupied land near railroad tracks and built a house amidst flourishing, lush vegetation, 100 yards from the next home. Tess is now silver haired. Her voice sings rich memories.

"Our house was very small," she says, "and the walls, we made them from rice sacks. We used boxes for a floor so that we could lie down to sleep." She says that two metal sheets made for a roof. "Just enough to cover our bodies."

Tess still lives in Balic-Balic, along with seven children and nine grandchildren who stay with her periodically. When she married Arnold, he renovated their home with wood. When he died a year ago of a heart attack, family and friends helped Tess pour a concrete floor in her home.

Tess's family grew *camote,* a type of sweet potato, bananas, melons, and other fruits and vegetables. They raised ducks, chickens, and goats. They caught fish from a nearby canal. "It was like a fish farm, and we looked for vegetables right in front of our homes. There were many plants here, different kinds of plants." Tess's family also sold *balut* in the city. A traditional Filipino food, *balut* is a boiled, half-incubated duck egg.

11

The canal, fifty feet down the tracks from Tess's home, "was clean before, very clean," she says, remembering water lilies and *kangkong*, or swamp cabbage, a leafy vegetable that overran the marsh. "We could take baths there. But now it's no good." Today residents of the Balic-Balic railway community use the putrid canal only to dump waste.

In 1963, just four families lived along the tracks of *barangay* 576 Z-56 and *barangay* 422 Z-42 (a *barangay* is a local municipal unit). Now an estimated 200 families live along this one-eighth mile stretch of tracks in Balic-Balic, and slum communities line most railways throughout Metro Manila.

During the 1960s, the population of Balic-Balic grew as relatives of residents migrated from the provinces—from the Visayas and the Ilokos and Bicol regions. "Owners of the homes here, they have relatives in the provinces. They tell them that they can come here to Manila because they can have a place here, build a house," Tess says. In 1967, the Philippine National Railroad, the owner of land adjacent to the railway, demolished rows of illegally placed homes, but residents simply rebuilt.

Then Balic-Balic became more violent as gangs formed around regional rivalries, which run hot in this fragmented nation of more than 7,000 islands and nearly 170 spoken languages. But in 1972, President Ferdinand Marcos declared martial law for the entire country, which would last until his downfall in 1986, and gang activity in Balic-Balic subsided.

Sammy Seares, a resident of Balic-Balic for twelve years, says ironically that now, "It's better . . . because [residents] are united with *shabu* [the local name for methamphetamine]. They are united by illegal drugs." Children wander the neighborhood with their hands covering their noses as they sniff solvent.

The Manila Railway Company began laying a pair of forty-two-inch-gauge tracks in 1887 until a line spanned 120 miles from Manila to Dagupan in the north.[1] "Riding a train passing the area," one researcher says of Balic-Balic, "is a frightful experience for the train sometimes touches the sides of the roofings of some dwellings . . . for the dwellers, however, the passing of the trains is as ordinary as their breathing."[2]

Trains rumble through Balic-Balic a couple of times an hour at full throttle, horns screaming for people to clear the tracks. Residents scatter, only to pour back onto the tracks in the train's wake, like ocean waves ebbing and flowing. Children's laughter and the meandering banter of adult conversation fill all remaining silence.

Trains, Tess notes, have always bisected the community. "They passed even faster [then]. They ran faster, because there were no houses." The few existing homes in Balic-Balic were also farther from the tracks, but now they're just a few feet and even inches from passing trains.

Today, Balic-Balic residents live side by side in two- and three-story homes made of corrugated metal, plastic tarpaulin, bamboo, plywood, cement, and even tires, with one to three small rooms per household, and in some instances multiple families share a home. Residents are known as *taga-riles* (from the railway tracks) who live among the *riles* (railway tracks). And the community is now a maze of impromptu homes and cramped walkways.

The train tracks serve as a front yard, informal market, dumping ground, and playground. Children set up basketball hoops between the two sets of tracks. Vegetation is absent. Many residents sprinkle water in front of their homes during the heat of the day to prevent railway activity from stirring up dust. The soil quickly turns to muck during the rainy season.

Tess's family had no clean drinking water. They walked fifteen minutes to a market to buy water and cart it home. Today many families in Balic-Balic have water piped into their homes, though it can be unreliable. Some people share communal spigots. Others illegally divert water from city pipes.

Tess's family also had no electricity, though today many homes do. In fact, hoping to mitigate the tropical heat and boredom of unemployment, many people enjoy the constant whir of electric fans, murmuring televisions, and, for a small fee, video games and karaoke. As they do with water lines, people run illegal electrical lines off of legitimate ones, creating a mangled mess of wires and transformers. Occasionally the electric company enters the community and clips illegal lines. Within a week, residents reconnect them.

The Seares Family

Sammy and Joanne Seares purchased their Balic-Balic home at the intersection of the tracks and canal for 35,000 Filipino pesos twelve years ago (about US$1,300 at the time), when their oldest of three children, Angelique (Gellie), was just a few months old. The couple had been living in a boarding house, and, after making a few minor improvements, Sammy had surprised Joanne with the Balic-Balic home, their first together.

"But she didn't like it," Sammy says. "She said that the people here are scary, that there's lots of drug addicts and sometimes they have riots." Sammy leans back in his chair and speaks slowly. He has dark hair clipped close to his scalp, and he's lean and muscular with a welcoming grin. Sammy seems a youthful thirty-five years old.

The Seares's two-story home provides their family of five, regular visitors, and relatives with less than 200 square feet of space. Whitewashed slats of wood crisscross the first-story façade. Several fragments of sheet metal cover and reinforce the lower half of these slats. Brown wood planks and lattice plastered with political campaign posters comprise the second-story façade. From both stories hang wooden rods that hold recently washed clothes. The roof is corrugated metal.

Joanne shakes her head and smiles. She wears a rust-colored, loose T-shirt and airy pink-and-white pants. Her black hair is shoulder length and straight. "I said to myself, 'I don't want to stay in this kind of place. There's lots of trouble here, lots of people,'" she says. "I knew God had a plan. There was a church here. But at first I didn't want to stay here. So maybe someday, if we have a chance to transfer to a nicer place, we will."

"I hoped that in this place," Sammy says, "our lives would be better, where we can have a house. Maybe here we could raise our children. Maybe our life would be better here. She just said, 'Look at this place!'"

Sammy recalls that when they first arrived in Balic-Balic, the last of the canal's swamp cabbage was dying, and crime, gangs, and pickpockets were even more common than today. Since 1990, Balic-Balic has had at least three major fires, and over the years passing trains have killed dozens of people, at least one or two a year within the immediate community, according to one resident.

The Seares considered participating in a mortgage program that would help them purchase a low-income home, but only in Cavite or Laguna to the south of Manila, "maybe a two- or three-hour ride," Joanne says. And besides, she explains, on Sammy's salary, they'd have no guarantee of making regular payments, and he'd be much farther from his job. "So we're prepared to stay here, with squatters, just because this is the center of the Philippines, Manila. But here in Manila there are no more houses to be sold. Just renting. Forever you rent." Joanne adds, "We own this house but the government owns the land."

Though Sammy and Joanne grew up in Cebu in the Visayas provinces, they met and fell in love in Manila. Sammy recalls their earlier days. "We were praying—we didn't know each other but we were both praying—to have a relationship, with a family, with a job. Sometimes, when you are young, it's hard. You wait for your love, your true love." A security guard stationed at the pharmacy where Sammy worked introduced him to Joanne, and they got better acquainted while attending the same church.

Then Joanne left to work abroad for six months as a nanny for a family in Singapore. Such work is common for Filipinos: of an estimated 90 million people, 7 million Filipinos live abroad.[3] During the second half of the 1990s, Filipinos remitted more than US$29 billion from foreign countries, the second highest remittance level in the world. Jose, a Balic-Balic resident, worked in construction in Saudi Arabia for a few years. Myla, a sixty-three-year-old widow, says her daughter works in Japan as an entertainer. Some years Filipinos have found more new jobs overseas than within their own country.

Sammy and Joanne wrote letters to each other frequently. Upon her return, the couple lived together for a time, and, just as Joanne was about to go work in Singapore again, she became pregnant. So Sammy and Joanne married at the city hall. Initially, Sammy worked and Joanne cared for Gellie. Then the pharmacy laid off Sammy.

So Joanne found a job and Sammy stayed home. "We don't want other people to take care of them," he says. "It's better for people to look after their own children." Sammy happily shares that he's learned to braid Gellie's hair and adorn it with ribbons.

For one six-month period Joanne worked in a pharmaceutical factory. "It was very hot. You just stand there, like this, no sitting down. . . . All day you stand. You only sit down when you eat or for a one-hour break."

Then Joanne sold shoes for a year at an SM Supermall, one of the many popular, multistory shopping centers in Manila that feature department stores, restaurants, and fast-food courts, gift shops, grocery stores, convention centers, twelve-screen cinemas, bowling lanes, carnival rides, and, most critically, air conditioning, all under one roof. SMs—as of this writing there are eleven of them in Metro Manila—and "malling" are a cultural staple here. Each day, an average 1.5 million people enter an SM Supermall in Manila.

Then Joanne became pregnant with Iren, their second daughter, and she quit selling shoes. They later had James (Jam-Jam), their youngest. Fortunately, Joanne's relatives sometimes help with cooking, washing clothes, and caring for the children.

With only an elementary school education, Sammy went to work in construction for 250 pesos a day (US$4.40),[4] demolishing buildings and salvaging debris. "It was hard on my body and the dust, your eyes. . . . It felt like you were working in a desert. I'd have blisters when I finished each day."

Sammy then received a job through a placement agency as a janitor. After two years, he became a security guard, a position generally requiring a high school diploma. He considered using a fake diploma created by a friend, but a personal recommendation landed him the job. He worked two years before receiving proper licensing. So Sammy has been a security guard for five years now, working for an armored truck company most recently where he earns 300 pesos a day.

He is fortunate. Most local men lack marketable skills, and most jobs are tenuous, without benefits, and on a contract basis lasting no more than a few months. Jobs at the local Jollibee, the largest Filipino fast-food chain and competition to McDonald's restaurants, are highly prized. In Balic-Balic, most men labor as construction workers, painters, carpenters, plumbers, and vendors.

Many also drive tricycle cabs or jeepneys. A major means of transportation in Manila, jeepneys are a colorful legacy of the thousands of vehicles that the U.S. Army left behind after World War II. With extended seating areas that, some claim, can hold up to three dozen people in a tight—very tight—pinch, jeepneys now look more like buses than jeeps, though they've retained their original boxy fronts and beady headlights. Drivers decorate their vehicles with an abundance of decals, chrome, and painted highlights and curtains and grotto-like altars with Mary or Jesus on the dashboard. About 70,000 men work as jeepney drivers in Manila, and nearly 50,000 more pedal tricycle taxis.

Sammy is also fortunate that he's the only guard in his truck who has not been shot. "The truck is like military armor," he says. "And it's kind of like a coffin." Sammy and his team transport cash from businesses to banks. He packs a handgun. At times he carries an M-16.

Joanne pipes up, "I'm always asking him to stop working that kind of job, it's very dangerous. . . . I don't worry every day, but I always pray. It's hard to find a job in Manila."

Sammy admires Joanne's work ethic. "Her mother got pregnant all the time," he says, noting that because her parents had nine children, Joanne, the fourth in line, was responsible for much of the housework and for helping provide for the family. "Her father was always going somewhere, working and other things, selling properties, and then he would go to drink." The family raised chickens, goats, cows, and pigs in Cebu. Joanne completed high school and wanted to continue studying, but her parents discouraged it. "That's why she chose to move here in Manila, from Visayas, to find work, though she stopped her schooling."

"In the provinces," Joanne says, "you can pay for a nice place, but there are no jobs. There's only work on the farm. I didn't want to always work on the farm. . . . In the provinces we didn't have much work. . . . So everyone wants to go to Manila to find a job."

The Seares often host Joanne's nieces and nephews so they can attend school or look for work in Manila. Some of her siblings also live in the city. One brother works in Singapore.

"We always get together to say 'Hi,' and we say 'Hello' by texting," she says. Cell phones are prevalent here, as they are in many countries in the global South, because they're relatively cheap and more reliable than landlines. While Joanne enjoys traveling to see family in the Visayas, it's an expensive journey, and, besides, she generally remains in Balic-Balic to host others. "This is like a dorm. But at a dorm, you pay. Here it is free!"

At Balic-Balic Christian Church, several homes down the tracks from the Seares, Joanne and several other mothers provide food and hospitality on special occasions. "I'm always ready to help with anything," Joanne says. For most events, such as birthdays, church celebrations, and to welcome visitors, the women cook large, multi-dish meals.

Though Sammy regularly attends church and reads the Bible, he hasn't always claimed or lived out a religious faith. "My wife," he says, "she got mad at me for being a drunk person," adding that Joanne experienced the pain of alcoholism as a child at the hands of her father. She helped Sammy put an end to his own drinking. "It was hard stopping. I drank after work. When I worked I got tired. I was used to drinking beer to relax. When we got married, I still drank." Sammy now relaxes with soft drinks.

Three-year-old Jam-Jam climbs Joanne as she talks. Gellie and Iren draw in notebooks. Sammy leaves for work.

Gellie is eleven years old and maintains little eye contact. Iren, just four years old but bold in her speech, has the wry smile of a teenager who knows something you don't know, though both girls are reserved and quiet. Jam-Jam's wiry frame, in white shorts and a white tank top that reads "Bear Bear" in pastel, building-block letters, moves perpetually.

Iren settles into a plastic chair, and Gellie, sitting on cracked and patchy, blue-marble linoleum, leans against a pockmarked, turquoise wall. Otherwise bare, this and the other walls display the tracings of children's stray pens and pencils. A three-foot-long plastic table dominates one side of the room and holds a rack with boxed foods and dishes. A second rack, loaded with an assortment of more dishes, hangs above the sink just below a ceiling of white wooden beams. A couple more chairs and two counters—one with a kitchen sink, another with a portable, two-burner gas stove—complete the room, which serves as both the living room and the kitchen.

Standing and swaying with Jam-Jam in her arms, Joanne laughs. "Everybody wants to stay here [in our home], but I don't know why. Staying in Manila is very hard. So everybody wants to go abroad to work. For me also, I want to go abroad, but I have three kids and I have a lot of nephews and nieces coming here to stay. One left yesterday and already another is here. This house has lots of people coming from the provinces to stay here."

Joanne then rests Jam-Jam against a ladder that leads to the bedroom and is of the same white wood as the ceiling. Jam-Jam screeches.

"He won't sleep," Joanne says. Jam-Jam makes motor sounds and smiles, writhes and escapes from his mother's grasp. He then pounds on the ladder with his fists. Plywood covering the backside of the ladder has several holes punched through it.

"He loves to play like a carpenter," Joanne says. Jam-Jam continues to beat the steps, the board. "He was using the hammer . . . but this is a little house, with lots of people."

Joanne lowers Jam-Jam from the ladder and then pours a baby formula canister full of small toys out onto the floor. "They are already destroyed, already broken," she says. Jam-Jam quickly scatters dozens of colorful yet scuffed and cracked plastic toys across the room. He fixes upon a plastic red-and-black bumblebee, the mascot for the Jollibee fast-food chain. The family sets undamaged toys and plush animals behind cellophane wrap on bookshelves upstairs, a museum of prized playthings.

Iren and Gellie, Joanne says, like to draw and watch cartoons on the television upstairs. "The TV shows are not good for children. So it's much better to watch cartoon movies," Joanne says. Gellie's favorite movie is Walt Disney's *Snow White and the Seven Dwarfs*.

"Iren can write her name. All day, they [draw] like this." Iren, with an ink pen, sketches birds, shoes, a tree, the flag of the Philippines, Jam-Jam. "But most of the time they are roaming around, inside the house, like this, not stopping. They stop only to sleep once a day." Joanne generally keeps her children at home, though they grow restless playing in its two small rooms, particularly during hot and humid days.

"The kids just stay home," Joanne says as a train passes outside the Seares's slatted front door. "I don't trust that they can go outside. The train comes by there. It's not good enough for the children. The train doesn't care who you are. And lots of the children just go outside, and lots of them are not doing good."

Across the canal, amplified singing serenades the railway community with "Killing Me Softly with His Song," the 1970s hit. Some locals claim that it was a Filipino—and not the Japanese, as others purport—who invented karaoke. Regardless, it's outlandishly popular here, even in the railway community where aspiring songsters pay five pesos a tune.

"It's very loud," Joanne says. "Also, many play the radio, that's very loud, on the other side [of the tracks]. And then they're watching movies. Very loud. We can't even talk. You can't even hear. . . . Always the karaoke.

"But my children, I don't let them go outside to do karaoke. But sometimes my husband and three kids sing upstairs. My husband loves singing." Sammy has learned, with help from a friend, to play the guitar. Though he only knows basic chords, he sometimes plays during church services.

It's the beginning of Manila's rainy season and the end of summer break. Gellie and Iren will begin school in two weeks.

During the school year, Joanne rises from bed at four o'clock and even earlier to begin chores and ready the children. Today, she washes three days' worth of clothes by hand in a tub of water in the kitchen sink, and then hangs them. She'd been unable to wash clothes for several days because someone had been tapping into their water pipes. The family buys water from a local vendor, for a couple of pesos for every two gallons, many times more than what they pay for city-supplied water.

"All day, [the children] keep me very busy," she says. "I work the whole day because when the children sleep, I clean the house or wash [the clothes]. I'm always thinking or doing. Sometimes I have time for reading the Bible. But always working is not good. I am always very tired. He is a very wild boy." Though Jam-Jam is only three years old, she laughs and threatens, "Next year I will send him to school!"

The bathroom, a tiny space behind the kitchen, is the only other first-floor room. It is partially tiled in white and blue and finished with bare cement. The toilet lacks a seat, and they flush it by scooping in several pails of water from one of two large barrels. They use buckets to shower. The family hides here when they hear gunshots.

The supply of electricity is similar to the water supply. "I always turn off the lights," Joanne says. "I turn off everything, but my bill is very high. Somebody told me that my line, my electricity line, somebody was using my electricity but not paying at all. A lot of people are using electricity illegally. . . . So I told my husband, 'Ah, with your salary we can pay the electric bill, then there's no more money left.'"

Iren and Gellie speak infrequently, so Joanne, after failing to coax them, earnestly speaks for the girls. Iren dreams of being a nurse someday. She also wants to see snow.

There was a time in the Philippines when snow was very much a part of children's learning. The *Baldwin Reader*, an early primer that American teachers used to "civilize" Filipinos during America's occupation of the islands, which began in 1898, taught that "A is for apple," though apples aren't native to the archipelago, and portrayed "John and Mary" playing in the snow. A few years later, new American governance replaced these images with avocados and coconuts and "Juan and María" strolling through rice fields, though overtones of racial inferiority persisted in the curriculum.[5]

Today, in part because of American influence, Filipinos view education almost as a basic need. Literacy among Filipino men is more than 92 percent and slightly higher among women.[6] Many homes in Balic-Balic maintain veritable altars to their children's schooling, with collages of school photos and medals hanging in the middle of their living rooms.

Joanne goes to an open-air market to purchase avocados, mangoes, beans, and fresh fish, "before it stinks," she says. But generally she buys canned food, canned tuna as a treat. She cooks on two burners connected by hose to a propane gas tank. The wall behind the burner is blackened. Many of the Seares's neighbors also use charcoal to cook in their homes.

"For my family," Joanne says, "we have expenses of 500 pesos a day. So you must try to buy only the things that you need. I don't buy anything that's not so important. So sometimes we borrow money, some from my brother or my sister or a money lender until [Sammy's] salary comes."

To wash dishes, Joanne pulls a barrel from the bathroom to the kitchen sink and ladles water into pans and other dishes and scrubs them. After pouring this water down a sink drain, she then slushes another cycle of water before dragging the barrel back to the bathroom. Some days, Gellie does this chore. Many neighbors sit on the ground next to the canal to clean dishes and clothes. Some women in the community earn a small income doing these chores.

To earn her income, Tess, the forty-nine-year-old widow who moved to Balic-Balic at age four, sits outside her home along the tracks and sells breakfast from eleven at night until four in the morning, "because the people here are not sleeping. They are always walking around," she says. Usually she sells fried rice or *champorado*—sticky rice with cocoa. Tess then sleeps for two hours before rising to ready her grandchildren for school. When possible, she naps later in the day.

Tess used to deal in drugs. "I would buy these drugs for [users]," she says. "I would run an errand [for a dealer], just so the kids could have food." She used to play card games and bingo frequently in hopes of making money. Tess also painted houses. "The children were always getting sick and going to the doctor, the hospital. So we needed to save money for medicine, and that's when I got involved in drugs." Tuberculosis, typhoid fever, diarrhea, and lung infections are widespread here, but without good preventative health care, people frequently die before anyone even knows they're sick.

Like the pervasiveness of drugs, rumors of forced evictions and demolitions constantly threaten Balic-Balic residents as well. But Tess laughs them off. "We have had many warnings," she says, "but always like that, it's almost every election. Then we get past elections and there's no more. We just go on."

Though carried out today much less frequently than a couple of decades ago, government evictions, here in the Philippines and throughout the global South, can be violent, even at gunpoint in the middle of the night. According to one researcher, "[D]ehumanization often begets dehumanization. Violent forced evictions are often carried out through intimidation and terrorization. In some cases, evictors rape or physically harass women and girls in order to break down a community's resistance prior to an eviction."[7] Officials have padlocked homes before families can retrieve belongings and burned or bulldozed entire neighborhoods. Without forewarning, they've forced residents to flee with nowhere to go and no help relocating. It isn't rare for several people to die in a demolition.

Over the years, many residents of Balic-Balic have protested against the threat of eviction by marching on Malacañang Palace, the nation's storied presidential residence. In doing so, they are battling eviction but also the fear of eviction, which can itself be debilitating. "The fear of eviction settles into the bones of squatter people, helping to destroy their confidence in themselves and their associations—'we're only squatters' they say, as if they had little value," says a report on evictions in the Philippines. "The fear of eviction helps make people fatalistic and puts an end to their determination to improve their homes and neighborhoods."[8]

According to Sammy Seares, "There were some protests because they were going to demolish." Early on he chose not to march. "I had just newly bought this house . . . so I was not participating in the protest, because it's a government's right to demolish."

He notes that Balic-Balic is unsafe not only because of the trains but also because of floods during the rainy season. He also recognizes that his home is, in fact, illegal, even though it's been here many years. But the demand for land and the value of urban land and housing is so great in Metro Manila that most low-income people, like the Seares, cannot afford housing in the formal sector. Land speculation puts additional pressure on land values as investors buy up plots but then hold them undeveloped.

Joanne says that talk of demolition is constant. She's also heard that a Japanese firm purchased the railway, that the company is privatizing it. "They're always saying, 'Demolish, demolish,' so maybe Gloria [Macapagal-Arroyo] is the one to become the president to fix the projects." Joanne describes rallies and protests that the community held. "Lots of people, everybody here went to the city hall to see the mayor."

According to the Philippines' Urban Development and Housing Act of 1992, "eviction or demolition as a practice shall be discouraged," though the practice is permissible in certain situations, including instances in which people build in dangerous areas, such as along railways.[9] Violent, forced demolition is much less common, in Manila and globally, than it once was. Law and international norms now require that governments follow certain procedures, such as providing adequate warning to residents and curbing violence or use of large equipment. Still, not all governments follow these guidelines.

Joanne has heard rumors that the government will relocate Balic-Balic residents to Cavite. If relocated, residents would lose most opportunities for work and experience disruptions in schooling and services, not to mention the loss of personal and social ties. To establish a new home, they would likely need to spend whatever meager savings they have. But, Joanne says, "Most people, they would come back again to Manila."

If the government seizes their land, the Seares will attempt to rent a home. "I am prepared because I pray that we can have a place to stay. I am not afraid of demolitions. You are not forsaken," Sammy says slowly. "You will not be left alone by God."

"I don't know where I will go [if displaced]," Joanne adds. "But a place like this is not good for children. Especially when they grow up."

The Philippine National Railroad has even asked Tess to sign a promissory note stating that she'll leave Balic-Balic if and when they ask her to leave, a request that she submitted to. "It's written there that [we] have to build a location like this in Laguna."

But Tess remains insouciant. "For almost forty-five years . . . no, it's not serious."

She adds, as if to bolster her own authority, "I am the oldest one here. You see, up till now I have lived here. It's God's glory. In God's glory I'm still alive and I'm very thankful."

Urbanization

Malays from the Malay peninsula and present-day Indonesia settled the Philippine archipelago more than 2,000 years ago. In the tenth century, the Chinese began trading with the islanders and settled into coastal enclaves. Muslims governed Manila, then a village known as Maynilad, before the arrival of the Spanish, who claimed to found the city on June 24, 1571. The Spanish then ruled Manila for more than 300 years, except for a short stint during the Seven Years' War when Britain occupied the city. Then came the Ameri-

cans for more than forty years, the Japanese for three, and then the
Americans for another year before Philippine independence in
1946. Metro Manila, with a population of well over ten million people in twelve cities and five municipalities,[10] is today an amalgama-
tion of cultures, American-molded legal and education systems, an
Asian sense of social protocol, and a national language, Filipino,
that has elements of Tagalog (sometimes equated with Filipino),
Spanish, American English, and various island dialects.

British imperialists, hoping to encourage more trade in its East
African Protectorate, birthed Nairobi in 1896 to connect Mombasa
on the Indian Ocean with Kisumu, Kenya, on Lake Victoria and
eventually with Uganda. A century ago, Nairobi, once advertised as
the "Green City in the Sun," had just 8,000 occupants. Today, 2.8
million people live in Nairobi and some say the city's population
will double by 2025, with most of the growth occurring in informal
settlements.[11]

In 1325, the Aztecs established Mexico City on an island in the
middle of a lake. They did so because an eagle, with a snake in its
beak, alighted upon a cactus, just as their religious myths prophe-
sied and just as the Mexican flag of today depicts. Almost 19 million people now dwell in Mexico City, many of them in structures
that lean dramatically as they settle into a massive, drained lake bed.

Bangkok—or *Krungthep* to the Thais, which means "City of
Angels"—was once renowned as the "Venice of the East" because of
its many rivers and canals. Founded in 1782 on the banks of the
Chao Phraya River, the city has the world's longest official city name:
Krungthep Maha Nakorn Amorn Ratanakosindra Mahindrayudhya,
Mahadilokpop Noparatana Rajthani Burirom Udom Rajnivet
Mahastan Amorn Pimarn Avatarn Satit Sakkatuttiya Vishnukarm
Prasit. More than eight million people now live in Bangkok.

Cairo, known as *Misr* and *um al-dunya* in Arabic, "the Mother of
the World," is an ancient city. Once a strategic urban center for the
Byzantine Empire and early Arab conquerors, Fustat (established
A.D. 642) and al-Qahira (established A.D. 969) comprise present-
day Cairo, home to ten million inhabitants.

Each city has an unparalleled history and character, and any survey of cities must consider these diverse backgrounds and on-the-ground realities. We may uniquely describe cities utilizing any number of indicators, including population, geography, economics, health, education, or religion, but most urban centers around the world have at least one thing in common—they are growing. For the first time in history, more people live in cities than in the countryside.

Metro Manila had just 460,000 inhabitants in 1918, 1.5 million in 1950, 5 million in 1975, and 8 million in 1990 before hitting today's mark of 10.6 million. Some say that by 2015 Manila will have nearly 13 million inhabitants, 28 times its population just 100 years earlier.

Around the world, the story is the same.

Eight thousand people lived in Nairobi in 1901, 343,000 at independence in 1962, 677,000 in 1975, and 1.4 million in 1990. A projected 4.2 million people will live in Nairobi by 2015.

In 1910, Mexico City had 630,000 people, 1.8 million in 1940, 10.7 million in 1975, and 15.3 million people in 1990. By 2015, Mexico City will have more than 20.5 million people, though by some measures the city has already far surpassed this figure.

Bangkok had just 170,000 people as recently as 1883, 1.4 million in 1950, 3.8 million in 1975, and 5.9 million in 1990. By 2015, some 9.8 million people will live in Bangkok.

In 1882, 375,000 people lived in Cairo, 2.4 million in 1950, 6 million in 1975, and 8.3 million people in 1990. An estimated 11.5 million people will live in Cairo by 2015, though, again, some claim the population has already surpassed that mark.[12]

Many of these figures are likely conservative because they may not account for all districts in cities comprised of expanding municipalities that bleed into one another, seemingly without end. And farmers and traders entering cities to buy and sell goods cause massive day-to-day variances. An estimated one million people enter and leave Metro Manila each day.

Urban growth leads to cultural vibrancy as well as to social stagnancy. It provides factories with workers yet leaves many qualified people without jobs. Enclaves representing various ethnicities and income levels insulate people in wealth and security or trap them within poverty. In the global South, poor enclaves, settlements like Balic-Balic, are particularly visible and growing more so in major cities.

According to the United Nations, *more than one billion people live in urban slums, and this figure will double in the next thirty years. Put another way, one of every three people in this world who lives in a city, lives in a slum.*[13]

During the last fifty years the world's population has more than doubled, and millions of people, in both rich and poor nations, have migrated to cities. Cities have long been places of trade and exchange, but today more than ever they serve as our nodes for cultural expression, commerce, employment, and the advancement of technology and services.

But most cities in the global South have been unprepared to accommodate people's many needs, so the poor resort to living in informal settlements where they access more affordable housing and food and find informal work. In the global South, 43 percent of urban residents live in informal settlements; and in several of these cities, including Nairobi and Cairo, slums represent well over one-half of the population, and most future population growth will be in slums. In sub-Saharan Africa, almost three-fourths of city dwellers live in slums.[14] More than an aberration, these settlements meet needs—albeit inadequately—unaddressed by formal sectors of society.

Though urbanization is a process that's occurred over hundreds of years, wealthy countries and cities that grew during the industrial advances of the early nineteenth century enjoyed the advantages of having a slower rate of population increase and more time to respond to demographic changes than today's developing nations, not to mention access to cheap raw materials and labor as a result of colonial, imperial rule. Today, facing even greater, more rapid demographic shifts, many poor nations struggle with unstable governments, depleted and unproductive agricultural lands, overburdened bureaucracies, and deficient legal codes.

As a result, people in urban slums live amidst garbage and human waste, disease spreads easily within dense settlements, and people fail to find jobs or adequate housing. The urban poor contend with overcrowding, poisoned water, evictions, flooding, and pollution.

So why move to the city from the countryside? The United Nations Human Settlement Programme (UN-HABITAT), in Nairobi, Kenya, reports, "Rural life is dull and backbreaking; there are few opportunities and little new arable land that can be developed, especially for women, who are often excluded from land occupancy upon death of, or divorce from, [a] husband. The cities are uniquely able to create jobs, and if the formal sector does not have them, the informal sector can produce them. . . . Cities are, in the end, a more controlled environment and life is less risky."[15]

Urban residents often enjoy the security of better food because they are less dependent on the weather and the health of farm animals. Because of crop failures and a lack of aid from overburdened NGOs and governments, famine and drought severely affect rural residents. Cities generally provide people, through both the formal and informal sectors, with higher incomes. Meanwhile peri-urban bands that surround most cities allow migrants to gradually transition to urban life and culture even as they continue to raise animals and farm small plots of land. Improved roads enable people to migrate to cities on a temporary basis, to vacillate frequently between urban and rural regions according to their needs.

While overpopulation because of migration is a major impetus for informal communities, it is not the only cause. New births still account for much urban population growth, and in many places people are simply living longer. International migrants and displaced refugees, often the result of war, add their own ethnic enclaves to city populations. Kibera, a Nairobi settlement, began as a refuge for Sudanese soldiers fighting for the British.

City systems—governmental, economic, legal, housing, educational and so on—have simply failed, in both scope and effectiveness, to keep apace with this growth. The formal sector cannot build affordable, appropriate homes quickly enough. Businesses and governments fail to create enough jobs or manage bureaucratic channels efficiently enough to enable social progress. Governments lack resources and stability. Most national officials lack the will to work toward solutions, and corruption undermines the efforts of more dedicated leaders. Many cities have been poorly planned, if planned at all, and they lack a plan for the future.

Urban Poverty and Globalization

Poverty is, of course, another major cause of informal settlements. People experience poverty when they have no true voice in a working democracy, when they cannot secure a job or basic education that might lead to a good job. The poor lack access to health care, decent living conditions, and safety. They enjoy few rights truly protected by law. In monetary terms, more than one-half of the world lives on less than US$2.00 a day and one in five people subsists on less than US$1.00 a day. Such deficiency drives people into informal neighborhoods.

Increased poverty often means increased inequality: disparity between the rich and poor has increased exponentially. Globally, average income levels in 1820 for the poorest region of the world, Africa, trailed the richest region of the world, Western Europe, by a ratio of only 1:3. Today, average incomes in Africa trail incomes in the world's richest regions by a ratio of 1:19.[16] After World War II, the world did experience an overall decrease in inequality between rich and poor nations, in terms of average incomes, but over the last thirty years the trend has again been toward greater disparity.

The story is the same within many countries, and wealth is unevenly distributed like never before. In Kenya, for example, the richest 10 percent of households controls 42 percent of the total income, while the poorest 10 percent controls less than 1 percent of the income.[17] Disparity is, of course, not limited to developing nations. Within the United States, the poorest tenth of the population controls less than 2 percent of the income and consumption. The richest tenth controls about 30 percent.[18]

Such urban poverty is self-propagating. Living in dilapidated housing, people face exposure to sickness, and they lack basic services and health care. Bureaucracy, transportation problems, and a lack of education have hindered the poor in gaining access to social services, especially if the government doesn't recognize a settlement's existence because of its illegal status. Some people don't have an established, legal mailing address and are therefore ineligible to receive help. With few marketable skills, overcoming these obstacles and finding security become nearly impossible for slum residents.

The complex causes of poverty are difficult to isolate, but many people blame trade liberalization and deregulation for recent increases in global poverty and inequality, particularly during the last couple of decades. World trade tripled in the twenty years following 1970, yet in trade deemed "free," advanced nations have an advantage because of tariffs, subsidies, and wealth. The recent boom in communication technologies has augmented these advantages.

To benefit from—and risk exposure to—outside competition, many governments in the global South have agreed to deregulate trade policies and fully privatize utilities, systems of transportation, banks, and various government-run bodies. Simultaneously, they have withdrawn state-run social safety nets as part of structural adjustment programs (SAPs), schemes that depend more on austerity measures, budget cuts, and free-market forces than institutional control and government spending. Meanwhile, these same governments have fallen into deep debt, a burden that continues to debilitate economic progress.

But this has led, one side of the debate claims, to the withdrawal of government without providing alternative forms of social support or even governance. A recent landmark report on urban settlements by UN-HABITAT says, "In the end, the growth in inequality has happened because national governments have abdicated their responsibilities to their citizens to promote fairness, redistribution, social justice, and stability in favor of a chimera of competitiveness and wealth for the few. It is also the outcome of international organizations that have adopted a dominant neo-liberal philosophy, which has failed to deliver on most of its promises almost everywhere that it has been applied."[19] According to this argument, economic globalization has weakened formal job markets and caused an increase in informal jobs, housing insecurity, inequality, environmental degradation, and social unrest.

The counterargument is that liberalized trade, privatization, and deregulation have worked in such places as Chile and South Korea because a freer economy attracts competition and investment, because private interests can more efficiently manage and provide services than governments saturated with bureaucracy. In addition, deregulated trade allows people to more easily exchange and disseminate know-how. "Government, including democratic government, is in this view always suspect, whereas markets are always benign," writes professor of political science and expert on democracy Benjamin Barber.[20]

Still, even in nations considered by many to be liberalization success stories, a purely laissez-faire approach does not exist. Regulatory lines continue to be drawn. "[N]ot even Adam Smith thought the market could do everything," Barber adds. The central question, then, is simply where to draw these lines and whether wider society or select elites will most benefit. But regardless of where we place the blame, poverty and economic disparity are real manifestations of a failing system of survival.

Globalization is not an inherently bad, nor a new, phenomenon. It's progressed for as long as people have reached across continents and oceans to exchange goods and ideas. Today, people in the global South enjoy greater access to aid agencies and NGOs and better, more holistic development programs. People in both rich and poor nations frequently laud the benefits of easily accessing foreign products and culture. Helpful technology is rapidly diffusing throughout the world.

It seems unarguable, though, that global trade and globalization directly affect the economic state of cities and nations in the global South, and therefore directly affect urban settlements. Because of foreign competition, an indigenously owned factory closes, and employees revert to street vending. Developing economies, dependent on a few agricultural products such as tea, coffee, rice, or cotton, enjoy qualified access to global markets yet depend on the vagaries of these markets, over which they have little control, while rich nations influence these markets through tariffs and subsidies. Men and women in a poor nation work at a foreign factory for good wages, relative to the region, yet owners, investors, distributors, and others beyond their country and national economy benefit most from their labor, thus adding to global inequality. Examples such as these are innumerable. We must continually, when studying urban settlements in the global South, consider the effects of global economics on this massive sector that comprises one-sixth of the world, as well as the effects of this sector on global trade and labor.

Poverty is not only a cause of urban settlements; it is also a symptom. Settlements are generally, by definition, marked by inadequate income levels and shelters and a lack of services, health care, transportation, law enforcement, and social safety nets. People usually do not possess legal title to their land and home. As illegal residents, they have little protection against crime and little say in government.

Often located in less desirable or even dangerous city districts, informal neighborhoods mingle with garbage dumps, sewage ravines, and industrial complexes spouting pollution and asphyxiating smells. In Manila, Smokey Mountain, an eleven-story landfill covering more than fifty acres, houses 25,000 squatters living amidst disease, methane, and carcinogenic emissions. The Mexico City settlement of Lomas de San Isidro rests on a cavernous strip mine that is, some believe, unstable. Railway residents in Pandacan, southeast of Balic-Balic, reside near oil depots.

Homes may have mud floors. Walls and roofs are made of found or cheap materials such as cardboard, corrugated metal, plywood, wire fencing, even box springs and mattresses. People live densely and multiple families sometimes occupy a single room. In regions of India, essentially homeless people rent portions of a shelter each day or night on an hourly basis so they can sleep while not working, saving themselves the expense of maintaining or owning a home. High density levels exacerbate the dangers of fire, especially when residents use gas and charcoal for cooking and heat, which can quickly wipe out entire neighborhoods.

Water is, of course, critical to survival, yet most settlements have neither good sources of potable water nor adequate drainage and sewage systems. In low-lying parts of Welfareville, one of Metro Manila's largest informal districts, disease-ridden pools of milky green and opaque yellow water surround and even engulf homes after rainstorms, forcing residents to hop on stepping stones rather than walk on pathways. Indoor plumbing may be nonexistent, as in Kibera where residents share pit latrines with dozens or even hundreds of other people. When settlements do have sewers, they are often open, narrow, and along unpaved pathways full of human waste that turns to mud during rain and to dust in sun and heat, which adds to air pollution in large cities already choking on traffic and industry.

Threatened by eviction and demolition, informal residents lack legal protection because they have no official documents proving ownership of land and home, though they may have lived in the same home for decades. Many governments are beginning to work with squatters to find collaborative solutions, to upgrade and transform neighborhoods rather than raze them. Governments are recognizing the contributions that illegal slums make to society in housing and employment as informal markets are succeeding where the formal sector fails.

The informal sector is not merely the black market populated by schemers who knowingly evade taxes and run illegal goods for personal profit. Rather, informal settlements represent a system of survival created by people who cannot afford the time and expense of working through massive bureaucracies or obeying the law when designing a home or business because the law is antiquated and ignores on-the-ground realities for poor people, though they may comprise a majority of the population. It is often the presence of these systems, rather than their absence, that hinders progress.

Informal settlements provide formal businesses with low-wage labor. In some cities, they house most residents and provide the majority of jobs. According to one development consultant, "Just as slums and slum dwellers need cities to survive, so do cities need slums to thrive."[21]

One in every three urban residents lives in an informal settlement. Over the next thirty years, the slum population will double to two billion. The systems of our urbanized world are failing, and we must learn another way.

Life in Manila

Centuries of colonial rule, war, and successive corrupt administrations have left the Philippines struggling for economic and political self-sufficiency. In May 2004, officials were unable to declare a presidential election winner for more than a month amidst claims of fraud, intimidation, and vote buying. Popular protests, celebrated widely among Filipinos as "people power," have ousted multiple sitting presidents in recent years.

Meanwhile, Muslim rebels in the southern island of Mindanao continue to seek independence, a struggle that has claimed 120,000 lives over three decades. Forty percent of Metro Manila's 10.6 million inhabitants live in informal settlements, in garbage dumps, along roads and waterways, wherever a sliver of land allows. And locally, residents of Balic-Balic live in constant fear of eviction and demolition in light of reports that President Gloria Macapagal-Arroyo and the Philippine National Railway plan to revamp Manila's rail system.

Amidst such insecurity, Bing Hornedo, a lifelong resident of Balic-Balic, pursues a college education. At twenty-three, he is studying mathematics at Jose Rizal University, named after one of the most revered national heroes of the Philippines, an intellectual and revolutionary whom Spanish occupiers executed in 1896. His death and writings spurred Filipinos to reject foreign rule.

"I started to study when I was seven," Bing says. His silver oval glasses sit low on his nose. "My memory was already good. The only subject that was really difficult for me was English, but I like mathematics and excelled. In my family, I'm the first one to go to college."

Bing describes his own childhood in Balic-Balic. "My mother, she is a lovely woman. But my father died when I was eight years old. He died of a crime, he was killed by an addict." Bing and his siblings went to work to support the family. "We used to get garbage that we sold at the junk shops. We sold cigarettes. We also sold peanuts, especially in restaurants."

Bing recalls playing on the railroad tracks and around Balic-Balic. "I liked biking, but the bike didn't want to play with me!" He laughs. "I always fell down. Later on I learned how to play volleyball. . . . I also play chess and am good. I like it. A good mathematician must be a good logician."

He hopes to finish college soon, though financing his education is, of course, difficult. When he was seventeen, Bing worked at a Jollibee restaurant for a short time. Upon graduation, he may seek work as a teacher or church minister. "My brothers and sisters already have their families, and some of them live in our parents' house, which is too full. So I sleep in the church."

As Bing speaks, he prepares to teach a preschool class at Balic-Balic Christian Church. He creates handwriting worksheets by lightly sketching letters out of dotted lines that children will later trace and connect. A workbook, open on the table before him, guides Bing. He must sketch dozens of worksheets, which teachers in wealthier settings could afford to recreate in a matter of moments with a photocopier. He's also taught children in Sunday school, summer vacation Bible school, and through Bukang Liwayway, a child sponsorship program. "I want [the children] to be responsible Christians. Becoming a responsible Christian is one of the most essential things.

"When I live for God, it seems very easy. Everything's kind of easy. That's for me. I don't know about others. . . . I have experienced contentment. For many other people, [discontent] is why they go out, to other places, because they seek their own desires, for things which God would not have for them."

In a recent presidential election, Bing voted for Eddie Villanueva, a preacher who, according to the final tally, received just 6 percent of the vote and placed fifth in a field of five. "Because of what I have heard and what I have seen on television, I think the [voting] process is not honest. [There are] reports coming from other countries that the counting system was not very reliable and true. . . . [Politicians] visit here when the elections come. But after the elections, they don't." To follow politics, Bing also listens to the radio and reads newspapers.

An elderly woman at Bing's church recently expressed gratitude to God because campaign workers visited the neighborhood and paid people 200 pesos (US$3.60) for their votes. She delighted in the financial windfall. Others expressed hope when FPJ—Fernando Poe, Jr., one of the Philippines' best-known actors—seemed to pull ahead in the vote counting. During the run-up to the election, fliers and campaign posters wallpapered the front of Balic-Balic homes and hung like laundry across pathways. Thousands of strings of campaign pennants made the streets a political mardi gras.

A month after the elections, officials declared Gloria Macapagal-Arroyo president for a second term, winning by more than one million votes, though her opposition sued in protest, claiming fraud. Joanne Seares plainly states her political views: "Gloria does a lot of dishonest elections. So she won again. We don't like her."

Families rule the Philippines. Gloria Macapagal-Arroyo is the daughter of Diosdado Macapagal, president of the Philippines in the 1960s, and is related to various other political leaders, both past and present. The Macapagals, in fact, have a family website celebrating their political pedigree. A 2004 study found that more than

60 percent of representatives in Congress had relatives in elected office, a figure that has actually increased since 1986 when democracy replaced dictatorial rule.[22] Such consolidation of power gives the elite little motivation to pursue progressive reform.

Select families control the business sector as well. Less than 10 percent of the 1,000 largest corporations on the Philippine Stock Exchange are publicly owned. When they are listed, a few major stockholders dictate decision making. While such concentration within firms isn't terribly rare, what's alarming in the Philippines is the concentration and ownership across firms: 15 families control 55 percent of all corporations.[23] Names such as Ayala, Lopez, Gokongwei, and Concepcion are regularly associated with family-based empires. Concentration of wealth encourages monopolies, weak corporate governance, and cronyism. Still, some investors believe these family monopolies are gradually breaking up, in part because of outside competition. Meanwhile, 40 percent of Filipinos live below the national poverty line.

Concentration of power, a legacy of Spanish colonial rule, has long been the norm in the Philippines. Early on, religious orders consolidated land into agricultural estates. As church ownership gradually waned, these holdings later helped powerful families create the nation's industrial and commercial corporations. American colonialists allowed elite families to retain control after World War II.

The Spanish named the archipelago after King Philip II, ruler of Spain for more than four decades. From the beginning of imperial rule, the church established a presence among the islands. Today, the Philippines is the only majority Christian nation in Asia, and Filipino piety and passion for Christian ritual remain. Religious orders, particularly the Augustinians, Franciscans, and Dominicans in the northern island of Luzon, held sway over the countryside.

Over time, the church ordained Filipinos as priests and when a native intelligentsia developed in the nineteenth century as Filipino elites studied in Manila and Madrid, and as the islands opened up to foreign trade and influence, the orders and the Spanish government maintained less and less control. Many priests agitated valiantly for freedom during this period.

Revolutionary leaders declared war on Spain in August of 1896, but shortly thereafter the Spanish-American war erupted as well. Spain, in the twilight of a centuries-spanning global empire, retreated from the islands after losing an infamously debilitating naval battle to U.S. forces. After much internal debate, American leaders decided to retain the Philippines. For the first time in history, the United States possessed an overseas colony.

Skeptics claimed that such imperialism violated basic, sacred American principles of self-rule. Expansionists considered the conquest proof of the nation's "manifest destiny" to expand and spread the good merits of American civilization. President William McKinley called U.S. rule in the Philippines a process of "benevolent assimilation."

Then in February 1899, war broke out between the United States and the Philippines. In fact, the first shots occurred not far from present-day Balic-Balic, where the major streets suffered the worst of America's initial artillery bombardment. At least 200,000 people died in the war, most of them Filipino civilians.

After years of neglectful Spanish rule, some Filipinos welcomed the American presence. Americans pursued land reform, improved railways, roads, and ports. They renovated financial structures and introduced a tax system. They strengthened education and health care. And, compared to their colonial counterparts in Europe, Americans allowed Filipinos much latitude in self-rule.

Still, the United States allowed power and control to remain with individuals and families who had enjoyed an elite status under the Spanish. America simply served as a conduit to greater prosperity for the privileged. Today, these same families rule the Philippines. After Japanese occupation during World War II, the Philippines finally celebrated independence in July 1946.

Filipino ties with America remain strong. American English is an official language on the islands. American commercial products are so ubiquitous that Filipinos refer to dish soap as *joy*, fabric softener as *downy*, bleach as *clorox*, and toothpaste as *colgate*. The Philippines enjoys one of the most vibrant free presses in Asia, another American legacy. Subic Bay Naval Base and Clark Air Base, once America's largest military installations outside the mainland, remain. Though stationed American troops left a few years ago, the bases' hazardous materials and air, water, and soil pollution linger on. Most Filipinos seem to have a relative working somewhere in the United States, and they consume American pop culture ravenously. "[Filipinos] love imported things from the U.S.," says Joanne Seares, "popular cartoons on TV shows and toys, too."

America's economic influence has long encompassed the Philippines. At the time of U.S. occupation, the Philippine government granted American investors equal rights and access to the nation's raw materials, inseparably intertwining the two economies. Meanwhile, the vast majority of land was public domain, and the agriculture-fueled economy depended on a limited number of products for export. According to historian Stanley Karnow, "[Americans] imposed trade patterns that retarded the economic growth of the islands, condemning them to reliance on the United States long after independence. The American monopoly on imports into the Philippines also dampened the development of a native industry. . . . The Americans shackled the country's economy to the United States in a quintessentially colonial relationship that continued, in modified form, long after the islands had gained independence."[24] Economic dependence on the United States has since lessened slightly, though some argue that these economic ties helped the Philippines survive the 1997 Asian financial crisis.

After World War II, and particularly during Ferdinand Marcos's protectionist rule, the Philippines' economy declined. But with political reform and democracy in the 1980s came economic reform. After Marcos's fall in 1986, the administration of Corazon Aquino set the groundwork, and the next administration, Fidel Ramos from 1992 to 1998, implemented more sweeping reforms and attracted direct foreign investment, reduced import duties, abolished trade restrictions, and deregulated and privatized industries.

On a level, reforms have worked. Between 1985 and 1997, the incidence of poverty was reduced from 44 percent to 31 percent. In 1990, 18.3 percent of Filipinos lived on less than US$1.00 a day, but by 2003 that figure dropped to 11.1 percent. Exports grew from US$5.72 billion in 1987 to US$25.23 billion ten years later, half of this coming from the export of electronic components, a signal that the Philippines is decreasingly dependent on agriculture. Still, about 12 percent of the nation's GDP goes toward servicing debt, and elite family conglomerates continue to benefit most from the Philippine economy.[25]

Since 1986, the nation has successfully held democratic, mostly nonviolent elections, albeit with no small amount of controversy. But overall, the Philippines has gained enough stability to attract the attention of some foreign businesses and investors.

As the economy grows, and as Manila secures its place as the "center for producer services—the command and control center of the Philippines," as one author describes the city, urban land values increase, and land and housing become even less accessible to the poor.[26] Just as Spain's powerful religious orders held land and power hundreds of years ago, and just as generations of elite families have since vied for the same control, today's power brokers are those who own land and monopolize economic assets. The poor remain marginalized.

Makati, one of Metro Manila's wealthiest districts with its modern architecture, gated subdivisions, high-rises, and contiguous commercial space, contains most of the nation's banks, insurance companies, and embassies. Initially emerging in the 1960s and 1970s as an international business district and then further developing in the 1990s, Makati is a deliberate city planned in detail, the antithesis of much of the rest of Manila, with one purpose in mind: attracting investment and business to Metro Manila and the Philippines.

Yet Makati is emblematic of a spatial paradox in Manila and other large cities in the global South. Worldwide, local governance, to attract and maintain investment, partners with private interests to create a city, such as Makati, with the most modern amenities, technology, and production services available, including quality telecommunications capabilities, design and development firms, ease in local and international transportation, and insurance, banking, real estate, legal, and financial services. Meanwhile investment and land speculation drives up the cost of living and the price of land throughout the city. While poor and working-class people are able to work as taxicab drivers, construction workers, restaurateurs, and hotel workers in these financial districts, they can no longer afford to pay for housing and land, and so they live in informal settlements. Therefore, the concerns of the working poor come into conflict with policies of economic reform and aggregate growth, with investors and the economically powerful.

Globalization is at the core of these conflicts. The demand for commercial land by international businesses—and accompanying housing, stores, and restaurants that accommodate particular tastes, felt needs, and cultural interests—pressures city officials to facilitate the development of a place like Makati if the country is going to participate in the global economy, while making the needs of local people for land and resources a lesser priority. The interests of global elites, both wealthy locals and noncitizens, take precedence over the needs of working-class and poor citizens. The idea is to attract this investment and trust that, eventually, the economic benefits will trickle into the rest of society.

Thus, Mexico City has Santa Fe, a shopping and business zone west of the city center populated by such companies as Kraft, Hewlett Packard, Columbia Pictures, Chase Manhattan, Mercedes Benz, and Philip Morris. Originally built on a garbage dump, Santa Fe is now a pristine complex encircled by urban squalor. Similarly, Bangkok, Thailand, has developed Rama III. Shanghai, China, has its Lujiazui Central Finance District, and Kuala Lumpur, Malaysia, is developing its Multimedia Super Corridor between its downtown and the Kuala Lumpur International Airport.

These cities compete to be *global cities*, centers of corporate strategizing, financial processes, and services necessary to conducting business, such as accounting and advertising firms, banking and investment services. In the past, cities formed around industry, but in recent years manufacturing has dispersed to the South. Industrial cities have declined in economic importance, and cities that serve as nodes of communication, decision making, and investment have replaced them. New York, London, and Tokyo are thus today's urban centers of power and control, whereas manufacturing cities like Pittsburgh, Pennsylvania, and Manchester, England, have lost prominence.[27] In addition to changing the urban landscape, globalizing cities tend to provide the working class with service-oriented jobs that are non-union, short-term, and insecure and have lower wages than manufacturing jobs of the past.

To enable the Philippines to compete in this global context, planners and investors have created Makati. "From the urban chaos of metropolitan Manila, a new global city is emerging," writes one journalist.[28] This assessment will likely prove overly rosy, and it is this competition against other urban regions that dictates the nature of development in this and other cities in the South.

Getting by in Balic-Balic

Bing, Sammy, and Joanne are just a few of the 4 million people living in Manila's informal settlements, beyond the bounds of Makati, laboring within these economic conundrums.

Raymund Cruz, a student in criminology, works on a small, local scale to help people. He is the accountant for a rice-purchasing cooperative, a strategy to affordably purchase the staple food.

"They order rice," he says, "and I record it. [Sellers] give the rice to members for a low price, about 600 pesos for 25 kilograms. And when we make twelve purchases, we get one free. So, it's a low price. Each participating member has responsibilities." Daily, ten Balic-Balic residents each contribute 20 pesos toward these large rice purchases. By organizing and buying bulk, each participant saves money.

Raymund also mixes and sells soap and fabric softener with Ernesto Galang, a tall, effusive, constantly joking seventeen-year-old. They mix *joy* and *downy* on the floor of Bukang Liwayway, the child sponsorship program, for about US$.35 an hour.

"We are the ones who make it," Ernesto says. "There are chemicals in the office and there's a procedure. First, you need distilled water for the dishwashing liquid—water, purified water. Then mix this with the chemicals. Then you stir it for a long time." *Joy*, Ernesto adds, is more difficult to make than *downy*. "The *downy* has only three things to mix: the perfume and the color [and the water]. But in the *joy*, dishwashing liquid, there are so many ingredients."

Together, they earn two pesos for every kilogram (about 2.2 pounds) of mixed and bottled dishwashing liquid, one and one-half pesos for every kilo of fabric softener. They then split the earnings. Ernesto gives an example: to make 100 kilograms of *joy* and pour it into small, individual bottles, he says, requires five to six hours of work. On such a job, Ernesto and Raymund earn 200 pesos, 100 pesos each (US$1.80).

Ernesto takes a break from making soap and shares that he most enjoys two things: eating and basketball. His favorite foods include *menudo* (pork with tomatoes, onions, and peppers in a thick sauce with potato cubes), *sinigang* (a sour meat soup with either tamarind or guava), and pork or chicken *adobo* (a particularly popular meat dish with soy sauce, peppercorn, and bay leaf). And then spaghetti. Basketball is wildly popular in the Philippines. Ernesto plays whenever he's able at a nearby community court. The Philippine Basketball Association sports such corporate-sponsored teams as the Shell Turbo Chargers and the Talk 'N Text Phone Pals.

Ernesto has also worked in construction. At home, where he's the oldest of four children, he cooks rice, hangs and folds clothes, and washes dishes. He's studying economics at the Polytechnic University of the Philippines.

Along the tracks, Yole Galang, Ernesto's mother, sells *bananacue*—fried, caramelized bananas—for five or six pesos per banana kabob, depending on the size of the banana. Ernesto peels the fruit for her. Other vendors sell *pan de sal* (Filipino bread), coconuts, mangoes, papayas, *kangkong*, cigarettes, candy, and various household goods. Many families find it more economical to buy prepared food, including rice, than to buy gas and expend time cooking, time they could invest in working, finding work, or caring for children.

Some men, in this and other areas of Manila, run junk shops that employ boys to gather scrap metal, newspapers, bottles, and plastic from around the city, which the shop owners then sell. These junk shops riddle city garbage dumps. Payatas, one such dump just northeast of Manila, is a landfill of more than 50 acres, which receives one-third of Metro Manila's 6,000 tons of daily garbage. Thousands of children and adults treasure hunt for anything they can sell. Many of them also live next to or in the dump. In July 2000, after weeks of torrential rain, a section of the dump collapsed killing more than two hundred people as a fifty-foot high tidal wave of rubbish crashed over their homes and workspaces. Thousands of people continue to call Payatas home.

Tess Esguerra resorts to gambling to earn income. Throughout Balic-Balic, intermittent groups of people huddle around bingo cards, paying one peso or fifty centavos per card. The rattle of bingo numbers tumbling within canisters is incessant. "For them," Ernesto says, "bingo is a pastime. And they gamble because they need money."

Some people train roosters to fight and win money in cockfights. Fowl in three-foot cages line the tracks in railway communities. Even before the Spanish, cockfighting was a national sport and pastime among Filipinos. In fact, by law, a municipality is only considered an official municipality if it has within its bounds a cockpit. Men in Balic-Balic and other railway communities breed chickens to sell or to compete at registered matches or at illegal ones, called *tupadas*.

Ronald Galang, Ernesto's father, works twelve hours a day selling tires, though he holds a bachelor's degree in commerce. After college, Ernesto hopes to "find a job because our family is struggling and because I am the oldest."

Raymund hopes to go into law enforcement. "I want to be a policeman because the police have a bad name here," he says. "I want to be a good model as a policeman. . . . I will do what I know is right.

"A lot of them will raid homes and they'll come with their guns, [causing] a lot of accidents. A lot of times, they're not really looking for anything specific, but they want money. The raids are very violent. They'll come into the homes with guns because they're trying to get money." Police frequently extort up to 50,000 pesos from drug pushers.

Drugs are prevalent in Balic-Balic. *Shabu* (methamphetamine), known locally as "poor man's cocaine," is particularly popular among students and youth. Many families support themselves through drugs, if not as dealers then as runners. Sometimes even mothers and their children prepare and sell the small, plastic packets of drugs. Most community members believe unemployment, hopelessness, and simple boredom among youth encourage the presence of *shabu* and other drugs. Because peer friendships are so fiercely valued among Filipino youth, most drug addicts become users through peer pressure. Alcoholism is pervasive as well.

Within the blue walls of tiny Balic-Balic Christian Church, Pastor Danilo P. Francisco—his congregates call him Pastor Danny—ardently relates his church's vision to transform the settlement of Balic-Balic. "We train urban poor church members to reach out to other urban poor, so they can start their own small groups."

Now twenty-nine, Danny left a pastorate at a large, middle-class church four years ago to serve in this railway squatter community. With a master's degree in community development, he is intense, with short, black hair and simple dress, a T-shirt and jeans. Pastor Danny adds, "We are not starting a church, as in a building, but as in believers. . . . We are just looking for families, small groups to start it."

The model contrasts starkly with most Filipinos' understanding of religion and faith. After more than three hundred years of Spanish rule, and under the influence of the enduring presence of the

Catholic Church, Filipino religion is today, for many Christians, a mixture of orthodox beliefs, animism, superstition, mysticism, and miracles. But as the Philippines becomes multidenominational—Protestant and independent church affiliation is growing by almost 15 percent each year—innovative church models seek to meet the unique needs of the poor in a nation burdened by poverty.

The aim, Pastor Danny notes, is to train poor people to serve and lead others. "[We] see advantage in starting a house church, and building it on relationship."

"Here there is no band," says Ernesto, referring to Sunday worship services. "But it is okay, because we have the powerful voices of our members." His words become faint as a train passes at full speed just a few feet from the church.

The two dozen members of the church participate and lead in preschool, Bible studies, weekly prayer meetings, and various social programs including the rice cooperative and life-skills training that teaches women to give manicures, sew cross-stitch, and create greeting cards to earn income.

Pastor Danny, who lives above the church, emphasizes that this happens through relationships and by sharing in a common cause. "I like living with the people. It's easier for me to relate to how it feels when the train passes, during rainy season, along the railways. They are teaching me how to be content."

Emma (Silva) Smith, who is 4 feet, 7 inches tall with a trilling voice, grew up in Balic-Balic and became a member of the church at age eleven.[29] She performed well in school and eventually earned a partial scholarship that enabled her to attend Central College of the Philippines, where she studied computer science though she didn't own a computer and had to borrow one while enrolled. "I think [school] is the only thing my Mom, my parents, are proud of. Me and my sister, we were always in the top section." Emma and Marie, the middle child, also have a younger brother named Paploi.

"[Our childhood] was hard," Emma says. "Everyone lives day by day. They don't know what might happen to them because the train company constantly threatens to move or demolish houses. Food is hard also. We didn't get enough nutrition because sometimes it would just be rice and soy sauce or rice and salt or sugar. Going to school was hard also because sometimes we didn't have money for food and transportation. We simply walked to school and didn't eat during lunch time."

Paploi, now twenty, still lives in Balic-Balic and often helps Emma with odd chores, fixing appliances or electronics or by helping host visitors. Marie lives in Caloocan City, part of Metro Manila, in a larger, legal home though still next to a squatter community. Like Emma, she successfully worked her way through college. Now Marie researches stocks for Thomson Corporation in Makati, an international business that provides other businesses with information on law, taxes, and other sectors.

Sally, Emma's mother, modeled a strong work ethic. "First she was a house girl in a guest house," Emma says, "cleaning the guest house, assisting families, cooking for them, doing their laundry. She also worked for Botika Binhi, a community drugstore." Botika Binhi, with outlets throughout the Philippines, sells affordable generic drugs. Sally traveled to various provinces to teach classes about drugs and the agency.

"I think that's one reason why my father and her quarreled a lot," Emma says. "She was gone for days, weeks sometimes, one month. So my father would be really mad. At first we didn't like it, but we got used to it. We were already grown up when she did that. My brother, I think, was really affected, though. He was still young."

Emma's father drinks heavily. He gambles. Emma has difficulty discussing him without crying. He tells Emma that he wants to change, and yet she is embarrassed to know that he spends many nights sleeping in a parked jeepney or on a public bench. She continues to see him on occasion.

A year after graduating from Central College, Emma accepted a job with a health insurance agency as a secretary. Then she helped manage a computer rental business. Eventually, she met and married Aaron Smith, a white American who had been studying in

Manila. "I wanted to marry someone who would understand Filipino culture. Aaron is really good. I think he adapted. He is like a Filipino."

The couple moved to Aaron's hometown in Virginia, where Emma worked in a department store, then as a bank teller. They lived with Aaron's family, whom Emma says is similar to Filipino families in that they gather together with family members who are sick or in need.

Still, she finds that crosscultural marriage has its challenges. "Filipinos, when we get angry, we just leave or we want time to pass by. We don't tell the person that, 'I'm angry with you.'" Emma laughs. "[Aaron] would always tell me, 'You know, I don't read minds.' I think for Filipinos, we do a lot of reading minds. I think we guess what the other person is feeling."

Together, after living in the United States for two years, Emma and Aaron returned to Balic-Balic to help the community, to serve their family and friends rather than just preserve their own comfort. The couple now works at Balic-Balic Christian Church and for Servant Partners, an NGO that develops holistic churches and programs among the urban poor.

In Virginia, the couple lived in relatively good health. In Balic-Balic, Aaron contracted dengue fever. Emma finds it difficult to return to such simple and uncertain living:

> In the United States, you don't need anything. In the morning, for breakfast, when you open the refrigerator, there's milk, there's orange juice, there's all kinds of cheese, there's all kinds of bread, there's all kinds of fruit in the kitchen. . . . But here it's always an effort to do something. But there, everything is there. So I feel that sometimes you forget God and then you forget to ask for anything, because whatever you ask for it's already all there. Here for breakfast, for lunch, for dinner, especially when I was young, we would always pray that we would have breakfast, that we would have lunch. You know, you're closer to God.

Emma recalls similar struggles in college. "There's pre-term, mid-term, and then finals, and I did installments on my college tuition. It's really expensive at college. I would always pray because you can't take exams unless you pay the tuition." On the verge of crying, Emma says, "I feel really that God has provided for everything." She concludes: "I think that's why the poor are really blessed. There's always a sense of need and God being there."

Josephine Garcia, a resident of Balic-Balic, has a clear sense of need. Even her favorite memory as a mother, she says, is steeped in loss. Many years ago, her two-year-old and six-month-old both went into the hospital with symptoms of leukemia.

"The first one died," she says, "and then the second one had only a fifty-fifty chance to live. But I thank God that he saved my second child." Today, Josephine teaches children, but, she says, "It's been twelve years now but it's still heavy in my heart. The other people here, they steal, they gossip. So I ask God, 'Why my child?'"

Joanne Seares frankly describes living in poverty, though she blunts the sharp edge of her words with a nervous laugh. "Life in the Philippines is very hard. If you don't know how to survive, maybe you'll die earlier."

Still, Joanne remains hopeful. "Sometimes I ask, 'Lord, I want to have things to do for *me.*' I am searching for the things the Lord wants for me. I am not satisfied with what I am doing now. I want more. When you're looking out there [at the tracks], I lose my hope. But I keep on praying, especially for my children."

The railway tracks of Balic-Balic are just a portion of Metro Manila's slum-lined tracks where families have created homes of found materials, on found plots of land, in neighborhoods that they or loved ones discovered. To roll along these tracks from community to community, young men have built tablelike, forty-two-inch-gauge wheeled carts. They push the carts much as they might a scooter or skateboard, with one foot as the cart glides forward.

Aaron Smith and a few friends ride a rail cart southeast from Balic-Balic toward Welfareville, an informal settlement in the city of Mandaluyong, part of Metro Manila, to visit another church. A large umbrella planted in the center of the cart shades the passengers. They each pay the driver seven pesos for a twenty-minute ride. When a train appears in the distance, the driver stops the cart, and the riders scurry away from the tracks. The driver hoists his cart onto his back and carries it to safety. Once the train passes, the ride resumes.

The tracks turn west, and Aaron motions to the driver to stop. The group walks to a busy intersection nearby, and Aaron hails a couple of tricycle taxis. They eventually transfer to a jeepney and then walk the final stretch. After an hour of traveling, they come upon the settlement.

Unlike Balic-Balic, Welfareville rolls among several hills and covers forty city blocks. But like Balic-Balic, residents here must deal with the prevalence of drugs, family disintegration, domestic abuse, and poverty. Aaron and his companions find the church and call on friends in the area.

In their two-story, two-room home atop a Welfareville hill, Cora Bicoy and her four daughters and one grandson rest after a long hot day. Cora and her daughters recall times past when they saw entire sections of the neighborhood burn in the valley below. Cora remembers how rapidly the fires spread.

The neighborhood has undergone many other changes, she says. The area was once infamous as a dump for murderers, and residents have found several dead bodies discarded along roads. Before the settlement developed, a rehabilitation center for delinquent girls operated here. The government continues to threaten eviction and relocation, and there are rumors that SM is going to buy up Welfareville and build a Supermall.

As Cora Bicoy and her family look out a window into the bleak night, fireworks sprinkle across the southern horizon above Makati's modern skyline. The date is June 1, and tonight Makati is celebrating its founding 334 years ago.

The Bicoys and other residents of Welfareville, from their dense, wooden homes, have a grand view of the celebration's display— shimmering whites, golds, emeralds, blues, and rubies cascading through the atmosphere. The thunder of explosions exclaims success above Makati's glass and steel towers.

Cora recalls her home in Laguna, south of Manila. She recalls the people and the splendor of the coconut trees, the *rambutan*, and mangoes. She looks at her daughters, watches the fireworks over Makati, and hugs her grandson as he climbs into her lap.

3

Nairobi

Colonial City, Then and Now

E VEN AS I ASK THE QUESTION I realize I've probed too quickly. Imbumi Makuku, whom I'd first met just moments earlier at a shopping center in western Nairobi, simply walks and smiles with his eyes alert to the passing landscape. He is bald, with glasses and a slight mustache. "There's no talking about Kibera," he says in a soft, unassuming voice, "when you're breathing all this fresh air."[1]

I withhold my checklist of questions and chat on more personal levels as we follow a worn, dirt path to Kibera, Kenya's largest informal settlement and one of the largest in all of Africa with at least 600,000 people, about one-fifth of Nairobi's 2.8 million residents, squeezed into just 300 acres.[2] Kibera—originally *Kibra* in the Nubian language—means "wilderness."

Three American college students, who refer to our common companion simply as "Makuku," stroll with us. They've been volunteering in Kibera for the past month and share an evident friendship with Makuku. As we pass hawkers selling maize and kale and several women selling used clothes and cloth on spools, I enjoy the students' good-natured cajoling and the rhythmic lilt of Makuku's laughter.

Eventually we come upon a landscape that I find threatening and unreal. Spanning the hillsides and horizon before us, corrugated metal rooftops, rust splotched and ragged, jam against one another, forming a quilt of shelter seemingly so tight-knit as to allow no space between structures for walkways or streets, much less public spaces or playgrounds for children. Mud and wattle walls form a maze beneath these contiguous roofs.

And while I stand in a place quite different than my own home and usual surroundings, the smell of Kibera is familiar to me. Garbage and sewage have a strangely universal stench. It's the rotten smell of things dead and finished, unwanted and wasted, stenches that cause me to recoil, reel, and pause a moment.

Makuku motions with one hand toward the landscape as if he's unveiling the settlement before us. "Welcome to Kibera," he says.

As we continue walking, we cross a set of railroad tracks and enter the slum by traversing a large pile of garbage. Islands of rubbish serve as stepping stones over a meandering, sewage-filled creek. We leap from garbage outcropping to garbage outcropping and skirt dangerously close to the water. As I jump, I hope that my worn-smooth shoes don't slip on the garbage and into the muck. I learn later that with heavy rains, these ravines become impassable. It's also during rainstorms that pickpockets and thieves go to work. According to one resident, "It's the noise . . . the sounds of rain on all those tin roofs. You can shout all you like, but no one will hear you."[3]

We delicately complete our crossing and pass a long, woven wire fence bordering a muddy playground. Within moments several children come running, calling out Makuku's name. They reach their arms through the fence in an attempt to grab at him and shake Makuku's hand as he gladly stops and returns their greetings, their words and smiles. He seems to have plenty of time for them, though I know already from our initial conversation he's only just begun a very busy day. I shake some hands as well, greet them in my minimal Swahili—"*Habari!*"—and discover that their small fingers are surprisingly cold.

More and more children come toward us, wave, and say "Hello" and "How are you?" fishing for a response from this *mzungu* (white person). I continue to respond in kind, "*Jambo*" and "*Habari.*" The children run along the fence as we walk.

We then pass through an endless stream of mud and wattle structures, lanes sometimes just a few feet wide, over canals of more sewage, and I catch distinct scents along the way: kerosene and wood fires, marijuana—known as *bhang* locally—frying grease, excrement. We pass a couple of men picking meat from bones in front of a butcher shop. Raw thirty- and forty-pound cuts of meat hang from hooks. I dodge various chickens and ducks underfoot, and we tiptoe through sewage runoff. Flies overrun the place.

We also pass a couple of barber shops, each in ten-foot by ten-foot rooms with reclining barber chairs, a mirror, hand-painted mannequin heads displaying sample haircuts, and people lounging, waiting. In another shop a blacksmith bends mangled metal. Along the way, vendors peddle maize, cabbage, onions, cilantro, kale, potatoes, beans, and peas. They grow some of this produce along the Motoine River in Kibera. Some of it comes from the country-side. Several slate boards announce, in chalk, the showing of American movies in people's homes for a small fee: the local cinemas. Children sell trinkets and newspapers, scavenge through garbage, and shine shoes. Unseen, prostitutes sell themselves. Men brew and sell Nubian gin or *chang'aa,* an illicit alcoholic drink made of maize, sorghum, or sugar cane.

Most people in Kibera work in some kind of petty retailing. Because of its close proximity to the Nairobi city center, Kibera is also a source of cheap labor. Many people walk several miles each day to work in the city. "I usually walk in to work in the mornings," says one man. "It takes me two hours, but it's downhill, and I save 10 shillings on the fare."[4]

Makuku stops frequently to greet friends and animated children. "When you carry a Bible around here," he says, "they'll know you're up to a lot of good. It's like a policeman in full uniform."

The slum has no electrical service, except that which some entrepreneurs pirate from beyond Kibera via ramshackle wire networks. Residents generally use candles and kerosene lamps, so the threat of fire is real. At night, Kibera is pure darkness, with intermittent glimmers of fire.

After twenty minutes of weaving through just a portion of Kibera, which is composed of ten neighborhoods divided along ethnic lines, we finally arrive at the church that Makuku and his wife, Martha, recently began, Kibera Reformed Presbyterian Church. The church has nearly thirty members, most of whom are young, in their early twenties, and of the Luyia tribe, though the church uses Swahili instead of the Luyia language, Makuku says, "or we will close out other tribes completely. . . . We have said that we are a church of Christ, and we want everybody to know that if they stop in here they are welcome. We want to transcend the tribal system that our political system thrives on."

The church building is an oblong, eight-by-thirty-foot room of mud and stick walls and a dirt floor. It contains a dozen plain, wooden benches and a table and it opens on one side into a narrow walkway through two wooden doors and a couple of windows. The other three walls are windowless.

In addition to this main sanctuary, the church rents six other rooms for 5,000 Kenyan shillings a month (about US$64), which they use for skills training and other ministries.[5] The vast majority of people in Kibera and throughout Nairobi—up to 90 percent in some settlements—are tenants rather than owners. Through a system of patronage, the government has allocated most settlement land in Nairobi to individual chiefs or even militias who, at their own discretion, allow residents to temporarily occupy the land.[6]

Sitting on the wooden benches in the dim light of the church, Makuku and I talk, though we're interrupted periodically by visitors. A young girl serves us hot tea.

A major problem in Kibera, Makuku explains, is that the slum has plenty of development projects and churches—according to one journalist, "It is often said that there are more churches than toilets in the slum"—but not enough training and effective leadership.[7] So he's forming his own nongovernmental organization, Daybreak Word & Deed Ministries, to train pastors and equip them with resources on leadership development, advocacy, church planting, and social justice issues. All of this, he says, "means being on top of things in Nairobi."

For ten years Makuku led a church in Mukuru Kayaba, an industrial region in southern Nairobi. Then, after training other pastors for a season, he felt he needed to return personally to a church-planting situation, while continuing to train other leaders. So he began this Kibera church and is founding Daybreak Word & Deed.

Kibera's Colonial Past

Except for the whims of colonizers one hundred years ago, Kibera wouldn't exist. The settlement, Makuku tells me, began in 1912, when the British colonial administration in Kenya, as a form of unofficial pension, settled Nubian military veterans from Sudan whom they had conscripted to fight in the King's African Rifles, Britain's East African colonial forces.[8] Prior to this, the Maasai used the region for animal grazing.

These soldiers guarded the new railway that connected Mombasa and the ocean to Nairobi and inland areas, and they protected other British interests in the region, fighting with Allied forces in World War I and World War II. Colonizers also regularly hired soldiers from one tribe to subordinate other tribes, "walls of pacification," according to Makuku. The Sudanese of Kibera, who to this day cling to their military identity and Muslim faith as sources of community pride and unity, were skilled and loyal fighters.

Kibera began as a temporary solution to placate retiring soldiers, but over the years the settlement became a source of political and social unrest. In the early 1950s, the Mau Mau freedom fighters, a secretive movement of Kikuyu militiamen bound by oath to force white settlers from Kenya, began agitating for independence and setting fire to homes of collaborating Kenyans. The British responded by decreeing a state of emergency, during which British soldiers pursued Mau Mau fighters and other members of the Kikuyu tribe, capturing and killing many of them. Thus Kikuyus, the largest tribe in Kenya, fled into Kibera and other informal settlements seeking refuge and a safe haven where they could securely organize.

City authorities failed to guide slum growth or control land use, and Kibera residents, including Nubians, held no legal title. Meanwhile, the land increased in value as Nairobi's city center extended ever closer to the settlement. Colonial administrators, concerned with containment, public health, and racial segregation, developed myriad schemes to relocate residents of Kibera. But the Nubians didn't die off or scatter as quickly as administrators had hoped. The expense of these schemes and the lack of suitable land for relocation, not to mention reluctance on the part of Nubians to move and the refusal of other tribes to accommodate them, repeatedly derailed administrators' plans. Thus, Kibera began haphazardly as an impermanent home to Britain's colonial conscripts, but it became a long-term solution for the city's lack of affordable housing.

In Nairobi, 60 percent of residents now live in illegal settlements though they occupy only 5 percent of the land.[9] For the most part, these settlements developed because colonial administrators developed Nairobi as a city, but to the exclusion of native Kenyans. Colonial officials allocated most land for personal benefit.

In Nairobi and throughout the country, Africans were not allowed to live in designated areas, including quickly developing urban centers that became loci of power, decision making, and economic gain. By 1948, colonialists had racially zoned Nairobi three times. Officials sequestered Kenyans who had migrated to the city in search of work to fringe regions, even then against the wishes of many colonizers who believed Africans should remain in rural areas and live in cities only temporarily.

Colonial perceptions and policies thus fostered deep inequalities in living conditions early on, the impetus for a legacy of poverty that still festers in Nairobi's informal settlements. According to one historical account, "The divide between the legal and illegal city owes its origin to the colonial period. . . . The two areas had different types of houses and services. . . . Africans were restricted to African reserves located on the urban fringe where the necessary infrastructure and services were not provided."[10]

Colonizers also attempted to limit Kenyans' freedom to move

about. The Vagrancy Act made it illegal to have "no fixed abode," to beg, or to have neither "lawful employment nor lawful means of subsistence."[11] Basically, Africans broke the law if they couldn't afford housing or find a job. Yet Kenyans still flowed into illegal settlements by the thousands to escape rural poverty. Like today, African settlers fended for their own housing, jobs, and services as informal settlements became their only means of survival.

Colonizers forbade Kenyans from growing their own coffee crops, lest they compete against settler plantations, and British settlers extracted any material or economic wealth generated within Nairobi, widening the divide between secure foreign settlers and dispossessed native residents. Illegal settlers, already at the bottom rung of society, had little hope of enjoying economic development. Commenting on colonialism throughout Africa, one author says, "[Africans] were denied access to their own land, could not grow certain cash crops, were limited in the ownership of property, were forced into unpaid labor. . . . Their powerlessness to legitimately control their own lives left them on the other side of a chasm whose expanse was as great as that between god and worshipper."[12]

Even the layout of Nairobi's streets is a colonial legacy. "The roads we have now were built during the colonial period to serve a small population that was only allowed to be at the city center," says a professor at the University of Nairobi.[13] The city's early developers configured streets according to separate enclaves occupied by Europeans, Indians, who served in lower-government and labor positions, and then the most excluded class, Africans. European settlers enjoyed easy access to major road arteries connecting the central business district to the white-occupied districts in the north and west, while roads bridging the African population to the city center were poorly maintained and less accessible.

Today, because of such lopsided, narrowly focused planning, Nairobi lacks adequate roadways between neighborhoods and from these neighborhoods to the city center. City traffic is stifling, and roads cannot physically sustain the ever-burgeoning mass of vehicles. Yet as Kenyans attempt to establish a greater presence in international trade, good roads can be the difference between vibrant economic development and stagnation. Poor roads mean less efficient and more expensive business transactions, while consumers have less access to goods and services.

But the opportunism of intruders didn't begin with the British. Arabs settled on the Indian coast of Kenya around the eighth century before the Portuguese gained regional control for almost two hundred years with Mombasa as their administrative center. During the 1700s, two Arab dynasties expelled the Portuguese. Then in the early nineteenth century, Britain developed commercial ties with these sultans of Zanzibar who controlled much of eastern Africa.

In 1887, after European powers sliced up Africa in the infamous Berlin Conference of 1884, the Imperial British East Africa Company gained full judicial and political authority over various coastland areas of present-day Kenya. They then penetrated further inland, designating certain land exclusively for European settlers and allowing native Kenyans to remain only on land that was occupied or clearly being utilized, according to British definitions and standards. They viewed everything else as Crown Lands or public lands.

In essence, colonial government officials discounted indigenous land rights, though local people viewed all land as essentially occupied. Such haphazard land grabbing, in addition to the development of railways, interrupted tribal trade routes and displaced communities. Europeans then commandeered land for cities and agriculture.

So the stage was set. British colonizers decided to create Nairobi.

Britain made Uganda a protectorate and then worked to connect that region to the coast, through Kenya by rail. Present-day Nairobi was a suitable midway point between Mombasa on the Indian Ocean and Kisumu, Kenya, a short distance from Uganda. So, as of 1899, Nairobi, at mile 327 on the East African railway, served as a railway depot. By 1906 Nairobi had 11,000 inhabitants.

Within a decade, the British effectively seized the most fertile highlands in the city and segregated Africans to designated regions. But not until 1948, when the city had a population of nearly 120,000, did officials develop a comprehensive master plan that even began to consider the needs of these fringe settlements and provide guidelines for their development, though little improvement in African settlements resulted. In general, white settlers occupied areas where rich, red soil could support coffee plantations. By 1963, the year of Kenyan independence, 70 percent of Africans in Nairobi were sequestered to the Eastlands, a municipality comprising just 10 percent of Nairobi's total land area.[14] Other Africans lived in Kibera and other settlements.

At independence, the Kenyan government—elite Kenyans who held some sway even under colonial rule—lifted policies of residential segregation. Thousands of people poured from the countryside into Nairobi, though the government did little to manage this migration, and settlements swelled and multiplied. The government eventually pursued strategies of demolition before early attempts at public housing. But, as is often the case with such schemes, the units they developed became too expensive for the poorest sectors.

During the 1970s, the government attempted to upgrade informal settlements with service provisions such as water systems and electricity, a process rife with political patronage. In the 1980s, the government implemented World Bank structural adjustment programs, which included the removal or lowering of subsidies on fertilizers, fuel, health care, education, and various public services. Illegal settlements and other low-income areas deteriorated as residents scrambled more than ever to pay for these services. In addition, a devaluation of the shilling led to a loss of income for informal workers and decreased demand for their wares and labor. In 1993, after the government moved from a one-party system to a multiparty system, the Nairobi City Convention provided a forum, for the first time, for citizens to express their views on city planning and management. The meeting resulted in a comprehensive city plan, though the government failed to act on it.

One result of poor city planning is an utter lack of clean drinking water in Nairobi's informal settlements. As early as the 1930s Kibera experienced a shortage of clean water as seasonal springs dried up while the population of the settlement grew. Rather than develop a permanent, public water supply the government used the occasion to encourage residents to relocate to more water-rich areas. "The administration began a policy of what can only be considered malicious neglect in an attempt to force the Sudanese out by rendering Kibera unlivable," writes one researcher.[15] The government further spoiled the water supply by oiling open pools of water to prevent the spread of malaria.

Kibera has since continued to experience intentional neglect. The government forbids residents from building with anything other than temporary materials. The community lacks full representation in government and benefits proportionately less than rich neighborhoods from city tax revenues, though Kiberans comprise much of Nairobi's workforce.

Today, where piped water is available in Nairobi, water infrastructures remain in tatters. In Kenyan urban centers, 40 to 70 percent of treated, piped water doesn't even reach targeted consumers because of illegal connections, burst pipes, and other leakage. Not only do people not receive water, but municipalities are also unable to collect money on resources they are failing to provide, thus perpetuating the government's lack of revenue. Like informal settlements, a lack of clean water isn't inevitable, some random inadequacy of nature. Kenya lacks the necessary finances and policy to properly manage the resource, this in a country rich with interior water sources and bordering an ocean and the second largest freshwater lake in the world, Lake Victoria.

Local leaders say that Kibera's most pressing needs are health care, hygiene, and safe water. People purchase water from vendors, often paying at least three times the municipal rate. The few latrines that do exist each serve hundreds of people. "Flying toilets," bags of human feces haphazardly tossed over roofs, into walkways or wherever possible, serve as a convenient but unhygienic method of waste disposal. Neighborhoods have poor drainage and pools of stagnant water. And the city is unable to easily collect trash from Kibera. These conditions breed the spread of skin infections, diarrhea, and worms. Eight of ten medically treated children in Kibera suffer from preventable, sanitation-related diseases.[16]

Common diseases include tuberculosis, malaria, hepatitis, cholera, respiratory diseases, and various STDs. According to Makuku, one of every three adults in Kibera has AIDS, as it strikes a disproportionate number of people living in poverty. In Kenya, one in every fifteen adults, ages fifteen to forty-nine, is HIV positive and 1.2 million people have the virus.[17]

Yet life-prolonging antiretroviral drugs are much less available in Kibera than they are in rich countries, even as the social effects of AIDS are arguably more severe here and in the rest of sub-Saharan Africa where the social safety net is already overburdened. AIDS is destroying families, leaving thousands of orphans to fend for themselves, sometimes forcing them into a growing sex trade which, in cyclical fashion, further propagates the spread of HIV. AIDS also depletes the nation of its most able workers.

Regardless of living conditions, Kibera grows at an annual rate of 12 percent. The settlement began with just 300 detribalized *askaris* (soldiers) but had more than 10,000 people by 1972 and has at least 600,000 residents today.[18] The settlement parallels national urbanization trends. Some researchers estimate that the majority of Kenyans will live in urban areas by 2015.

Meanwhile, the settlement's land area has gradually diminished. In 1918, 4,198 acres comprised Kibera. In the 1950s, the government converted sections of Kibera into housing estates and the Royal Nairobi Golf Course. By 1971, Kibera had dwindled to 550 acres and to 300 acres by 2002.[19]

But even as Nairobi's impoverished informal settlements grow more crowded, they provide people with affordable housing alternatives. "I have been forced to live in this environment since this is where I can afford rent," said Otieno Oyoo, a metal welder in Kibera. "With my meager income, I have to support my family and siblings back in the village."[20]

Urban migration has made Kibera more ethnically heteroge-
neous, and, amid poverty and the increasing demand for housing
and land, ethnic tensions have grown. In late November and early
December 2001, Makuku tells me, rioters ripped through the narrow paths of Kibera looting, burning, and destroying homes. At
least a dozen people died, and hundreds of people were wounded
or raped. In response, police simply "went on their own rampage,
raping, beating, looting, and destroying property," according to
Human Rights Watch.[21] Residents fled from the settlement by the
thousands, taking only what they could carry.

The cause of heightening tensions and violence, Makuku says, is
twofold: tribal disputes and rent hikes. Tenants used to pay an average of about 300 shillings per month, but this figure has quickly
risen to 750 shillings.

One source, which sets the death toll as high as fifty, claims that
"political hirelings" were responsible, that they had each been paid
250 shillings (about US$3.00).[22] Others point directly to then-
president Daniel arap Moi, who publicly denounced high rents in
Kibera just one month earlier, comments which knowingly
enflamed ethnic divisions between Nubian landlords and mostly
Luo tenants. One of Moi's cabinet ministers repeated these sentiments the week preceding the riots. Moi publicly demanded, without offering alternative plans or meeting with local authorities, that
rents be cut in half.

According to one report, "Such mayhem spurs Kenyans to vote
along tribal lines, which, in turn, allows KANU [Kenya African
National Union] to stay in power so long as Mr. Moi gives cabinet
posts to members of each major tribe."[23] But Moi has since been
voted out of office. In December 2002, Mwai Kibaki became only
the third Kenyan president in forty years of independence.

For these and many other reasons, Makuku's Daybreak Word &
Deed Ministries encourages Christian leaders and others to personally transform their communities. But while signs of Christian
influence abound in Nairobi—Christian newspapers, churches,
posters by the thousands announcing prayer rallies—most Kenyan

Christians are leery about getting involved in politics or social issues. They fear compromising their spiritual message with earthly, temporal affairs.

"For us to be salt and light in Kibera," Makuku says, "we will need to overcome that sort of fear and come to a better understanding that life for the Christian is not dualistic, but an integrated matter." Makuku has begun inspiring others to write letters to public officials and to seek creative ways of positively influencing their communities. "We're enabling the Kenyan church to have an impact on urban society."

Makuku, in partnership with other NGOs, is lobbying the government to truly recognize and service Kibera and other slum communities. They are asking that informal settlements, most of which are on public land, be granted regular tenure, basic amenities such as safe water, and community services at standards that affordably meet the needs of low-income residents. They are encouraging government bodies and NGOs to use local resources and labor in development. And they are calling for the removal of institutional bottlenecks and bureaucratic inefficiencies, including prohibitive policies and building codes that don't suit the needs of slum residents.

Makuku and his colleagues would also like to see Nairobi's transportation infrastructure become less dependent upon *matatus* and other forms of transportation that converge so overwhelmingly in the city center. Wildly painted and decaled vans, notorious *matatus* boom with musical beats both Kenyan and foreign and treat sardined riders to breakneck rides on potholed roads. Some have names such as Death Wish, Death Warrant, or Kosovo Conflict, to cite a few.[24] Many people advocate for an improved, affordable regional train system. For slum residents, decentralized transportation could create job opportunities outside the city center.

Foremost, Makuku wants the government and development agencies to heed the input and needs of slum residents. This seemingly simple approach would reverse a century-old strategy of neglect and disparate city planning aimed initially at serving the interests of British colonizers and, later on, African urban elites. It would empower the very residents who have labored to construct and provide for their struggling communities.

As Makuku and I conclude our discussion, he speaks with affection about the people he serves. "Once you get beyond the dirt and squalor and filth of the slum culture, you see the dignity of people. Once the people know you do not look down on them and you're not patronizing them, they will accept you . . . once they know you're with them when they're hurting."

We leave Kibera by a different path, for my sake, Makuku claims. He encounters the same handshakes and personal greetings as we exit the settlement.

While crossing a ravine that's even more precarious than our pathway into Kibera, I slip and immerse my right foot, over my ankle, in sewage water. For a moment I want to cry out and complain. But instead I decide to quietly retain the present feeling of disgust, to simply dwell on it and keep it as a memory, as fodder to feed my own sense of compassion for people living in Kibera. Makuku had, in fact, chosen our path for my sake.

The Dignity of People in Mathare Valley

She goes by "Jane." And while her last name isn't Doe—it's Matiba—she is anonymous to the world outside her slum.

She lives in Mathare Valley, a settlement of a few hundred thousand people in northeast Nairobi, though no one knows the real population in a place that's tax-dollar deficient and unworthy of a census, a place of illegality that, by definition, is excluded.

Amidst mud and wattle walls enclosed by corrugated metal roofs that, Jane says, are in constant danger of being stolen by thieves, Jane and her family of seven live in a single room. Bandits, brash and desperate enough to displace her roof, would exchange it for cash and leave the Matibas to face the relentless sun, heat, and rain of Kenya's highlands. As it is, her roof leaks. "At least stealing has reduced over [the past] two years," Jane says, "but money is getting rarer by the day."

Two of the five Matiba children are in school. According to Vicky Birir, a law student at Moi University in Eldoret, Kenya, who taught briefly at Mathare Community Outreach, a local school, "[T]he cry of the people in Mathare is not so much to get out of Mathare but that their children may go to school."

Jane washes clothes by hand, cooks, and, of course, tends to the sundry needs of her children. She buys food on occasion, though usually this is her husband's responsibility. Jane also plaits women's hair for money.

Each week she contributes 30 shillings (US$.40) to a savings group for women, and each week one woman receives this windfall of pooled money so as to purchase more expensive items. Jane patiently awaits her turn for the windfall. Sometimes she borrows money from her husband if he "gets good money and he agrees to lend me some." His trade is construction.

Jane believes she could improve her family's situation if she had enough money to start a small business selling roasted maize or *mandazis*, local doughnuts. "I take each day as it comes," she says. "I don't know whether I'll be here tomorrow. I just hope I will be here."

Jane and her husband moved to Mathare 4A, the division in which they now live, from the countryside in 1991. Like many of her neighbors, Jane grew up in Nyakach, in the Nyanza Province in western Kenya. The Matibas made a down payment to secure their small home and pay 600 shillings in rent each month, though they have no deed or paperwork confirming the transaction. "Sometimes we are threatened that the owners are coming to take the land, and many times people fight over ownership of the land here," Jane says.

When asked who owns the land in Mathare, Jane responds, "I don't really know. Sometimes we are told it's the government, sometimes some companies claim it. Sometimes my landlord claims it. I am confused."

She fears daily that fire will break out and destroy the settlement. People use kerosene to cook in tight quarters and, when tensions rise over landownership in Nairobi's settlements, stakeholders have been known to burn homes to smoke people out.

In light of such fears, Jane embraces a faith of hope. "I believe in God," she says. "I know God loves me, but I can't go to church because of my husband." Some of Jane's neighbors are part of the *mungiki*, a mysterious sect that, she points out, practices female circumcision. *Mungiki* combines traditional African beliefs, Islam, and secret oaths.

She states that most residents have either bought land from illegal residents or are squatters themselves. "Most of them grabbed the land. They just woke up one day and said, 'This is my plot.'"

In Mathare Valley, as in most Nairobi settlements, residents only have the option to rent. Landlords subdivide and sell their land, but without titles or government paperwork. These informal processes feed misunderstanding and corruption. And with tacit support from the police or government, landlords become warlords.

Confusion persists as to who owns Mathare Valley. Some say the police own division 4A, that descendents of Mau Mau freedom fighters own 4B. A private corporation, Moroto Company, purportedly owns Mathare Moroto. Though officially the government still owns most of the settlement, many speculate that some landlords are actually members of parliament.

In one subsection of Mathare, a German development agency legally purchased land from the government, leveled houses occupied by members of the Luo tribe, and built new homes as well as streets with lighting. But the agency disregarded the Kikuyu landlords who complained. The courts must now clean up the muddle.

Jane says that having the right connections is critical. "People are not allowed to build permanent houses though some people have done so, especially those who are friends to the village elders. If you have a good connection with the village elder, you are better off. . . . When the village elder speaks, it has to be so."

Much like in Kibera, people in Mathare Valley live in dense, deplorable conditions and neighborhoods developed along tribal lines. Here, well-established landlords are Kikuyu, and more recent tenants are Luos of the Nyanza Province. Luos comprise the majority of the settlement, and women head most households.

Mathare Valley materialized as nine villages merged around the Mathare and Gitathuru rivers. Early on, in 1954 when only a few hundred people lived here, the colonial government razed the densest section of Mathare Valley seeking to flush out and disenfranchise Mau Mau resistance fighters. Some residents eventually returned to Mathare. Unplanned development and people relocating from other slums fed intermittent surges in the settlement's population over the next decades until in 1970 about 20,000 people called Mathare home. Today, population estimates range from 300,000 to 500,000 and even higher.

One 1971 study, noting Mathare's suitable land for building, its somewhat central location, and its proximity to rivers and roads, optimistically proclaimed, "In view of Nairobi's predicted expansion in the direction of Thika, Mathare Valley is assured of a prosperous future."[25] But, as with urban settlements throughout the world, Mathare Valley is now infamous for squalor, crime, poverty, and drugs and alcohol, including *chang'aa*.

Cheaper than store-bought beer, *chang'aa* concoctions sell for about US$1.00 per liter and may contain methanol. Some people die drinking the brew. And desperate to earn an income, some women entertain men with *chang'aa* and sex, even as their children sleep in a corner of the same tiny room. "*Chang'aa* is turning men into zombies and wrecking families," says Father Peter Kihara, Catholic bishop of the Murang'a diocese in central Kenya.[26]

Still, "the dignity of people" that Makuku champions endures and through various projects and strategies residents retain hope. Community members have come together to dig pit latrines and to unblock clogged, above-ground sewage trenches. They've established schools, churches, and NGOs. They've even formed sports and service organizations and art exhibits.

At Mathare Community Outreach, a six-room school that some-how serves lunch to more than 600 children every day, students eat the usual Kenyan fare, *ugali*, a cornmeal porridge, and *sukama wiki*, a green leafy vegetable. Teachers and students scoop the *ugali* and *sukama wiki* from twenty-gallon vats onto aluminum plates held by a line of energetic though polite children. Shifts of several dozen students cycle through the room as school staff quickly wash the plates before each class arrives. For some children, this is the only meal they'll eat all day. While not much larger than the lunchroom, classrooms of just 150 square feet hold up to forty desks and a chalkboard. Children learn arithmetic, language skills, and other basic subjects.

Mathare Youth Sports Association (MYSA), which includes more than 1,000 sports teams and more than 17,000 boys and girls from Nairobi settlements, is another local initiative. To play soccer at certain levels, children must volunteer to coach, referee games, or teach AIDS awareness and prevention. The majority of MYSA's league officials, coaches, referees, and linesmen are about six years old. On weekends, teams gather to clean streets and walkways around their homes.

The agency has been recognized worldwide for these efforts, and MYSA soccer teams have won international tournaments, including the Norway Cup, the world's largest youth soccer tournament. Mathare United FC received a nomination for the Nobel Peace Prize in 2003. Though most Mathare youth begin playing the sport with balls made of bundled plastic bags and twine, Mathare United FC was the first nonpremier team in Kenya to win the annual Moi Golden Cup and go on to represent Kenya in Africa's Cup. Thus soccer and service provide Mathare children with hope and a venue to dream of being future soccer stars, as well as doctors, lawyers, and leaders.

Francis Kimanzi, once a striker and captain with Mathare United FC, teamed up with photographer Lana Wong to teach children about photography and writing. Their collaboration resulted in *Shootback*, a collection of images created by Mathare youth that express the realities of slum life from their points of view. Wong writes in the book's epilogue: "[W]e watched shy kids bewildered by these strange plastic machines transform into confident young photographers, emboldened by their new talent and the attention their pictures have generated in Kenya and abroad."[27] *Shootback* photographs have appeared in galleries all over the world.

According to Kimanzi, "Older kids who have been involved since its beginning have become leaders and role models in the community, and [soccer] has catalyzed their social, physical, and intellectual development."[28]

By empowering children through education, by accentuating their skills and unique perspectives, by enabling them to enjoy nutritious meals, these and other interventions are combating legacies of poverty and disenfranchisement. But within the global context, formidable economic forces continue to adversely impact Jane Matiba and other people in Nairobi's settlements. An analysis of these forces and their effects may help describe what some consider to be a present-day form of imperialism.

Economic Colonialism

If Nairobi represents Kenya's urbanization over the last one hundred years, the benefits of which have been unavailable to most native Africans, economic globalization represents the new center to which many Kenyans are hoping to migrate.

Just as Nairobi settlements are the result, in part, of colonial dictates, so too is Kenya's current economic state partially the result of foreign policies and control.

The creation of Nairobi resulted in Kibera, Mathare Valley, and other informal communities of exclusion and poverty for the benefit of the British Commonwealth. Kenyans lost control of their raw materials and land. Similarly, economic globalization has disenfranchised Kenya, rendered the nation incapable of fully participating in and benefiting from today's global economic prosperity, even as rich nations import Kenya's produce. Global markets most benefit prosperous nations, while Kenyan labor and products flounder and fetch too little compensation. Yet Kenyans and other people in the global South wish to distribute their wares and services to the economic center, the markets that rich countries and corporations design and control to their own advantage.

Consider Kenya's renowned commodities, tea and coffee. As of this writing, Kenya is the largest exporter of black tea in the world and tea is by far the nation's most critical export commodity, though Kenyans didn't even drink tea, much less grow it, before British occupation.

The good news is that, yearly, Kenya produces about 300,000 tons of tea and earns some US$440 million on tea exports.[29] And it's now a popular drink in Kenya. In fact, most Africans and Kenyans drinking tea are drinking Kenyan-grown tea.

The bad news is that a large portion of this tea goes, in bulk form, to richer nations where manufacturers process and package it before exporting it back to Africa for local consumption. The United Kingdom, for example, grows virtually no tea, yet it exports million of pounds of processed tea each year.

"It is frustrating for Kenya," editorializes one Nairobi newspaper, "that its leading contribution to consumers' wants in Western markets is not generally acknowledged because of the way tea is blended and marketed there."[30] Echoing these sentiments during a visit to the United States, Kenya's Minister of Trade and Industry said, "We want Americans to consume Kenya tea as Kenya tea and not as English breakfast tea."[31]

Kenyan companies generally do not have the resources or capital to build processing plants, and they face punitive tariffs for selling value-added tea to many rich countries. So they only have significant access to bulk-tea markets, though some claim that processing tea at home could reap Kenyans up to ten times what they now receive for raw tea leaves.

Other obstacles facing Kenyan tea growers include the simple fact that the international price for tea is set in U.S. dollars. Thus Kenyan earnings are intricately tied to the fluctuations of American currency. Meanwhile, the world is producing more tea than it consumes, driving prices down. Kenyan tea producers also face formidable challenges within their own country, including the high costs of energy and technology when dealing with terribly poor infrastructure and inefficient export and regulatory bureaucracies.[32]

Many growers pursue niche markets based on high-end specialty or quality teas such as orthodox teas, processed tea leaves that retain more of their original taste and aroma than the usual cut, fermented, and dried leaves. Others lobby for export processing zones subsidized by the government to allow producers to package and sell value-added tea within Kenya more cheaply.

The song drones on, in much the same tune, for coffee. During the 1980s and early 1990s, coffee comprised more than 40 percent of Kenya's export earnings but just 7 percent by 2003.[33] Coffee prices have dropped, due in part to competitors' strategy of dumping tons of cheaper grade coffee onto the world market—more than fifty nations now produce coffee. Like tea, coffee processing companies blend premium Kenyan beans with poorer quality beans, from Vietnam, for example, and producers have learned to better utilize lower-grade beans.

Coffee processors in America and Europe have the added advantage of being closer to affluent final customers. In America alone, 108 million people drink coffee each year and spend more than US$18 billion on coffee at stores and restaurants.[34] And coffee processors in rich nations have the power to negotiate and relate with coffee retailers. Internally, Kenyans struggle with corruption in coffee cooperatives and a lack of good marketing at the national level.

In response, many Kenyan coffee growers, like tea growers, are focusing on quality control to produce a premium coffee bean for a niche market, though coffee beans are not, for the most part, processed and packaged within Kenya because of many of the same obstacles facing the tea industry.

But coffee isn't even popular in Kenya. Kenyans consume only between 1 and 5 percent of the nation's coffee produce, and most

Kenyans cannot afford to drink coffee regularly.[35] It's a drink of the elite and for foreigners. In fact, coffee farmers are more apt to consume tea—arguably their competition—than coffee. Meanwhile, the nation imports basic foodstuffs.

While blame and root causes are debatable and complex, what's clear—and this is the main point here—is that Kenyans are not the real beneficiaries of their produce, finely cultivated beans and leaves that stand among the best in the world. Just as under colonialism, outside interests are able to extract the wealth of Kenya's industry and, try as they might, Kenyans have too many disadvantages to compete globally.

So, what do the informal settlements of Nairobi have to do with the price of tea in Kenya? General conditions of severe poverty and inequality drive people to create homes and jobs for themselves, beyond the bounds of formal structures. When the national economy suffers from unfair trade practices, poverty grows, and access to formal jobs and markets dwindles. So poor farmers and villagers enter cities; they begin their new urban lives in settlements and hope for something better. "[A]t the end of the day," writes urban theorist Mike Davis, "a majority of urban slum-dwellers are truly and radically homeless in the contemporary international economy."[36]

Actually, one might blame cows for Kenya's lack of trade leverage. Cows living in the European Union enjoy a daily government subsidy of more than US$2.00, which is more money than half the world's people live on each day. Put another way, the yearly EU cow subsidy is about $913, while the per capita gross national income (GNI) in sub-Saharan Africa is $500 per person. In Kenya it's only $400.[37] These are culpable, miserly cows.

While I write somewhat facetiously on this point, these are the kinds of disparities that make Kenya's participation in global trade—and that of many other poor nations—troublesome. As a Nairobi newspaper editorialized in the run-up to the September 2003 World Trade Organization (WTO) Cancun trade talks, which ended in dissent and disagreement, it's not as if developing countries and their businesses are against economic globalization and free trade. What many nations want is simply free trade that is truly free, on a level playing field:

> If all the states "liberalized" their economies by opening them up to foreign trade and investment, they would all end up benefiting. For in the liberalized global marketplace, each country would focus on those economic activities in which it has a competitive advantage. There would be free movement of resources, personnel, capital, and even ideas, and this would lead to prosperity all round. . . . That's the theory of it. The reality, unfortunately, is somewhat different. . . . When it comes to the poor countries of this world, the effects of globalization has [*sic*] been quite different. Their experience is not one of fair trade, diminished tariffs, and free movement of goods and services. Rather, globalization means the rich countries with strong economies do as they wish, and the poor countries suffering what they must. . . . From the perspective of poor nations, globalization as it currently exists is nothing less than a policy of economic tyranny.[38]

Rich nations impose tariffs against developing countries that export raw materials and commodities. They use subsidies to prop up their own farmers and producers, creating advantages that make it nearly impossible for their stakeholders to lose. Many farmers in rich nations sell their product for less than what it costs to produce, and taxpayers basically make up the difference. For Kenyans and other people in the global South, these structures dictate how they're able—or not able—to sell coffee, tea, and many other commodities on international markets.

Then there are U.S. cotton growers, 25,000 of them. The U.S. government subsidizes the cotton industry with several billion dollars each year, enabling American cotton farmers to dump their produce on the international market and drive cotton prices down. Without subsidies of their own, other cotton farmers around the world cannot compete. Yet the scale of American farmers dedicated to cotton growing compared to many other regions is incongruous to say the least. While the United States tends to the needs of 25,000 cotton farmers, in the tiny nation of Burkina Faso two million people depend on cotton production and sales for survival, though they lack similar government support.[39]

Such self-protective practices serve a purpose. They preserve domestic jobs and secure domestic well-being. One may argue that these practices reasonably preserve a way of life, a culture, and stable economic order. In the United States, whether it's corn farmers in Iowa, dairy farmers in Wisconsin, or cotton and catfish growers in Mississippi, subsidized trade not only maintains jobs but it also perpetuates tradition.

The reality, though, is that other farmers suffer the consequences. According to one editorial, "American farm subsidies, like those in Europe and Japan, are intended to support a traditional way of life and save farmland from either development or abandonment. If city-dwelling Americans think of the subsidies at all, it is to complain about their cost, or to express a vague sense of satisfaction that we are protecting what seems like a wholesome part of Americana. The idea that we might be inadvertently ruining the chances of small African farmers never occurs to us."[40]

In light of such inequalities, the U.S. Congress approved the African Growth and Opportunity Act (AGOA) in 2000. AGOA reduced or eliminated tariffs and quotas on more than 6,000 items exported from Africa. By some estimates, AGOA has produced more than 45,000 new jobs in Kenya alone, attracted more outside investment to the continent, and spurred productive labor disputes and internal debate over fair wages. Asian producers are now outsourcing their textile labor to Kenya, where it is cheaper, and they'll no longer face quotas when exporting to the United States directly from Kenya rather than Asia. Apparel exports to the United States from Kenya more than doubled after Congress approved AGOA.

But AGOA, touted as an attempt to establish freer trade, isn't permanent, not all African nations are eligible and those nations that do qualify must eliminate protective barriers to trade with the

U.S. and not participate in "activities that undermine U.S. national security or foreign policy interests."[41] Congress may rescind provisions in the coming years, and WTO policies could yet undermine the act. In the end, AGOA remains contingent upon American magnanimity.

Meanwhile, African countries risk alienation if they don't walk lockstep with the United States politically and economically. For example, certain developing nations that banded together at the September 2003 WTO talks fell into disfavor. According to one report, "Trade officials in the Bush administration are upset at Africa's defiant stand against trade subsidies at the recent trade organization talks in Cancun, Mexico. Enhancing AGOA is not on the fast track, officials say."[42]

Even under a seemingly progressive act, the insatiable drive of rich nations for profit and security inevitably leaves poorer nations with little control, even over their own business affairs. The powerful dictate the rules of the game. While self-preservation is reasonable and necessary, it's a relevant matter that depends on context. The meaning of survival and security for most Americans is much different than it is for most people of Kenya and Burkina Faso.

But this is, of course, why rich nations provide developing nations with aid to the yearly tune of US$70 billion in development assistance. This is a massive figure. But it's critical to consider these gifts within a wider context. These same rich nations allot more than US$300 billion a year for domestic farm subsidies, more than four times the amount of money given in foreign aid. And even monetary aid can exclude the poor, "leaving them in a state of permanent dependence; even stigmatized; isolated from the mainstream society and without hope of re-integrating with it," according to a report on cities.[43]

Other forms of charity, which may help rich citizens feel we're doing our part, can also be misleading. As noted previously, AGOA is helping provide thousands of Kenyans with textile jobs. Yet donated, second-hand clothes are proving detrimental to Africa's budding textile industry. Used clothes from Europe are, according to Norway's main trade union, "breaking the back of the textile and ready-made clothing industry in Africa's poor countries," even as it emerges.[44]

In Kenya alone, used clothes are worth US$74 million, making them the nation's seventh largest import. Used shoes are affecting the leather industry as well. The government recently imposed a 200 percent import duty on second-hand clothes to protect the domestic textile industry.

Meanwhile, Kenya faces almost $7 billion of external debt. Because of corruption in Kenya, the International Monetary Fund (IMF) has at intervals stopped lending to Kenya. By cracking down on some crooked judges and initiating probes into a few widely known wrongdoings, the government is ingratiating itself into good standing with the IMF, which is in turn allowing Kenya to borrow more money.

It would, of course, be myopic to view Kenyans as mere victims. Corruption pervades every sector, from judicial decisions to land usurpation to trade practices. In the early 1990s, a scam in which dead police officers remained on the payroll cost taxpayers about US$3 million. One investigation found that only 3 of 310 judges were "neither corrupt nor incompetent."[45] Transparency International, a German agency that monitors and combats corruption worldwide, once ranked Kenya the fifth most corrupt country in the world.[46] Particularly at the local level, as Jane Matiba in Mathare suggests, personal connections are critical.

President Mwai Kibaki, elected in late 2002 as the first president in Kenya's forty years of independence who was not a member of the KANU party, vowed to end corruption at all levels and initiate judicial reform in hopes of attracting further investment, an effort that has, in fact, enticed some investors to return to Kenya. But allegations of corruption within the Kibaki administration are beginning to surface.

The government hopes to bolster Kenya's economy and trade through a regional trade block with Tanzania and Uganda. By working together, these neighboring nations can work toward common economic goals and wield more leverage globally. Kenya also hopes, under AGOA, to reach tea and coffee markets with processed products. Many people are calling for reform in the Kenyan tax code and trade laws and for improved roads and electrical networks to lower production costs.

Powerful foreign interests have thus inhibited Kenya's physical and economic development, through both urban planning and global trade. Kenya's current structures and leaders perpetuate this maldevelopment. Outside parties have dictated living conditions and the rules of survival. Kenyan elites rely on these rules to maintain their own prosperity. It's no wonder that most people must live beyond the bounds of the law in Nairobi.

They set up informal housing. They create informal jobs as vendors, cleaners, day laborers, and drivers. They practice informal lending. When all else fails, they resort to violence and crime. When so few people benefit from certain laws and policies, on both local and international levels, these laws and policies cannot adequately apply to them. Most people in Nairobi must live in illegality, and if a policy or law adversely affects a majority of people, then it is, democratically speaking, likely illegitimate or, at the very least, useless.

Reform, of course, stagnates because the minority that does benefit from the rule of law has little motivation to relinquish control. Colonialists had little reason to plan for or truly accommodate informal residents, just as today's Kenyan elites, legacies of the British regime, can blithely maintain the status quo and enjoy the benefits of corrupt power. And rich nations have little motivation to rescind trade policies that impede poorer competitors.

Recall that colonial administrators decided the exact location of Nairobi, its layout, its beneficiaries, and, foremost through acts of omission, the conditions of its informal settlements. As a result of colonial rule, more than one-half of all people in Nairobi now live in settlements, marginalized and insecure.

Recall also that trade rules designed by rich nations dictate that Kenyans depend on the export of basic commodities. As a result of these unfair trade rules, wealthy foreign interests now maintain unbeatable advantages.

Unfortunately, Kenya is not a lone model. Similar forces are at work, for example, in the Philippine economy, "a vital supplier of cheap raw materials; cheap human labor; and cheap economic resources such as land to foreign investors wanting to expand production and economic control," says one researcher. "As in any Third World country, [the Philippines'] agriculture is devoted to supplying the production needs of the industrialized countries."[47]

Around the world, colonizers needed places to administer their empires. Similar to Nairobi, they established new cities and planned them only enough to accommodate colonial settlers. They relegated local people to havens of informality that lacked services and infrastructure and attracted poverty. These colonial forerunners to today's urban conglomerations include many Asian cities, nearly all national capitals in sub-Saharan Africa, and most large cities in Latin America.

Many people now fatalistically assume that informal settlements are inevitable, that they're simply the result of rapid urbanization, a necessary, even if unfortunate, byproduct of economic development. Informal settlements, however, are not inevitable. The conditions of slums have causes. Slums have a history, a beginning.

Likewise, our global economic systems are not inevitable. They have histories. They have designers and decision makers perpetuating a legacy of dominance.

Colonialism Today

This is the context within which Kibera and Mathare Valley and so many other informal settlements in the global South have developed and continue to grow. Any analysis of slums must consistently acknowledge the impacts that colonialism and economic globalization have on residents of informal communities.

Of course, imperial legacies are more than economic or municipal. Colonialism invalidated the lifestyle and language of Kenyans, and consumer technology and pop culture from rich nations continue to overrun Kenyan society. When poorly administered, even aid from governments and NGOs can feed some Kenyans' sense of helpless dependence on others.

Colonial influences remain visible in countless cities in the global South—Manila, Mexico City, Cairo, Cape Town, Dar es Salaam, Algiers, Dakar, Tunis, Mumbai, Kolkata, Yangon, Singapore, Ho Chi Minh City, Hong Kong, Jakarta, Santiago, Rio de Janeiro, and the list goes on—in their particular locations, in their street layouts, architecture, land tenure laws, district and street names, public spaces and squares, the placement of hospitals and schools, in the allocation of green space, in disparities in the quality of infrastructure such as water supplies and roads, and in zoning and segregation by race and class. Additionally, foreigners now pervade their popular music, television, radio, and other media, home and hygiene products, advertising, food and beverage selections, shopping centers, and clothes. In Kenya, people purchase these goods with a currency called the shilling, and news broadcasts cover British current events and weather. Everyday apparel includes dress slacks and button-down shirts for men, dresses for women.

When people in wealthy nations think of Kenya and East Africa, they likely think of poverty, safaris, and wild game. Americans may recall the rugged exploits of Ernest Hemingway and Theodore Roosevelt. A favorite destination for safari-goers hoping to mingle with lions, giraffes, and elephants, the Kenyan landscape features wilderness and game reserves like none other and safaris remain critical to the Kenyan economy. Tourism is, behind agriculture, the nation's second-largest industry. But as with urban settlements, many safaris are fraught with colonial legacies.

One prominent, present-day safari company plugs its out-of-the-way wedding ceremonies in an airline flier stating that, for a fee, the outfit will arrange for catering, an outdoor chapel, native music, and a Maasai choir with traditional *Chukka* drummers. Brochure photos depict a bride in full bustle feeding a rhinoceros. It reads, "For those who are seeking the 'Out of Africa' experience under canvas, with four-legged witnesses presiding, then let the Governor's Family of camps in the Maasai Mara recreate the bygone days of the pioneering colonials with their luxurious tents, old fashioned grace, and classic safari style."

The bygone days of the pioneering colonials?

Such sentiments completely disregard the disturbing realities of life, now and in the past, for the vast majority of Kenyans. These images are caricatures of life in Kenya and have more to do with colonizers' stereotypes than with the local people.

Kenyans and people of other nations in the global South aren't just victims, but people from rich nations must keep in mind that colonial legacies are inherent to these and other distortions as well as to the ways we think about developing nations and the problems they face. We must continually labor to transform mindsets and structures that, even if subtly, depend on images of *bygone days* or *pioneering colonials* or the assumed supremacy of today's Western experts, ideas, culture, and technology.

Even well-intentioned aid and development efforts can engender assumptions of patronizing superiority. And by throwing poor nations lifelines of debt that send them deeper into dependence on foreign assistance, rich nations rob people of their self-sufficiency, dignity, and any semblance of economic independence. Instead, we should value the laws, cultures, ideas, and contributions of Kenyans and others in the global South, work with them to formulate a viable means of becoming financially secure, and then provide resources, training, and funds in ways that empower rather than disenfranchise.

We must appreciate precolonial histories and cultures and then recognize, persistently, the ubiquitous influence of colonialism that remains today in urban settlements through trade policies, city planning, legal codes, politics, development efforts, and so on, so that people of rich nations can more effectively and fairly—and contritely—learn to partner with developing nations to negotiate fair economic policies and together create better cities that enable people to live productive and healthy lives.

Slums are the result of particular causes. They have complex histories, beginnings. We can help ensure that they also have an end.

4

Mexico City
No Title, No Land, No Home

IN THE CORNER OF A SMALL, dusty shop in Lomas de San Isidro, Letty sells powdered laundry soap, rice, eggs, vegetable oil, soy nuts, cornmeal, candy, and various other foods and household items. She slouches into a white, wooden chair with her daughter, Navy, on her lap. The shop interior is painted purple-pink but lacks other decoration. Letty has been in business only eight days, and it's been good, *más o menos*, "more or less." As she speaks, Letty seems older than her age of thirty years. "All my life has been the same as it is now," she says.

Navy crawls up and down Letty's lap while making frequent eye contact with a couple of visitors. She is curious yet wary, seemingly unconscious of the sucker in her mouth.

Letty describes the childhood she shared with eleven siblings in the southern state of Oaxaca, Mexico. "My family was so poor, some days we had food, some days we didn't have food." Nagging her mother for food was of no use. Their family simply didn't have money.

Letty attended school until she was fifteen, but then her father said she couldn't enroll any longer, that they couldn't afford to support her studies. Letty had aspirations of studying law or computers and working with prisoners in some way. She told her father, "If you don't allow me to study more, I will leave this house."

So at fifteen, Letty left for the State of Mexico. She lived with her cousins on the outskirts of Mexico City where she resumed her studies through government subsidies until school authorities apparently "lost my papers," she says. Letty then began working in a factory making cinder blocks and sending money back to her family in Oaxaca whenever possible. She met her husband, Leonardo, in the factory. They now have three children and live in Lomas de San Isidro.

The Land of Cartons

Known by locals as Lomas or Cartolandia, literally "Land of Cartons," Lomas de San Isidro is a *colonia* in the municipality of Chicoloapan, a southeastern region of the urban agglomeration of Mexico City. This hillside of lean-tos and cinderblock homes has earned the nickname Cartolandia because most homes utilize thick, corrugated cardboard, a relatively cheap material that's readily available to people like Letty. Paths and roads in Lomas are unplanned, unpaved, and passable only by the most rugged vehicles. Erosion scores ravines into the hillside.

Lomas was a privately held strip mine rather than what the government refers to as *ejido* land, communally held land designed to benefit rural *campesinos*, which comprises much of peri-urban Mexico City.

Several years ago, the owner of the strip mine began subdividing and selling plots for homes. Sensing an opportunity for land and potential security, hundreds and then thousands of migrants arrived as *paracaidistas*, or squatters—literally "parachuters," those who drop-in seemingly out of nowhere to claim the land. As one of Letty's neighbors states it, "When they sold the land a few people came at first, then the rest came like bees." Letty and her family squatted on their 1,500 square feet of land twelve years ago.

Lomas is one of numerous *colonias* that help make Mexico City one of the largest cities in the world with almost 19 million—some claim as many as 25 million—people. Mexico City spans the Federal District (the national capital) and now bleeds into the State of Mexico to the east, west, and north. During the 1950s and 1960s, urban growth ballooned throughout Mexico, by 70 percent and 84 percent respectively.[1] Today, some three-quarters of all Mexicans live in urban areas.[2]

Letty has no formal deed to her land. The ownership of Lomas remains in dispute. Though most residents have little knowledge of such processes, the original owner is trying to evict Lomas's *paracaidistas* through judicial means. CRESEM, (Comisión para la Regularización en el Estado de México, Commission for Regularization in the State of Mexico), a government bureaucracy that surveys and titles land, is also involved. Complicating matters, some people have squatted, like Letty, but many have unwittingly bought their land from original squatters. Though they paid good money, these buyers still don't have formal ownership of the land.

Letty admits that she fears for her family's well-being. Living without secure landownership, without utilities in the arid highland heat, as the fledgling neighborhood leadership and the owner squabble, Letty and her husband seek work and hope to provide for their children.

Life is hard in Lomas. But Letty proclaims her personal strength and determination. "I've told myself, I won't lose my land. I am stronger now. I have my business, and I have my land."

Because eviction is a real possibility, residents make few improvements to their homes. They have no sewage systems, no water except that which expensive tanker trucks ship in on occasion. Residents run their own wires 900 yards into the valley to divert electricity to their *colonia*. "Now we have light, but I don't know if we'll have it later," one resident complains.

To change their fortune, Letty's husband, Leonardo, wants to travel to the United States to work. He plans on going to Piedras Negras, a city in the northern state of Coahuila. From there he'll walk for six days through the desert along the border of Texas before crossing the Rio Grande. Each year, an estimated 400,000

Mexicans enter the United States illegally, most of them like Leonardo seeking work.

"I'll feel good if my husband has the money, of course," Letty says, "but I'll feel bad for there's no security." Letty has backup plans in mind in case something goes wrong and she doesn't hear from Leonardo. "If you aren't able to send money," she told him, "I will sell this and move to Oaxaca and live with my parents."

José is a forty-year-old resident, with a green parakeet named Coti, short for *cotorra*, a type of parakeet that mimics words and sounds. *Coti* is also, José notes with a smirk, slang for a talkative woman. If he's evicted from Lomas, José will destroy his home rather than leave it for corrupt leaders or the government to use or sell. With some 2,000 to 3,000 families in the settlement, he says, the government would have to warn people of a demolition ahead of time.

José wears blue flannel, and his wide smile reveals gleaming metalwork in his teeth. He and his family moved here because of rising rent levels in nearby Valle de Chalco, a more developed *colonia*. He gradually builds on his home with cinder block and cement. There's a mound of cement mix in front of the house, gravel and dust everywhere.

Three years ago, José paid 3,000 pesos (about US$330)[3] for his land. He does fear eviction but continues to build anyway. He believes the government has an obligation to help the residents of Lomas. José also believes he possesses credentials for living here: a mailing address. He notes that his identity card bears the Lomas de San Isidro address. And every two weeks, he earns a 2,800-peso paycheck bearing his name and address. José works as a police officer in Mexico City.

Ana, a neighbor who lives down the hill from José, is a mother of twelve children, eleven of whom still live with her and Brijido, her husband. If they have to leave Lomas, the family doesn't know where they'll go.

"I'm not afraid. I won't resist," Ana says. "If the government says to go, I'd go, but we don't know where we'd go." She then compares her plight with the Exodus of the Israelites out of Egypt. She points out that they, too, wandered in the desert without a home and without rest.

Most of their children work—one is in construction, another is a seamstress, another is a factory worker—and a few of them remain at home with Ana during the day. Ana and Brijido don't have the necessary documentation, birth certificates, to enroll their younger children in school. They had a window of opportunity during which the government issued certificates free of charge, but they missed the deadline.

On this day, one of Ana's sons, Pablo, wears a University of North Carolina ball cap and lounges in the afternoon heat. His younger brother, in a Georgetown University T-shirt, copies his lassitude. Yet another son, sitting attentively next to Ana, wears a light Dallas Cowboys vest.

As a teenager, Ana journeyed alone to Mexico City from the central state of Querétaro. She cleaned houses and then met Brijido. He worked construction in Valle de Chalco, which he continues to do, though on occasion he contracts independently in Mexico City.

Brijido and Ana moved to Lomas, like José and others, from Valle de Chalco. They purchased their one-room Lomas home and land for 4,500 pesos. And they received no documentation except for an anonymous green CRESEM sticker.

"I don't know if [the sticker] is true, though," Ana says. The document is about three by five inches, a glossy green with black lettering and a couple of handwritten codes, apparently designating Ana's plot. The document lists neither their names nor their signatures. "I have the sticker, but I don't have another form. The sticker is my security. I own this land, me and my daughters."

Brijido, she says, contributed little to the family's purchase. Instead, Ana and her daughters paid for most of it, though they'd fought with the owner over the final price, insisting that she'd originally asked for only 3,500 pesos. Still, Ana considers the former occupant a "good woman" and is sure she's willing to return to help deal with CRESEM officials if necessary. The dispute, it seems, arose primarily between this woman and Brijido.

Isaura, another neighbor, is forlorn. "We'll stay here," she says, pulling her long dark hair into a pony tail, "and if the government says to go, we will go. But I hope to stay here."

Much like Letty, Isaura has been in business for herself for a short time. For ten hours a day, she sells candy, shaved ice, soda, and various other snacks outside of her home. For several minutes, she runs a metal ice shaver over a two-foot block of ice until she fills a plastic cup with ice chips. She adds mango flavoring and, with a smile and a nod, hands the cup to a customer. Her husband, Alfonso, like José, works as a police officer.

Isaura and Alfonso feel they've been duped. The local government, Isaura says, and even the governor of the State of Mexico once proclaimed that residents of Lomas could remain in their homes, on their land. In 2001, just before elections, he promised to hand out one thousand land deeds. After winning the election, he never followed through on his promise, a frequent political tactic in informal settlements.

The couple also trusted a man by the name of Augustin. For five years they paid him 5 to 10 pesos each week for their home and land. They understood him to be in business with the original owner of Lomas, and they believed that eventually they'd own the land themselves. But then Augustin stopped coming to collect payments, and they never heard from him again. Isaura doesn't know how much money they lost, but they weren't the only Lomas residents to fall victim to Augustin's deception.

They've lived in Lomas for nine years now, along with their three children. Isaura calls this land and home her own, and the family has another house down the lane that she says is Alfonso's. They are reluctant to build on these homes because they fear the government will evict them or alter their homes to accommodate a paved street. She's unsure where the property line falls or how much of her land a street would require. The family makes no house payments, no utility payments, and once a week a truck fills a large yellow tank outside Isaura's home with water for a fee.

CRESEM has, according to residents, told them that the land

may one day be theirs if the government successfully brokers a deal with the owner. In some informal neighborhoods, people organize and tackle these issues as a unified front. In Lomas there's little leadership, but some say it may still be in the government's best interest to make the current occupants the formal owners, for relocations can be equally problematic, expensive, and have little chance for success. Besides, the government would face the challenge of establishing another site in the area for a new settlement.

Isaura baldly claims, "Now, we are the owners. . . . I think the owner doesn't want to come back to the land. He and the government need to negotiate. They don't want to give us papers because the government says it's dangerous because it was a mine." She'd like officials to conduct a study before deciding the livability of Lomas. According to Alfonso, Augustin collected 40 pesos from each household for such a study, but this too never came to fruition.

A year ago, CRESEM officials visited Isaura and Alfonso and provided them with a coded green sticker. Isaura believes this paper is part of the regularization process, the means by which an illegal *colonia* transforms into a formal settlement with water, sewerage, paved streets, and security, but she doesn't see the sticker as an official document. Feeling bamboozled by Augustin and then the government, Isaura puts little stock in promises.

Several people have heard rumors that the owner originally planned to use Lomas for burial crypts but that he'd had a change of heart. One woman, María Elena, quips, "Better for people to live here than to die here."

María Elena works with AMEXTRA (Asociación Mexicana de Transformación Rural y Urbana, Mexican Association for Rural and Urban Transformation), a Mexican nongovernmental organization working locally to provide savings and loan programs, skills training, day care, and elementary school. The agency provided both Isaura and José with small loans, Isaura for her business and José to develop his home, loans with reasonable interest rates and repayment plans, unlike those proffered by local loan sharks.

Isaura says residents aren't unified, that they "don't have ideas," and therefore aren't able to pressure the government. Even within the community, she complains, people will not respond unless it's in their own financial interest. Isaura has seen multiple self-appointed *colonia* leaders discuss organizing, only to back away when they realize there's no money in it.

Isaura planned to make her home into a church. Several neighborhood families and some organizers from outside Lomas were, in fact, going to renovate it, but the two leading couples—Ana and Brijido, Isaura and Alfonso—had a falling out. Isaura changed her mind, and the organizers stopped visiting. In particular, a Presbyterian, seminary-trained pastor, who also works as an acupuncturist, had encouraged the families to work together, but he eventually left in frustration.

Reflecting on the episode, Alfonso complains that, "God is not for politics. God is for prayers." Now, where this group of friends once envisioned a place to worship and organize, Isaura sells her candy and shaved ice.

Community organizers inevitably encounter the will of the settlement underworld, the local crime syndicate. Leonardo once had an encounter with a female member of the neighborhood syndicate. They had argued over market space, and she struck Leonardo. When he, fearing the syndicate, refused to retaliate, Letty fought the woman personally. Fortunately, nothing more came of the incident. Rumors of robbery, embezzlement, personal vendettas, and even attempted murder are rampant in Lomas.

Yet, Lomas is home to people, to Letty and Leonardo and thousands of others. Like millions before them, they've chosen to make the most of the few, even if illegal, opportunities they have in Mexico City. They're clinging to their Lomas homes and land and hoping for the best.

Tierra y Libertad

Land has forever been central to the dynamics and evolution of Mexican politics, economics, history, and daily life. As one researcher writes, "To the Mexican, a plot of land always has meant liberty and the ability to control one's destiny. The *conquistadores* understood this when they took land and demanded tribute, and the intellectual Antonio Díaz Soto y Gama understood this when he provided Emilio Zapata with the slogan *Tierra y Libertad* [Land and Liberty]."[4]

Lomas de San Isidro is no exception. Disputes over landowner-ship prevent the entire settlement from progressing, prevent people from controlling their own destiny. Instead, residents live in in-security and fear. Conflicts over land rights are in fact simmering within most slums throughout the global South.

Conquest and colonialism began an unrelenting land grab in Mexico. Conflicts over land have repeatedly pitted the elite against a disempowered majority, federal law against pragmatic, local real-ities, national interests against trade policies aiming to reconfigure Mexico to participate in a globalized world. For some people in Mexico, land has been a source of security, for others a means of control and appeasement. While multiple Mexican administrations have made attempts at land reform, the *campesinos*, the peasants, are consistently left on the periphery of governance and wealth. Today, land disputes remain commonplace in Mexican cities.

Mexico City is, like many places in the global South, living out the wounds of conquest. After various nomadic bands forcefully occupied what is now Mexico City, the Aztecs overcame the Mayans and other tribes in the thirteenth and fourteenth centuries, appro-priating much of their culture, including the Mayan language, pyramids, and calendar. According to some accounts, the Aztecs settled in the Valley of Mexico when they saw an eagle alight upon a cactus while carrying a snake in its beak, an image that their reli-gious prophesies claimed would mark the land that they should occupy and settle, an image that is now emblazoned on Mexico's flag. Upon witnessing this eagle, the Aztecs founded Tenochtitlán (Place of the High Priest Tenoch, named after their leader) upon a large island in Lake Texcoco, which would later be fully drained for the continued construction of modern-day Mexico City.

Even then, land was a matter of "paternalistic reciprocity" and clientelism, a system in which the government or political parties set themselves up as gracious parental figures kind enough to grant citizens such services as roads and sewage systems, rather than viewing these things as government responsibilities.[5] Many officials manipulate their public service so as to grant favors and in turn gain support from people. Recall, for example, Isaura's complaint about the governor's campaign promise to give land deeds to Lomas residents.

The Aztecs concluded that the responsibility of land regulation should fall to a highly centralized government that, at least by design, pursues the corporate good of a diverse public. The government granted people, generally groups of people, the right to possess and work land, though usually within a quid-pro-quo relationship in which peasants gratefully served their gracious rulers.

Two centuries of Spanish colonial rule further ingrained in Mexicans deference to a ruling executive office, as well as state control of private and economic affairs, including the distribution of land, which a few select leaders administrated.

After gaining independence in 1821, Mexico faced incessant economic hardship and political instability, which led to years of foreign intervention and, among other things, the loss of roughly half of Mexico's land to the United States in the Mexican-American War. The 1853 Gadsden Purchase added to this American seizure.

Under *La Reforma* (the Reform Era), the government banned collective landownership. Then the 1857 Constitution enabled the government to dissolve *ejidos*, communally held lands designed to provide farmers with security and a safeguard against land hoarding. This push toward privatization aimed primarily to dismantle the Catholic Church's intimate ties with the government and political power, but these reforms also caused *campesinos* and Indian communities to lose possession of their land.

Then came the *porfiriato*, the dictatorial regime under Porfirio Díaz, whose excesses eventually led to the Revolution of 1910. Large *haciendas* forced small farmers off of their land, and they became common laborers. Land usurpation became a normal part of social progress. Meanwhile, if landowners didn't have their legal title in hand, their land was technically vacant and therefore available for others to occupy.

With 90 percent of the rural population living as landless peasants by 1910 and a growing lack of food and security, Díaz had undercut Mexico's social stability. Emiliano Zapata led a revolution seeking, among other aims, to reinstate a system of communal landownership based on the nation's indigenous past. The resultant 1917 Constitution again legalized collective ownership and made limitations on the accumulation of property.

In short, the government reinstated *ejido* landownership and also claimed final sovereignty over all resources and the right to expropriate them. This made the government responsible for land distribution and prevented the amassing of land into *haciendas* or *ranchos*. Still, while the revolution won new leadership and a reformed constitution, real reform didn't come until the presidency of Lázaro Cárdenas in the late 1930s.

Under Cárdenas, peasants organized, petitioned for land rights, and became communal owners, known as *ejiditarios*, who possessed and worked the *ejidos*. Law dictated that *ejiditarios* pass land on from generation to generation, and they had no right to sell it. The government provided *ejiditarios* with agricultural inputs such as fertilizer or credit, which, when viewed as favors, garnered greater support for the ruling Partido Revolucionario Institucional (PRI), the political group firmly institutionalized as the nation's ruling party during the years following the revolution.

During the 1950s and 1960s, many rural Mexicans migrated to urban centers and squatted on unoccupied land. The government intervened minimally, allowing *colonias* to develop spontaneously and illegally. In 1952, illegal settlements comprised almost a quarter of Mexico City's developed area. Within two decades, this figure increased to between 40 to 50 percent of the city.[6]

The government finally resisted land invasion in the 1970s by developing an extensive bureaucracy to facilitate the enforcement of land laws and, in some cases, formally deed land to claimants. The government has since employed land reform as a means of political mediation and control, a means of delivering payoffs to political allies.

Due to reforms under President Carlos Salinas, from 1988 to 1994, *ejiditarios* may now convert *ejido* land into private land, and the government doesn't limit ownership. But poor records and a backlog of petitions have made this bureaucratic process terribly slow. Only about 1 percent of all *ejido* land was officially privatized by the end of 2000.[7] Also, most *ejiditarios* choose to forgo government channels and instead sell off their land independently, leaving land registrations in even greater disarray. Owners and buyers agree on a price, and money changes hands without public record.

So while on paper *ejiditarios* seem uneager to privatize, in practice they are informally selling or renting it to speculators, squatters, and *hacienda* owners. Meanwhile, economic deregulation and free trade push Mexico's markets toward greater privatization as well. These pressures, combined with population growth and land scarcity, render customary, communal land rights irrelevant.

As in much of the global South, overburdened bureaucracies, conflicting land claims, and poor records impede the Mexican government's efforts at land reform. In Lomas and other *colonias* in peri-urban Mexico City, ineffective reform engenders confusion and litigation. But Mexico's tenurization program, which records landownership and issues deeds, is one of the largest in the world. So bureaucratic structures are, in fact, in place, and Mexico is attempting to make land legally usable for commercial development and private ownership. But the systems are inefficient, and the demands are just too great. Poor rural residents experience the brunt of these failures, and then, in search of security and work, they migrate to Mexico City, Monterrey, Guadalajara, and other cities.

Land disputes often turn deadly. In Chiapas in December 1997, PRI-backed paramilitary men killed forty-five Tzotzil Indians said to be in alliance with the Zapatistas, rebels championing the legendary Emiliano Zapata's quest for land for indigenous peoples and peasants. Most people attributed the mass slaying of twenty-six people in June 2002 in the state of Oaxaca to land disputes between two villages.[8] That same summer, violent protests by poor residents forced the State of Mexico and then the federal government to cancel plans to develop a new airport northeast of Mexico City. The project would have required farmers on the city periphery to cede land.

Opting for nonviolent means, dozens of farmers stripped to their underwear and staged a protest in one of Mexico City's busiest intersections in June 2003, claiming that the former governor of Veracruz had ordered unjustified land seizures and mass arrests. "We are stripping because it is the only way to get attention," said one forty-five-year-old farmer. "We don't have money to buy an ad in the newspapers."[9]

American retirees have even found themselves in the fray. Some 300 of them discovered that the land they purchased and developed in the Punta Banda region of Baja California turned out to be *ejido* land. Their case reached Mexico's Supreme Court, and, in 1999, the original owners won back their land. As is often the case in such conflicts in Mexico, many speculate that corruption also buoyed this boondoggle.

Over the years, land reform in Mexico, even when supposedly aimed at helping the poorest *campesinos*, has failed to serve the people most in need. While the central government has occasionally led successful land-redistribution schemes, more often it has enabled the elite to manipulate and control landownership for their own benefit. Even today, while legal statutes dictate particular rules, on-the-ground realities don't reflect the law.

Land Reform in the Global South

Like Mexico, most nations in the global South have weathered redistributive land reforms over decades and centuries, many of which have led to violence and even deeper inequality. Yet, in agrarian societies, land is critical as a primary source of wealth, culture, and continuity. As the global South populates and urbanizes, as both rural and urban societies battle poverty and faltering economies, land-ownership systems, often complicated and archaic, are failing to meet current demands.

In the Philippines, previous to Spanish rule, municipal governments owned land, and people enjoyed the right to use it. Spanish colonizers introduced individual land titles, which allowed people in power to accumulate land and create huge coconut and rice plantations. The Philippine government has since attempted to implement various reforms, including the Comprehensive Agrarian Reform Program (CARP), established by President Corazon Aquino in 1988 and undergirded by the 1986 Constitution, which emphasizes agrarian land reform as a matter of social justice. Many of today's rural landowners, bolstered by their own elitist pasts, blatantly mock reform and prevent land transfers by burning crops and threatening and murdering farmers. Thus, the majority of farm laborers remain landless, and, according to one researcher, large sugar plantations remain the "last bastion of feudalism in the Philippines."[10] Judges are ignorant of agrarian reform, and the government's bureaucracies aren't prepared to facilitate redistribution. In the end, for land reform to be successful in the Philippines, the government and law enforcement agencies must have the will to implement policies.

The first president of Kenya, Jomo Kenyatta, proudly stated in 1964, "Our greatest asset in Kenya is our land. This is the heritage we received from our forefathers. In land lies our salvation and our survival."[11] Kenya initiated one of the first and most sweeping land reform programs in Africa. Aiming to survey and register all land with individual titles, the government now contends with increased litigation as a result of land disputes and confusion over conflicting rules based in either current law, which favors individual ownership, or tribal custom, which favors communal ownership. As a result, most land transactions continue to occur under technically illegal customary principles that ignore national policy, legal frameworks, and expensive bureaucratic requirements. Even so, Kenya has been an incubator for various experiments with models of communal landownership.[12]

In Bangkok, Thailand, possession of individual land titles is seemingly less important to slum residents than having a general sense of security. In a city choked by traffic, and where location and proximity to employment can be critical concerns for people in informal settlements, maintaining flexibility by informally renting a home rather than owning it is helpful. In fact, formal, regulated landownership can actually cost residents more money and elevate the threat of eviction. Many residents are happy to maintain the status quo, continue to negotiate unwritten rental agreements with landowners, and simply focus on improving services such as water and electricity.

Geoffrey Payne, a leading authority on urban land rights, defines land tenure as "the mode by which land is held or owned, or the set of relationships among people concerning land or its product."[13] As in Mexico, proper systems of land tenure are in fact central to the material development of these and other cities and nations in the global South. Yet, most settlements, including Lomas, Kibera, Mathare Valley, and Balic-Balic, remain mired in disputes over land rights.

Land as Political Patronage

Juan Luis and his wife, Rosa, gradually renovate their home in the *colonia* of Ilhuicamina, just southeast of Mexico City. They began several years ago with the tough, corrugated cardboard that residents of nearby Cartolandia now use. But in stages they've built with cinder block, poured concrete floors, and enclosed walls. They've obtained electricity and water and sewage pipes, for which they pay monthly fees to utility companies. They hope to put in a toilet soon. The entire settlement of Ilhuicamina is building and improving. Meanwhile, most surrounding *colonias* struggle.

Residents have the Antorchistas to thank for their good fortune. An advocacy group associated with the PRI, the Antorchistas bought up land a few years ago and divided it among poor buyers, asking only for a down payment and no rent. Utilizing substantial political clout and money, they then pressured government leaders to provide the residents with services.

To obtain their 1,300 square feet of land and participate in this relative prosperity, Rosa and Juan Luis first put their name on a waiting list. After three years of renting elsewhere, the Antorchistas gave the couple land for a down payment of 3,300 Mexican pesos (about US$360), but then they had to wait another three years for documentation, which even then consisted only of a sticker with a number on it, hardly a legal document. They worry, for they still don't know how much the land will cost in the end, though they guess between 11,000 and 15,000 pesos. They have no contract stipulating these details.

In return for their services, the Antorchistas expect the entire *colonia* to attend regular meetings and rallies. They tell residents where to stand at rallies and even what to say: the rallies are entirely scripted, a sham. Rally chants, according to Lourdes, a resident, include, "We're one man! We're one ideal! Forward, Antorchistas, until we triumph!" and "Let it rain, let it rain! We're not going to move!" (*¡Déjele llover, dejarle llover! ¡No vamos a movernos!*) On election days, the Antorchistas send buses to transport everyone to the polls. It is, of course, expected that they will cast their ballots for PRI candidates. "They're good for those of us who don't have much money," Juan Luis says of the Antorchistas. "We come together as a group."

Still, the couple has no deed to the land. Their housing investments are not their own. They cannot build credit, take out a mortgage, or own their home if they wish. They are in possession of their land and home, but the Antorchistas continue to make the decisions and retain the deed. While eviction and demolition at this stage are unlikely, residents do not enjoy the security provided by strong judicial systems and freely-agreed-upon contracts. They've also forgone the freedom to choose leadership. Juan Luis notes that he knows people who've been "kicked off" the *colonia* for not voting. But in return, Juan Luis and Rosa gain stability and better living conditions.

The Antorchistas—and by extension the PRI—and other similar groups are thus able to advance their own interests as well as maintain social control. They have socially constructed utilities and other services as resources to be paternally withheld or granted, contingent upon support and negotiation, rather than as responsibilities of governing bodies populated by elected officials. The Antorchistas control Juan Luis and Rosa, who have no contract for their land and housing payment. And even if they do eventually establish ownership, the couple will likely still be subject to desultory fees and taxes.

Fortunately, this kind of paternalistic practice is slightly on the wane in Mexico. Various bureaucracies are documenting and registering land, Mexico is becoming more democratic, and people are demanding greater transparency by the government. As the PRI's political monopoly weakens, citizens feel safer to speak out. Newer models of regularization are moving away from clientelistic practices.

Still, the case of Juan Luis and Rosa is indicative of the ways in which the control of land is and has always been a political matter in Mexico. Residents of informal settlements such as Lomas and Ilhuicamina will remain vulnerable as long as they lack secure land rights, community leadership, and economic clout, as long as they are unable to be part of an oppositional voice in a true democracy.

So how do slum residents, at risk of living in destitute poverty on the streets, live securely if they lack legal rights to their land and homes? When they cannot afford rent or ownership in other locations, when they lack other options, how can they live within the dictates of the law? They only have the option of choosing the illegality, ambiguity, and insecurity of squatting. Or, in the case of

Ilhuicamina, they can enjoy a modicum of security and receive basic services such as water and sewerage from political honchos, yet sell their civil souls.

Spontaneous Property Lines

Isabel, a Mexican, and Jared, her American husband, purchased land in Ixtapaluca, a municipality near Lomas and Ilhuicamina, at the current edge of the Mexico City metropolitan area. They know that the final cost for their small grassy plot of undeveloped land is 55,000 pesos (US$6,100), a principal which they gradually pay along with a minimal interest rate. A woman named Susana receives their monthly payment and brokers the sale of about sixty such plots for the owner, a former *ejiditario* who is selling his land privately as allowed by recent reforms. Susana will receive a commission once she sells all the land.

Isabel and Jared aren't certain how they'll use this land. They may eventually move here. They may give it to her mother. Isabel wants her three daughters to have this space to run and play where it is, in her estimation, cleaner and quieter.

Along with a couple of friends, Isabel drives to Ixtapaluca to give Susana a payment. The group begins in a *colonia* with paved roads, but eventually they drive up country hills and on dirt lanes along barbed wire fences, safeguards against invading squatters, before parking in a field overlooking the urban valley. By public transportation they're more than two hours away from the city center. In a matter of months, this peri-urban edge will give way to even more settlements.

Isabel steps out of her car and sees several half-finished cinder-block structures, not yet a story tall, a few cacti and trees, and an unfinished electrical tower.

The group walks for ten minutes over a couple more hills to Susana's home. Upon making the 1,200-peso payment in cash,

Isabel receives a receipt. Susana slings a machete into a leather sheath and over her shoulder. It reaches to her knees. She then escorts the group to see Isabel's land.

They return to the same hill where they parked the car and, after confusedly studying a small map and the terrain, Isabel and Susana believe they've located the correct plot, though initially Isabel was unsure which one was hers. Other landowners—future neighbors—dig into the dry soil and relocate piles of rubble nearby.

Tire tracks have worn a lane into the grass in front of Isabel and Jared's plot. At the far end of this lane, about thirty yards away, a man maneuvers a bulldozer and another man directs him. Three other construction workers sit and watch. One smokes. The crew begins grading the dirt into a workable road, lifting and relocating and pushing soil around until it's flat and fairly consistent in width.

The other land owners who had been working nearby—a couple of men in white ten-gallon hats, a woman in sandals, pinafore, skirt, and ball cap, and several other men—suddenly scramble with a measuring tape in hand to designate their property lines. A couple of men unroll a line of twine and sprinkle lime powder along it and onto the grass to provide the crew with guidelines. The surveying work for this neighborhood, it seems, is as simple and haphazard as that: measuring tape, lime, twine. These guidelines will, in the end, dictate property lines.

Initially, Susana tells Isabel she's merely given the construction workers a few sodas to perform this friendly favor. Only later does Isabel discover that Susana has paid them 800 pesos to bulldoze the street while on their break from other work for their company.

One of Isabel's friends takes photographs until the workers ask him to stop. They ask him if he's some official, whether he'll report their extracurricular work to their company or boss. They fear they could go to prison. He refrains from taking more photos and insists that he's no official. They continue bulldozing.

One of the landowners that helped mark the guidelines tells Isabel and her friends that he worked illegally in California's San Fernando Valley. After five years, he returned to Mexico and bought this land in Ixtapaluca. He proudly points out his wife and "bambinos" and then a twenty-nine-inch Trinitron television box.

"My baby is in the box," he says in English. The child has a birth defect and cannot walk so the family uses the box to hold and move him. The man's wife eventually calls to him to ask for help moving soil and building supplies out of the lane before the bulldozer reaches their plot. The man's television-box-baby remains out of sight.

Those neighbors who don't happen to be here this day will soon discover that their lane has been leveled, and they may or may not agree with the placement of the road in relation to their plot of land. As she watches the boundaries shift, Isabel knows of one neighbor in particular who will likely become angry over this.

Two weeks from now, at Susana's initiative, the landowners will have a meeting to discuss piping water in from the city. The project will require an assessment of 500 pesos from each landowner. They're hoping to have electricity available within a month. The streets will remain unpaved for several years. The land, Isabel believes, will be "official" once electricity and water are in place. These are critical steps in the regularization process.

Fortunately for Isabel and Jared, they're able to afford monthly payments on their land, land that's among those few settlements going through enough of the right channels to obtain legally secure land rights. But they're an exception. And even when land is legally subdivided and sold, much of the process is still ad hoc. Even with the best of efforts, rarely is selling land in Mexico City completely legal or efficient. Just on this day in Ixtapaluca, as Isabel drops off her monthly payment, Susana's map is questionable, a construction crew provides cheap, under-the-table labor, and landowners improvise plot boundaries.

Urban Land Tenure

For as long as people have farmed and settled into homes, villages, and cities, we've been renegotiating our relationships to land for, according to one author:

Land is the source of all material wealth. From it we get every-thing that we use or value, whether it be food, clothing, fuel, shelter, metal, or precious stones. We live on the land and from the land, and to the land our bodies or our ashes are committed when we die. The availability of the land is the key to human existence, and its distribution and use are of vital importance.[14]

As our world urbanizes, our relationships to land and to one another become more intricate. "There are few more contentious and complex problems in the world than those dealing with land and secure tenure," says a UN-HABITAT report on slums. "Many religions have firm rules on land and inheritance, most local com-munities have deeply engrained cultural traditions, and every gov-ernment faces the challenge of land differently with its own vast array of laws."[15] Meanwhile, inequality grows, and a small segment of society maintains dominance over the majority of land and material wealth.

We negotiate claims to land, individually and corporately, for-mally and informally, by law and by custom in ways that enable us to control, use, and exchange land and record expectations. Some people create systems to track land rights using detailed surveys and maps. On the other end of the land tenure spectrum, other people create less stringent and less expensive systems that rely simply on landmarks such as trees, hedges, or rivers to determine boundaries. Societal values, culture, economics, and laws heavily influence the nature of these systems in a given context.

However people manage property rights, agreement among all parties and an efficient, appropriate system for acknowledging these rights are vital. Yet, in many poor nations, land tenure policy is ambiguous, nonexistent, or grounded in colonial bias, and gov-ernments lack the resources necessary for adequate land reform.[16]

Few investors will build or support projects on disputed land. In informal settlements, residents living under the psychological duress of daily uncertainties will not invest in their own homes when eviction seems imminent. Governments without proper land administration and registration cannot levy taxes. They can't efficiently provide services such as water, electricity, and sewage systems. Real estate markets cannot readily function. But with agreed-upon land rights, owners can plan for the future, sell land, and access formal credit. Land rights are so crucial to economic development that UN-HABITAT has made secure land tenure the focus of a global campaign, one of only two campaigns the agency is promoting as of this writing. Indeed, without secure land rights, no real economic development is possible.

Insecure land rights make women and children particularly vulnerable. If formally titled, land owned by a married couple is generally registered in the man's name. If her husband dies, a woman often loses possession of her home. In cases of eviction or land disputes, women's rights are more frequently violated. Children face similar dispossession, particularly those orphaned by violence and the AIDS epidemic. "'[T]here is the issue of property rights,' says Roselyn Mutemi, Kenyan program officer for HIV/AIDS for the United Nations Children's Funds. 'If the children leave their homes, they will lose their claim on their land, and it will be taken by relatives or other unscrupulous people. And in Kenya, if you have no land, it is like having nothing at all.'"[17]

Land tenure takes many forms, including individual land rights backed by formal statutes, which evolved in developed nations, or customary rights based on family or traditional ties with their origins in agricultural societies. Most cultures recognize some form of public tenure to enable the state and populace to hold resources in common. Religious tenure systems base ownership on religious guidelines. Islam, for example, provides for private, communal, state, and religiously derived land rights. The majority of urban settlements rely on informal land rights that provide varying degrees of legitimacy through squatting, illegal subdivisions, and various informal rental agreements. In some cities, through a process known as adverse possession, residents may informally occupy land until, after a legally defined period of time, they automatically gain titled rights to the land.

Under secondary land rights, the right to own land may differ from the right to use land and its resources. In many urban settlements, residents purchase the right to build a home, though landownership remains with the government or some individual.

Tenure systems frequently coexist. Land rights recognized by the law (de jure land rights) may in fact conflict with how people recognize land rights in day-to-day practice (de facto land rights). One author labels these multilayered, often contradictory systems "confused land tenure."[18]

Indigenous claims to land, based in a people's culture, history, and identity, may conflict with municipal efforts to title and regulate land for commercial purposes because officials may leave "gaps" in their definitions of land use or ownership that don't allow for indigenous ideologies.[19] For example, they may set up a false dichotomy between developed land and unused land and appropriate all unused regions, as the British did in Kenya, as if soil must host buildings, infrastructure, roads, or cultivated fields for someone to justify a claim, whereas indigenous people may base ownership definitions more on trade or grazing routes or familial tradition.

Vital to creating a workable land tenure system is accurate, current information on landownership, existing conflicts, geography, and natural resources. But gathering and managing this information to create maps, plans, files, and databases is expensive and time consuming, not to mention teeming with political conflict and corruption in some places. In most poor nations, official records don't account for more than 70 percent of the land.[20]

The majority of countries have attempted to implement land reform at various points in their history, some with more success than others. In Asia, Japan, China, and Korea have enjoyed the benefits of recent reform, while many Latin American reforms have failed to meet their objectives because of resistance from rich landowners and institutional barriers.[21] During America's first 100 years, the United States Congress passed more than 500 laws reforming property systems as squatters pushed westward. Over time, politicians had no choice but to recognize squatters' claims and either write new laws or let the squatters reside illegally, a concession made frequently today by leaders in the global South.[22]

Many land reform programs fixate on individual private property as the end goal and ignore existing property rights. Most planners and governments simply assume the superiority of individual titles while letting economic interests and politics dictate the nature of reform, though some are beginning to experiment with other models that accommodate communal and customary land rights. In Kenya, community land trusts are enabling some people to jointly own and control land, while retaining individual use and building rights. Such models champion indigenous traditions of common property.

Hernando de Soto, economist and founder of the Institute for Liberty and Democracy in Lima, Peru, says that poor people own the material means necessary to prosper but that they simply need access to the formal sector—in land, employment, housing, and education and so on—to participate fully in society and economic progress. Reformers should, in de Soto's estimation, work with local, informal systems already in place and integrate them into the formal sector: "Creating one national social contract on property involves understanding the psychological and social processes—the beliefs, desires, intentions, customs, and rules—that are contained in these local social contracts and then using the tools that professional law provides to weave them into one formal national social contract."[23]

As informal settlements integrate, they enable local authorities to plan development efforts better, they contribute to a city's tax base, and they improve the efficiency of land markets. Residents with formal land rights have more incentive to invest in their property and to utilize their assets as collateral for credit. In most places, these arguments have convinced officials to establish tenure systems that provide formal individual titles.

Many argue, though, that formal ownership of land and other property is not an adequate solution. Geoffrey Payne counters that Bangladesh, for example, has a higher level of formal landownership than Switzerland or Germany and that the poor generally lack easy entry into formal systems of ownership because they are expensive to administer and therefore expensive to access.[24] And though the poor cannot use formal credit and banks, they do in fact borrow money and resources from family, friends, and neighbors and may not trust formal institutions. And some residents simply prefer the mobility of informality.

In terms of land, formal individual titles—otherwise known as freehold tenure—are an option, and often a good option, but they are not the only option. Freehold titles can provide standardization, efficiency, and clarity and can even maximize land's commercial value. But automatically defaulting to this form of landownership may be inappropriate in some settings.

In the Philippines, the Kabalaka Homeowners Association, a network of community-based organizations, helped households organize and collectively save money, purchase a plot of land, and then negotiate with the Philippines National Housing Authority to help develop the new settlement. Collectively, they enjoyed greater leverage and security than they did as individual owners.[25] In Cairo, bureaucratic processes make legal, individual landownership virtually impossible. Intermediate tenure solutions, such as temporary rental agreements in Bangkok, which give squatters security and landowners income, provide flexibility and enable people to adapt to economic and social changes without facing a violent, disruptive eviction.

These arguments represent just some of the international debate over urban land tenure. For the purposes of this book, they begin to provide a context for understanding issues of land rights in informal settlements.

Joanne and Sammy Seares cannot purchase their home in Balic-Balic in Manila, yet they want to make it comfortable and safe by painting the walls, securing a front gate so that Jam-Jam doesn't wander outside and onto the train tracks, and fixing the roof if it leaks during the rainy season. Yet if they're evicted, they have nothing to show for their improvements, and they could, in one night, lose everything.

In Mexico City in Lomas de San Isidro, the local government will likely not provide Letty, Ana, and other residents with running water and garbage removal as long as the neighborhood's land rights remain in question. Juan Luis and Rosa will not make free election decisions as long as they're dependent on the Antorchistas for the right to build a home. Isabel and Jared will patiently watch their neighborhood develop through haphazard planning until the municipality and landowners can afford to create better maps and replace corruption with adequate employment.

Residents of Kibera in Nairobi will continue to live in fear of violence as long as the allocation of land depends more on illicit favors, bribes, and ethnicity than on fair, legal land rights.

More than formal land rights, though, slum residents need security from eviction. They need the assurance that they can upgrade their homes and neighborhoods. They need the time that security provides to negotiate with landowners and governments to find solutions to land conflicts.[26]

They gain security when the government implements upgrading schemes or provides a few services, implicitly recognizing a settlement's legitimacy. Also, when residents occupy homes for several years they develop this sense of security.

In many instances, residents do receive rights to their land but then face market evictions: they receive land titles, but suddenly they cannot afford to pay the accompanying taxes or utility fees, and they quickly lose their homes. They need security before legal ownership, because once their land and home are formal and legal, people with more money and power can easily justify a seizure of their property. But security gives residents a chance to improve their neighborhoods and begin working their way out of poverty.

In Nairobi, for example, temporary-occupation licenses allow some residents to build semipermanent structures by paying the government an annual fee. Though originally intended for commercial use, residents are using these licenses successfully to establish homes and stabilize their lives. While these homes remain temporary, they are secure, and residents can get on their social and economic feet without the daily fear of eviction.[27]

Therefore, many people are now advocating for slum upgrading schemes and alternative titling programs and encouraging governments to phase out eviction and relocation schemes.[28] Governments and NGOs must learn to work with slum residents, within informal processes, rather than against them, by helping people formally participate in market and government processes, but only incrementally, over time. They must recognize on-the-ground needs for security before thrusting programs on residents that simply endanger what little security they enjoy.

Security in Valle de Chalco

While visiting people in various *colonias* in Mexico City, I stay with Aline and her sons, Denzel and Gustavo, a working-class family in Valle de Chalco, just a few miles from Lomas. After many interviews and much travel, I hit a wall: I want rest and I want to hear English and I want to be alone. But at the behest of Aline, we all pile into a car at nine o'clock in the evening and head off to a children's birthday party. We're joined by Paloma, Aline's sister from Acapulco, and her three year-old daughter, Fatima; Angie, a friend of Paloma's; and Jared and Isabel and their three young daughters.

Birthday parties in Mexico are very much about the guests. After stepping into a ballooned and streamered courtyard, meeting the cheerful hosts, and finding seats at a table, we settle in to enjoy some gifts, though we discover that we've missed the breaking of the piñata. We begin with a spicy barbequed meat sauce over rice before feasting on birthday cake. The children each receive wrapped boxes of candy and then a cartoon-character plant holder, Barney, Winnie the Pooh, Tigger, and others. The father of the house wanders by our table, a bottle of tequila in hand, and offers it to Jared and me. Salsa music flits from a radio, into the cool evening.

As one of only two gringos among some forty people, I arouse from my earlier fatigue and attempt to salsa. Paloma and Angie laugh as they dance and watch my syncopated wrangling with rhythm. I lose this struggle with my own body and desperately turn to teaching those around me how to swing dance. Other partygoers stare. My friends show me, once again, how to celebrate.

When we return home at midnight, everyone is ready to sleep. Aline and the others had spent much of the last twenty-four hours cooking for more than one hundred people at a regional meeting for AMEXTRA, the development NGO that works in Lomas. Returning from the market yesterday evening with bags of peppers, cilantro, limes, tomatoes, beans, chickens, eggs, and tortillas, Aline and company had diced and simmered their way long into the night.

On this, the final night of my stay, after overcoming their insistent refusal, I take the floor, and Angie, Paloma, and her daughter, Fatima, all snuggle into the bed, a bed I'd previously had all to myself while they slept on the floor and on couches.

It's in Chalco, after losing support here in the 1988 presidential election, that the PRI launched a new initiative entitled Solidarity to bring running water, electricity, and paved streets to what was then a mess of muddy lanes and tin and wood structures, much like present-day Lomas. Also hoping, of course, to regain political support, then-president Carlos Salinas announced the ambitious Solidarity program in a Chalco plaza amidst much political pomp. He then toured the nation, handing out land titles, listening to people's concerns, and promoting the program.

At its peak, the program sank US$3 billion a year into more than thirty programs in an attempt to alleviate rural and urban poverty.[29] Many people in Chalco hailed the program's involvement of local residents who dug water lines and prepared streets for paving. But by 1994 the PRI had regained political support in

Chalco. The PRI successor of Salinas, Ernesto Zedillo, dismantled Solidarity and reallocated the budget to state and local authorities.

María Elena Martínez Garcia of AMEXTRA tells me that Chalco developed after residents received secure land rights, as well as the support of lawyers to continue applying pressure on the government to install and upgrade services. To her knowledge, Lomas de San Isidro doesn't have this kind of political leverage to work for regularization.

Many residents complain that the Solidarity program used cheap materials. Water lines have since cracked and broken frequently. According to one forty-five-year-old widow, "When it rains, the water doesn't work and the lights go out. The sewage system has never worked."[30] A canal floods on occasion, leaving many homes saturated in untreated sewage and causing people to become ill. At one point 90 percent of illnesses in Chalco were intestinal infections, generally caused by polluted water as well as by air pollution that settles in the water supply.[31]

I discover that most streets in Chalco are paved and homes have been upgraded to concrete. Numerous stores and tiny restaurants thrive. Though living conditions still leave many people without reliable water and electricity, conditions are better than a couple of decades ago, before Solidarity.

Quite possibly, Lomas, which is today what Chalco was in the late 1980s, will someday experience similar improvements, though currently Lomas serves José and Letty and others as a lower, more affordable rung on the housing ladder.

Aline's home has a courtyard, three bedrooms, a small common room with a television, and then a bathroom and a kitchen. Curtains serve as interior doors, so when the television comes on much earlier than I would ever hope, I wake each morning. We watch *telenovelas*, ultradramatic soap operas, as well as a day of funeral proceedings and interviews commemorating the life of a Mexican movie sensation who passed away this week.

While here, I stay in Gustavo's bedroom, which likely resembles many American eight-year-old boys' rooms: a plush, orange

Garfield, a Woody doll and a Buzz Lightyear–quilt wall hanging celebrating the *Toy Story* movies, a Mickey Mouse poster, sailboat wallpaper, a remote control dump truck, and Old Spice deodorant. A placard hangs above the bed depicting an angel watching over two children. The prayer reads, in Spanish, "Guardian Angel, my sweet company, do not abandon me, neither by night nor by day."

Aline's family has other appliances, more than I'd expected, including a stove, microwave, refrigerator, and a washing machine, though I find I must add extra water from a hose for the washer to work properly. The kitchen is fairly bare, with a painted cement floor and walls, plastic patio furniture, and a table for food preparation. The only wall hangings are merely functional, a pot holder, an umbrella, a bag full of serving spoons.

Like many families in Chalco, Aline and her husband, whom I see only a couple of mornings during my time here, keep two guard dogs on the flat roof of their home. But while their bark is fierce, they turn docile once scolded.

The bathroom, also like many area homes, is a work in progress: a new, blue ceramic toilet, but without a seat; fashionable blue tiles with a water-puddle pattern—but only on half of the walls; a sink, but the pipes leak directly onto my feet and the floor. To keep the dogs out while in the bathroom, I must tie the door closed.

Several mornings in a row I turn the "C" knob on the shower but only get hot water, no matter how long I wait. One tired morning, just as my thoughts begin to condemn the shower, the piping, the lousy plumber who installed them, the manufacturer of the pipes, Aline and her husband, and even the president and the country and culture of Mexico, who seem to have no notion what cold water is and why someone taking a shower might desire it in such torrid weather . . . I finally contemplate the "F" knob and want to smack my forehead in wonder at my own ineptitude and poor penchant for making cultural assumptions. I recall that the word for "cold" in Spanish is *frío* and "hot" in Spanish is *caliente*. The "C," I finally conclude, means *caliente*. I take a cool shower and later feel myself work even harder to ingratiate myself to my hostesses who know so much more than I about navigating life in their context.

Each breakfast and dinner, Aline, Paloma, and Angie cook up simple and wonderful meals, always with beans and tortillas. We relate while we eat, and I hone my Spanish and they their English. We enjoy honey out of a five-gallon bucket that Paloma brought from the coast, from Acapulco. My favorite culinary discovery is *napoles*, a sweet cactus that cooks rather like okra, gooey and stringy.

Paloma, who is twenty years old and sells automobile parts, is visiting for the month so that she can see a doctor in Mexico City for a shoulder injury. She translates some of our group conversation as she speaks some English, and she gracefully corrects me with good natured giggling when I bungle my Spanish. Our conversation ranges from the kids to Mexico City to food to Paloma's tropical home.

"Why do you choose Mexico?" Paloma asks me.

I tell her of the short distance I needed to travel, the relationships I already had in Mexico.

"You come to see the poor people," she adds.

"Yeah, like most any country Mexico has poor people, but I'm traveling to many different countries to study neighborhoods like Cartolandia."

Paloma takes in my response, then asks, "What do you think of Mexico City?" I share my thoughts about the places I've already visited, some of the usual cultural hot spots in the city center, the Zocalo, the Templo Mayor, the murals of Diego Rivera. Paloma responds with tales of Acapulco, the beautiful lagoons, the rivers, the beaches where she lives, the "tranquility." She wants me to know that Mexico is about more than poverty, about more than poor people. In my own words, I, too, celebrate the people I've met, the culture, the food, the landscapes of Mexico, but I fear this fails to assuage her concern.

A few days later, Aline and Paloma offer to sell me silver heart earrings from the southern state of Gurrero for 110 pesos. They're pinned to plain cardboard and priced in handwritten ink. I quietly hedge for several moments. I don't know if I should bargain or whether it would be more culturally sensitive to purchase the earrings as a means of reimbursing them for my stay. I also fear that my cash for this trip is dwindling. Finally, I sheepishly blurt out, in broken Spanish, "I have a budget for my trip, and I do not have much money."

Paloma shakes her head. She is quietly passionate. "You have a budget," she says, "Mexicans have nothing."

I fear I've lost their trust. It requires impossible vigilance to prevent my affluence from affecting my relationships here. It is, in fact, impossible, and I'm saddened by this wedge between us. Days later I purchase the earrings and give them to my fiancée. They break before she can don them.

I become more concerned that this wedge is growing, but by the end of my stay we're enjoying our final meals together and dancing at the birthday party. I realize that their hospitality assumes friendship, regardless of economic or political wedges beyond our control. They've taken me in as a friend of a friend, and while they may wonder about life in the States, the ease and opportunity of America, they hold no outward resentment, only acceptance and warmth. Yet, it's terrible irony that they should put themselves out so selflessly, offering me the best of what they have, even while I come with a mission to serve. I need their help as much as they need mine.

One night the electricity goes out during a thunderstorm. Veiled light cast by candles and flashlights helps us relax with one another even more than usual. We break into spontaneous singing and a game in which each person must sing a solo, after which everyone else, in turn, scores the singing on a scale from zero to five, five being the highest of scores. If every member votes with an impassioned "Cinco!" then everyone leaps out of his or her chair and dances around the room. I know few songs, but I sing "Amazing Grace" and earn a resounding "Cinco!" across the board. Jubilation ensues.

We then play the same game while performing impersonations. Gustavo stoically rises from his seat, his chest puffed out. Awkwardly gesticulating with his hands, as if responding to a cheering crowd, and in a gruff voice, he says, "Yo soy Vicente Fox!" The room explodes in laughter, and though he earns a high score, no one is composed enough to stand and dance. We eventually do the limbo and then another Latino dance, all of this in the comfort of their simple kitchen.

Aline, through her hospitality and obvious affection for Gustavo and Denzel, and Paloma, proud of her Acapulco homeland, tacitly proclaim that Mexico is about more than illegal immigration, poverty, or squabbles over land or free trade. Mexico City is about more than squatter families subsisting on basic food staples in makeshift lean-tos. So much more than being a social problem, Lomas and Chalco and other *colonias* are, simply and foremost, home.

Aline and her family live in relative security because social and legal forces have, over time, come to ensure this security. After years of settlement regularization and progress, systematic seizure of homes in Chalco seems unlikely. But in nearby Lomas, Letty and other residents have little security and, in the event of eviction, little recourse, but they have no better options for shelter.

By not properly managing urban land and making it equally accessible to all, our world dispossesses millions of people of the right to lead a secure, healthy life on unpolluted soil in safe shelters. Such dispossession brings desolation to people's sense of place and even wounds their self-worth and identity. Then, by overburdening the land, we also pollute water tables and rivers, create massive landfills, and degrade general living conditions.

In the Bible, land is part of God's creation, a source of wealth and empire, a personal entitlement for the Israelites, and many other things, but, most importantly, land is a gift from God for human tenants to steward justly and wisely. Thus while people do own land, this ownership is not absolute: "The land shall not be sold in perpetuity, for the land is mine; with me you are but aliens and tenants" (Leviticus 25:23, NRSV). And consistently in the Bible good stewardship involves ensuring that individuals not hoard land and riches.[32]

We must properly steward land to ensure fair distribution and enable urban residents to participate in society through impartial, legal means that affirm personal dignity. And we must celebrate the intrinsic value and social importance of land, beyond its market values and pragmatic uses.

Without good, fair land management, we cannot create equitable, life-giving cities.

The Seares family home along the railway tracks in Balic-Balic.

Jam-Jam and Joanne Seares in their home.

A train rumbles through Balic-Balic.

Payatas, a garbage village near Metro Manila.

A vendor sells vegetables in a Nairobi slum.

Mathare Valley, Nairobi.

Children play in a walkway in one of Nairobi's informal settlements.

Children attend class in a Mathare Valley school.

Lomas de San Isidro, near Mexico City.

Residents near Mexico City quickly mark their property lines as bulldozers approach.

Electrical lines in one of Mexico City's informal settlements.

Letty and her daughter, Navy, in Lomas de San Isidro.

Klong Toey, Bangkok.

A cockfight in Klong Toey.

A major street in the Mokattam garbage village.

Zabaleen sort trash in Mokattam.

Women weave rags into rugs at the Association for the Protection of the Environment in Mokattam.

5

Bangkok

Life in the Shadows

JIAP DANCES IN A TINY BIKINI and sells sex to foreign tourists.
Family members, including her mother, herself a sex worker during the Vietnam War servicing soldiers in Bangkok, encouraged Jiap to leave their rural village in northern Thailand to earn money in the sex industry. Jiap began her career as a prostitute in Bangkok at the age of fourteen.[1]

She worked in a massage parlor for three years and paid off some debts. Then she moved up in the sex-trade ranks. "Because the customers like me, and I give good service," she says, "I got a better job in a bar, and I entertain a lot of foreigners." Jiap has also worked in Pattaya, Thailand, and Japan.

Bangkok is infamous for its trade in sex. In Patpong and other red-light districts, local and foreign tourists visit bars named Super Pussy, Lucifer Disko, and Supergirls that feature pole dancers, sex-show menus, and women for sale in rows of glass showcases. Like Jiap, many women are poor and come eager to earn good money in sex. Others are trafficked from the countryside or other countries, duped into believing that they'll work as a housemaid or waitress only to find themselves in debt-bondage to a brothel owner.

But the vast majority of sex workers in Bangkok service local clients in massage parlors and back rooms in clubs scattered throughout the city, away from concentrated districts like Patpong. Pink and red neon lights, evocative names like New Love and

Perfect Place, and lingering women in short skirts identify the establishments. Though the sex industry is difficult to track, some researchers say that as many as 2.8 million people are involved in the sex trade in Thailand.[2]

"This is good work for me," Jiap concludes, "because I can send money to my family. My brother has a motorbike and perhaps one day we can buy a car. My family has already made another room in the house with the money I sent them. They are very happy and proud that I am more successful than other girls in my village."

For half her life Ploey has run drugs in Bangkok. She's "walked" a few pills, three or four times a day. She's also moved larger hauls of hundreds of pills across the city, making her a legend among her peers. Ploey is petite, intelligent, and charming, and, because she's female, cops are reluctant to body search her. So she's good at walking drugs from dealers to buyers, and in Bangkok business is good, though for each shipment, worth anywhere from 25,000 to 50,000 baht ($575 to US$1,150), she earns only 20 baht (US$.50).[3]

But Ploey is only twelve years old, and her dealer is her aunt, Moe-li, who lies to her, insists that the drug money is going to support Ploey's parents in prison. Moe-li, along with her boyfriend, doesn't allow Ploey to leave their home except to run pills. They refuse to let her sleep under their mosquito net, but instead tell her to save up her drug earnings to buy one for herself. Ploey no longer attends school. Ploey has no friends. She does have a younger sister, Ying, but she lives with other relatives and is dying of AIDS, which their mother passed on to her at birth.

Ploey learned the drug trade from her heroin-addicted parents. She learned that she shouldn't bargain with buyers, talk to strangers, or reveal routes and customer names to friends. She learned that if she's in trouble while making a delivery, she should stash the pills and run. If apprehended, she should claim complete ignorance and deny everything. She's learned that children her age can go to prison for walking drugs, but only for three years, whereas adults, such as her parents, risk much longer sentences and even death. Fortunately, Ploey hasn't learned drug dependency.

And, fortunately, the police caught Ploey on a routine drug walk one day as she exited a settlement. She'd asked her taxi driver to stop in a secluded area, and, as she relieved herself by the side of the road, Ploey dropped her stash of pills. Police trailing Ploey nabbed her and the pills and refused to believe her protests exonerating Moe-li and her boyfriend. They went to prison.

Ploey went to the Mercy Centre, a temporary home for street kids in Klong Toey, a large settlement in southeast Bangkok where Ploey was born and raised. Fortunately, Mercy Centre helped Ploey return to school. In Klong Toey, drug runners like Ploey aren't rare and school is a luxury.

"Many young lives are being destroyed," says Rotjana Phraesrithong, a social worker for the Duang Prateep Foundation, a Klong Toey–based agency that provides residents with education and community development. While many people deal in heroin, the drug of choice is amphetamines, Rotjana says. "There are dangerous things in them that make people go crazy. We found that many families use the children, the younger children to send the amphetamines and other drugs to people because the children, they are innocent. They don't know how to say no and they don't know what they do."[4]

The government has in recent years made a point of cracking down on drug dealers and users in Klong Toey, sending more than one hundred police officers on raids and seizing firearms, millions of dollars worth of drugs, and logs listing dealers' clients. During a ten-month nationwide campaign in 2003, thirty-five police officers and almost two hundred suspects died in the government's highly controversial war on drugs, though many people, critical of the government's heavy-handed abuse of residents and lack of due process, claim that thousands of people actually died in the violence. Police arrested 90,000 drug suspects and seized 40 million amphetamine tablets, and, claims one local activist, they removed more than 90 percent of drug abusers from Klong Toey.[5] But drug dealers and buyers quickly returned, and drugs are still a major problem in the settlement.

Through the Foundation, volunteers and police have coordinated drug watches, though dealers have threatened Prateep Ungsongtham Hata, the foundation's director, and others. One activist, Chusi, her face bloated and stitched together, says she almost lost vision after some men beat her. Each Saturday evening, brave volunteers and police officers patrol a different neighborhood in Klong Toey to campaign against the use of amphetamines and heroin.

"Our patrols give people in the community a chance to see that we are actively fighting this terrible problem," says the director.

And also for the people who are selling drugs when they see our movement some of them slow down their business a little bit. . . . And some of the people who have money in this business they are against me. They do all kinds of things to scare me. They telephone me. They send someone to my house at night. Not just only me though. Other community leaders are also in the same situation. But I told them, don't be afraid, because everyone sooner or later has to die. But if we die, the [fight will] carry on.[6]

The Informal Sector

Drug running and prostitution are just a few of the illicit informal businesses prevalent in Bangkok. Other activities include money laundering, smuggling stolen goods, and fraud. But most informal work occurring beyond the watchful eye of government regulation, in Klong Toey and other settlements in the global South, is less antisocial. Unable to access the formal sector because of a lack of education, money, or connections, and because the formal sector suffocates under bureaucratic largesse and corruption, millions of people set up their own means for making a living. It's this informal sector—not only in work but also in housing, finance, travel, and various other arenas—that comprises the backbone of economies in developing nations. "Indeed," says one urban theorist, "the global informal working class (overlapping but non-identical with the slum population) is almost one billion strong: making it the fastest growing, and most unprecedented, social class on earth."[7]

The informal sector, also referred to as the underground, parallel, or shadow sector, defies a stringent definition, but it involves activities beyond the reach of government regulation that are both patently illegal, such as drug dealing, and legal, such as selling newspapers, repairing a roof, or constructing a home. Foremost, people work and live in the informal sector because they lack the skills, training, connections, money, or even the ability to read and write, which can be necessary to secure a formal job, begin a formal business, or build a legal home.

In 1973, anthropologist Keith Hart first noted the concept of an informal sector, which has grown rapidly as cities have grown, particularly in the global South.[8] After initial battles to eradicate the informal sector by rounding up street vendors and evicting residents of squatter settlements, governments are beginning to partner with the informal sector to improve homes and working conditions and reform markets to better accommodate the urban poor. Governments are recognizing the informal sector as a legitimate, even if incomplete, response to societal needs.

In terms of employment, informal workers, unlike formal workers, generally do not enjoy set wages and hours. Their working conditions are not regulated for health and safety, and they lack insurance, credit, job security, long-term contracts, and opportunities for professional development. For the most part, they don't have union representation. Neither do informal workers pay taxes on their earnings.[9]

Yet people with little education can easily access informal jobs. They're often family-run, and they allow people to maintain mobility and flexibility. The very young, very old, and women dominate the informal workforce. Often self-employed, people labor outside the letter of the law and on a small scale, strategizing just to survive.

Street vendors are the most visible of informal workers in developing nations.[10]

Other informal workers include brick makers, construction workers, cleaners, pedicab drivers, small artisans, furniture makers, and home-based workers who cut hair, butcher animals, and repair appliances, just to name a few. The informal workforce has, in fact, built the cities—the skyscrapers, highways, and infrastructure—of the global South.

In Balic-Balic, Manila, Yole Galang sells fried *bananacue* outside her home, and farther down the tracks men provide rides on improvised table-carts. Young boys in Kibera, Nairobi, shine shoes for a small fee, and Letty in Lomas de San Isidro, near Mexico City, sells rice, cornmeal, and soap.

These entrepreneurs aren't just setting up lemonade stands and depending on the magnanimity of passersby to earn a little extra side money. They're working long, hard hours, often in difficult conditions and at great personal risk, just to earn enough income to eat and pay the rent. They've created a parallel, informal sector adapted to their needs, resources, and capabilities, in employment and housing, transportation, credit and lending, governance, and other areas. Yet, they have few opportunities for improving their living conditions, getting higher paying, more secure jobs, or furthering their educations.

Even so, the informal and formal sectors aren't exclusive of each other. A mother working out of her home may earn cash for assembling a product that a registered, tax-paying company then legally sells to formal, registered business outlets. Informal vendors rely on formal shops and market trends for their products and business strategies. Day laborers make a major contribution toward constructing skyscrapers, offices, homes, and roads in the global South. Hotel housekeepers who lack formal work contracts depend on tourists visiting local, government-funded attractions. In Nairobi, the informal sector, or *jua kali*, provides the formal sector with manufacturing and repair services and welders, metalworkers, mechanics, carpenters, and construction workers generate value-added goods.[11]

In basic commodities such as coffee, tea, and bananas, or manufactured goods such as computers and sports shoes, informal workers may earn just a fraction of what formal employees earn to do the same job. Regional companies and transnational corporations subcontract with companies that subcontract with companies that subcontract with informal workers who don't work in a regulated environment, making labor conditions difficult to monitor.

Informality also complicates brands and intellectual property rights. Current technology allows bootleggers to reproduce CDs, DVDs, and computer software without inhibition, and myriad shoppers in the global South don sweatshirts with home-sewn Adidas or Nike emblems.

The informal and formal sectors do not represent a linear progression in which people simply work their way up from the informal to the formal. Often workers and residents shuttle between the two sectors, or simultaneously work and live in each of them. And by some estimates, fully two-thirds of money earned within the informal economy is spent in the formal economy.[12]

The informal sector isn't exclusive to developing nations, though it is much smaller in rich countries. When a skilled professional, construction worker, or computer technician performs off-the-clock duties for untaxed, cash income, he or she is participating in an informal economy, as is the drug dealer, prostitute, and pimp.

Nor is the informal sector completely free from the tethers of regulation. Trust, violence, and social sanctions motivate people to behave according to the local rules, whatever they may be. By building trust and social capital among associates, people ensure future business, security, and help in times of need. When squatters forcefully take over land or a sidewalk plot for vending, they rely on violence to grab what they want, and the threat of violence to maintain control. Local sources of informal authority, such as neighborhood bosses, vendors' associations, or police officers acting beyond their formal duties, may exact bribes or exclude people who disrupt the local rules of business. Ethnicity, caste, gender, and age also reinforce social norms that regulate life in informal sectors. People employ these regulations according to their context. In most cases, for example, violence can have costly consequences that outweigh any benefits, so people use force sparingly.[13]

In fact, to function properly, the formal sector actually relies on informal regulations. For contracts and other formal structures to operate, they require trust, relationships, and networks, interpretations of law, reputation, collective experiences, and general morals and ethics. Without these, even the most thorough regulations will prove powerless. Informal sectors rest on these same foundational precepts. To be successful, any outside interventions must, therefore, negotiate with regulatory frameworks already in place in informal sectors.[14]

In sum, when we talk of informal and formal sectors, we must view them not as two exclusive options for workers or residents or shoppers, but two nodes within a complex societal web, nodes intricately connected by various means of earning an income and setting up a home. Most people in the global South, particularly the poor, aren't focused on linear career trajectories. Nor are most of them pining for careers in illicit, antisocial work in drugs or illegal money-making schemes. They're just trying to make a living using whatever means—formal or informal—happen to be available to them.

We should, therefore, discuss the informal sector in terms of degrees of illegality or legality, rather than through either/or scenarios. José works as a policeman in Mexico City, yet he's building a home in the squatter settlement of Lomas, where he'll purchase water from a private company yet steal electricity from metered homes in the valley. Jane Matiba earns money by plaiting women's hair, and she lives in Mathare Valley, an illegal settlement, though she shops at stores in downtown Nairobi for certain goods, and two of her children attend a state-sponsored school. Juan Luis and Rosa, in Ilhuicamina near Mexico City, enjoy relative security, metered utilities, and community organization on land owned by the Antorchistas, yet they lack political voice or a contract that formally ties them to their home and land. These residents live in both formal and informal sectors to survive.

Klong Toey, Bangkok

Yung lives in a crawl space. Though she is tall, thin-boned, and gray haired, she has about four feet of vertical living space, from the linoleum ground to the house's floor beams. For twenty years now she's endured beneath this home on the fringe of Klong Toey. Her sister and brother-in-law and their four children live upstairs. He works as a crewman for the Port Authority of Thailand (PAT).[15]

Piles of clothes and boxes squeeze into nooks in the foundation walls. A cockeyed mirror reflects the smiling images of Yung and her niece, Tasanee, as they sit in front of a screaming television. Yung, after reluctantly leaving a factory job in another part of Bangkok, originally moved here so she could help raise her younger sibling's twins.

But recently Yung and her family received notice that they have two months to vacate their home. Their landlord, who lives outside of Klong Toey, has apparently decided to sell the building, and the family must leave. They know of no way to stop him. They have no lease agreement to which they can hold the landlord accountable.

Until now, their working agreement has benefited both parties: Yung's family rents a home they can afford; the owner receives income while investing virtually no maintenance or repairs in the property and making no official, long-term commitments.

For two decades the family has paid rent as well as monthly water and electrical bills issued by the government. They've also made all structural improvements, including a new roof. If evicted they'll see no return on these investments, and because they don't own the home or land, they cannot use them as collateral to access formal credit. Attempts to borrow from local banks have been fruitless.

Yung prays, and when she prays, she cries. Her greatest dream is to see her twin nieces, who are eighteen and in school, secure good jobs.

With well over 100,000 residents, Klong Toey, in the city's southeast region on the Chao Phraya River, is Bangkok's largest settlement, a bit of an anomaly here, as most settlements are smaller with only a few hundred residents squeezed between dense roads, canals, and buildings. The Port Authority of Thailand, a state agency, claims control over most of Klong Toey and determines which sections of the settlement are slated for demolition and commercial construction. The PAT dictates the speed and force by which people are evicted.

Residents of Klong Toey are victims of a civil bait and switch. In the 1930s, the government made the land of present-day Klong Toey available to low-income renters, many of whom moved here and helped build the port. At the time, land was abundant in Bangkok. But then the government created the Port Authority and, in effect, abolished its land-rental agreement with the people of Klong Toey. Legal renters became illegal squatters.[16]

But people continued to flock to Klong Toey because of its proximity to the city center and its ideal location for informal work in Bangkok. Residents of the settlement have long worked in construction and as taxi drivers, in slaughter houses and in the sex industry, cleaning streets, recycling garbage, and as vendors. Many residents also worked, as they do today, for the Port Authority and other shipping companies. Ironically, when the creation of the PAT terminated the rental agreement, more people moved to Klong Toey because they could occupy vacant areas rent-free.

Today, the heart of Klong Toey is fairly well established with a few two-lane, paved roads that guide cars and motorcycle taxis past restaurants, groceries, 7-Elevens, electronics and film-processing stores, and various other merchants on the first floor of four-story buildings. Vendors sell fish and watermelon. They fry rice and vegetables and meat. A banner, sponsored by Pepsi and spanning the main street, welcomes visitors.

Off the main road, though, paths are narrow, and they wind between homes of wood and corrugated metal abutting one another. The tight quarters and incessant sounds of dogs barking and people arguing, laughing, yelling, and cooking make one feel that a visitor is always at your doorstep in Klong Toey. Flooding is a regular problem here, and wood planks traverse standing water and plastic jugs, soft-drink bottles, snack wrappers, styrofoam food containers, and other garbage. Electricity lines run along roof edges.

Aran Kaenboon, fifty-seven, recalls flying kites and hearing birds in the Klong Toey of his childhood. He recalls open spaces and high-growing grass, fishing in a clean canal by his home and accompanying his father to scavenge and sell scrap metal by boat. Along with his parents and six siblings, Aran lived where a highway now bisects the district, having moved here from the countryside when he was a small boy. Today, Aran lives in the center of the Klong Toey settlement. The canal of his childhood is now sewage ridden, though children still swim in it to cool off.

Sitting in his family's Klong Toey bakery one muggy morning, Aran takes a break from work. His wife, Vanida, decorates the cakes, he says, and he tends to other "bits and pieces" of the business. Located on the settlement's main thoroughfare, the bakery has cases of cakes, wooden tables and chairs, and large windows so that passersby may gawk at his wife's handiwork.

Aran bemoans the crowds and squalor in Klong Toey. "It was difficult because most people came from other provinces, because a lot of people have left their wives, families, and parents to look for jobs. If the government provided enough to survive in the provinces, enough help so people could grow food to eat and use and sell, they wouldn't need to come here."

The railway tracks that course through the poorest part of the settlement have been here for many years, he says. Concrete has replaced some of the wood walkways. Though at times the PAT has uprooted people from their homes, residents generally find their way back.

Fires have destroyed buildings on all three sides of Aran's bakery and home. Initially he was alarmed, but over time he became used to the fires. He blames them on his neighbors' carelessness with candles and gas within highly flammable homes. He, however, is careful to turn off gas lines when they're not in use and ensures that rats don't chew through them.

Aran describes working various jobs as a young man. When he met his wife he was selling rice. Aran then turns in his chair, calls behind the counter and into the kitchen. A woman's voice responds. She was twenty-five. He was a few years older.

Aran admits that he and his family are not normal in Klong Toey. Most people here marry at an early age and, he emphasizes, have few skills and won't work hard. "Selling drugs is easy work."

Growing up, he watched his parents, who married young, struggle to raise their children, and his father drank heavily. Aran determined early on to do better. And he wouldn't marry just anyone. His bride had to be a good person, and she also "had to be pretty." When he met Vanida, she was a seamstress for fashion shows and pageants.

He considers himself a Buddhist, though Aran doesn't take the gold amulets around his neck seriously. "My parents believed and so I followed," he says. Aran, in fact, has another store where he sells amulets.

Aran again calls into the kitchen. Again a woman's voice responds. Their children are thirty, twenty-seven, and twenty-four years old.

Aran boasts that although he only finished the first year of primary school, their oldest child works for Epson, the printer and imaging company. The middle child, their only daughter, works for a chemical company, and their youngest is studying interior design. He attributes his children's success in part to their upbringing. Aran and Vanida instilled in them a strong work ethic. "And you have to know yourself," he says.

To guarantee the security of his family's home, Aran wrote a politician several years ago, asked him to quietly help the Kaenboons purchase their land and home. The politician contacted the PAT, which agreed to help, though Aran had to make a rather exorbitant down payment. Aran won't reveal how he persuaded this politician to help them or why the politician responded so positively. But unlike Yung and Tasanee, Aran had a political connection and knew how to use it.

When asked if there's anything else he wants out of life, Aran initially shakes his head, but then laughs, smiles, and says, "Another wife!" A woman's laughter floats from the kitchen.

Growth and Crisis in Informal Bangkok

More than one million people live in Bangkok's informal settlements. The majority of slum dwellers here have land rental agreements, though they're not officially sanctioned and legally registered. Landowners simply allow residents to remain on their land on a temporary basis and pay rent. And in accordance with a Thai culture of hierarchy, landowners and residents take on patron client relationships. For a semblance of security, residents give owners and others money and political support. And in deference to landowners, slum residents are more apt to work out rental agreements than openly squat on vacant land and instigate outright conflict.

Residents' sense of security rests heavily on these client-patron relationships. It also depends on their particular settlement's characteristics, including location, the quality of homes, living conditions, and access to services. The more a settlement parallels a developed, formal neighborhood, the more secure its residents feel.

Because of migration from the countryside, by the mid-1980s, 40 percent of residents in informal settlements and the majority of household heads had been born outside of Bangkok. By 1990, the city had became three times as dense as it was just thirty years earlier, fifty times larger than the nation's second largest city, Chiang Mai, and Bangkok claimed 57 percent of Thailand's urban population.[17]

Klong Toey residents actually faced greater insecurity in the 1980s and early 1990s than they do today. During that period, the Thai economy grew at an incredible annual rate of 8 percent, hit-

ting 13.5 percent in 1988.[18] Construction of infrastructure, housing, and commercial space boomed, which put pressure on Klong
Toey and other settlements as demand for land increased.

As land prices rose, development of low-income housing became
unfeasible and slum evictions increased. The number of settlements in the central business district dropped in the early 1990s but
increased dramatically during the same period in suburban outer
rings of the city. Residents of informal settlements found themselves pushed out of the city's core and into the periphery, upsetting
many of their connections to work and school.[19]

The National Housing Authority estimates that at least 13 percent of poor households are under "imminent threat of eviction,"
and settlements have faced heightened threats of demolition
because of expanding road and highway networks that planners
hope will alleviate infamous traffic bottlenecks.[20] During Bangkok's
boom years, some landowners pressured squatters to leave for spec-
ulative reasons rather than because they had concrete plans for construction. Meanwhile, most evictions and commercial development
projects diminished an already inadequate low-income housing
supply.

Prosperity in Bangkok brought household appliances and consumer goods to Klong Toey and many other settlements. And in the
years leading up to the 1997 Asian financial crisis, a precipitous
decline in the region's stock markets and currencies, the number of
people living in economic poverty in Thailand dropped from 18
million to 7 million.[21] Overall, inequality and the severity of
poverty also diminished.

But then the financial crisis hit and the number of people living
in dire poverty increased by more than 16 percent in two years,
another concrete example of how the global economy affects individual households within urban settlements.[22]

Informal workers experienced a cut in their earnings. "I sell
food. . . . In the past, selling was good," says one Thai vendor. "We
got about 1,000 (baht) a day. All day and all night we fried food
until our hands got hardened. Now selling is not good at all. We get
only 200 to 300 (baht) a day."[23]

According to a neighborhood leader in the province of Khon Kaen, "The crisis has happened so quickly it has left us confused, puzzled, and let down. We have lost our jobs but are given no explanation. . . . It was the rich who benefited from the boom . . . but we, the poor, pay the price of the crisis."[24] Many children dropped out of school and went to work. According to one report:

> Since 1997, the poor have experienced loss of jobs and falling household incomes, while the cost of essentials like rice, vegetables, fish, transport, fuel, electricity, and municipal water has risen 15 percent to 20 percent. People are making less, surviving on less, and borrowing more to stay afloat. Virtual enslavement to informal loan-sharks has skyrocketed in the slums. . . . Many who've lost their means for survival in the cities have been forced to take shelter with rural relatives, stretching already-stretched family resources.[25]

Ironically, while the 1997 crisis made life more difficult for many people, including poor residents of Klong Toey, it curtailed evictions in urban settlements. Countless unfinished cement structures, sprinkled throughout Bangkok with rebar (reinforcing bar) protruding from columns and beams, testify to the halt the crisis put on building and real estate development. With less lending, investment, and new construction, came less demand for land, particularly as Bangkok already had too much middle- to high-income residential and commercial space. Even as residents of informal settlements struggled more to make a living, they gained a greater degree of land security.

In Klong Toey, many long-time residents have multiple rooms, electricity, and running water in relatively well-constructed homes. Most households have refrigerators, CD players, television sets, and oscillating fans. Some have couches and chairs. Homes are built with permanent materials, and owners and renters have developed strong patron-client relationships. Settlement leaders and government officials have developed mutually beneficial relationships, and community organization is fairly strong, all of which buttress the residents' sense of security.

Yet in Nairobi's Kibera, several people may live in one small room on a dirt floor under a leaky roof, without running water or electricity, and with little between them and the weather, thieves, and the authorities. Jane Matiba fears having the roof stolen right off of her home.

Klong Toey is larger and better off than most of the other settlements in Bangkok. Most residents in Klong Toey have more material wealth and consumer goods than slum residents in Manila, Nairobi, and Mexico City. Most have a home, and people aren't sleeping on the streets. But residents still don't hold titles to their land. Owners, if they wish, can still evict residents without breaching a legally enforceable contract. And poverty is real here.

"Almost everybody in Klong Toey works, but they earn very little money," says Rotjana Phraesrithong, the social worker with the Duang Prateep Foundation. "Most work for themselves. They are vendors or [day] labor. They earn enough to keep their family alive. But at the end of the day they are back where they started. They have no money."

While a lack of adequate income, housing, and food are marks of poverty, we must, when gauging need, also consider people's access to formal sectors. While not all informal residents and workers are financially poor, most lack the freedom to access formal lending agencies, legal help, housing markets, jobs, and education. They may be unable to pay fees for school or to officially register a business. They may not know how to navigate complicated government bureaucracies and paperwork. Unlike Aran, they may not have key personal contacts. They may never have an opportunity to dwell in hygienic living conditions, free of disease and pollutants. Their home may be under constant threat of eviction. They may lack formally contracted mortgages. This insufficient access to the formal sector is also a form of poverty.

Even by lacking simple things such as identity cards, school uniforms, and documentation—the accoutrements of formality—the poor may experience ostracism. Ana and Brijido in Lomas, for example, didn't register their children in school because they didn't have their birth certificates. They didn't have birth certificates because they couldn't afford the government fees. These simple transaction costs and documentation can be the greatest barriers to accessing the formal sector.

It's this lack of freedom to participate in wider society that not only prevents the urban poor from flourishing in the formal sector but also leaves them vulnerable and insecure. According to a World Bank report,

> Lack of documentation creates a "precarious illegality" that is widely tolerated, but leaves the poor vulnerable to the exploitation of more powerful groups. In urban slums in Brazil, Kenya, Vietnam, Mexico, India, and Pakistan, the lack of identity cards or clear titles to land exposes the poor to the tyranny of "slumlords"; lack of land titles and food ration cards also lead to increased commodity prices for the poor, which in turn lead to dealing with money lenders and rich landlords, from whose clutches the poor often have great difficulty ever extricating themselves.[26]

Scale and Causes of the Informal Sector

By definition, the informal sector is terribly difficult to measure. When businesses, housing markets, and transportation systems function outside the reach of regulation, statistics are not easily available. Many people operating in informal sectors are glad to remain invisible.

Still, the International Monetary Fund estimates that in developing nations the informal economy accounts for between 35 to 44 percent of the gross domestic product (GDP), whereas in the United States, for example, the figure is 10 percent. Informal businesses in Thailand account for a higher percentage of that country's GDP than any other nation in Asia, an incredible 70 percent. Egypt's informal economy accounts for 69 percent of its GDP. In the Philippines, the market share of the informal sector nearly doubled in less than two decades. In Kenya, at least 38 percent of urban residents work in the informal sector. And at least a quarter of residents in Valle de Chalco near Mexico City work informally, at least part-time, as *tianguis* or "moving merchants."[27]

Figures are just as high or even higher for informal housing. As noted previously, one in every three urban residents around the world lives in a slum. In some cities in developing nations, as many as 85 percent of residents live in the informal sector. Meanwhile housing and real estate can be a key investment for financial security. About 20 percent or more of any nation's GDP comes from land, property, and construction. For most people throughout the world, housing is their greatest source of prosperity.[28]

While specific causes of informality in the global South have been the subject of much debate, one fundamental cause is the inability of a large portion of society to influence policies and laws. When housing and work regulations are impossible for most urban residents to satisfy, they have no option but to live illegally, not because of antisocial leanings but because the laws and policies are impractical. Most government systems of legal ownership in developing nations remain inordinately burdensome or rife with corruption. In Egypt, for example, gaining access to desert land for construction and properly registering property rights requires anywhere from six to fourteen years or more and up to thirty-seven bureaucratic interactions with thirty-one different entities.[29]

Yet, the poor lack the financial and political influence necessary to help reshape laws. Therefore, they do not live in a free and democratic society, and their obligations to the rule of law become, at the least, tenuous.

But creating laws that account for all sectors of society is difficult. "It is easier for city governments—through 'bad governance'— to destroy the livelihoods of the poor than it is to create, sustain, and enhance them," according to one development sociologist.[30] And in some countries, policy makers must take great personal and financial risks to administer equitable governance.

In Nairobi, not only does the government refuse to provide residents of Kibera with basic services because of the settlement's illegal status, but it also bans people from taking certain initiatives to help themselves, such as building homes with permanent materials or building pit latrines. Law dictates that they use waterborne facilities to remove waste, but such systems require much more money than local residents have, and pit latrines, properly built and serviced, have proven to be a safe, cheap alternative. One NGO ignored government guidelines and successfully created ventilated pit latrines and a latrine-emptying service that has benefited more than 20,000 slum residents.

"In my opinion," writes a Kenyan journalist, "only brave moves like these—side-stepping archaic by-laws that stifle innovation—have the potential to improve degraded slum environments. Besides, such moves put the destiny of the slum-dwellers in their own hands."[31]

Other factors that influence the growth of informal sectors include a country's economic development and politics, a city's growth and size, the availability and status of land in and around a city, and a government's ability and willingness to enforce laws and policies. Taxes, regulations, and bureaucratic corruption can also drive activities underground. According to the International Monetary Fund, countries with relatively low tax rates, fewer laws and regulations, and a well-established rule of law tend to have proportionally smaller informal sectors.[32]

Overcrowding, migration, trade liberalization, and structural adjustment programs overburden local governments and social service agencies as they attempt to provide essential services such as education, health care, water, and sanitation. As local communities grow but fail to administer these services, residents develop or obtain them on their own.

Some researchers say that labor markets dictate the nature of the informal economy. Companies facing heavy tax burdens, government restrictions, and substantial payments toward employees' social needs may have difficulty formally employing people. There-

fore, they provide few regular jobs and instead contract with informal workers.[33] With a large supply of cheap, itinerate, and short-
term informal labor, employers invest little money in the
development of these workers' skills or their safety. And without
resources to upgrade equipment and technology, business owners
in developing countries remain uncompetitive and wages remain
low.

The general public suffers because the larger the informal sector,
the smaller the tax base. Governments are left to apportion dwindling revenues to provide services, leaving the private sector and
NGOs to tend to shortfalls.[34]

Informal Employment

While in Mexico City, I ride the underground metro. It's prime
market space for hawkers because buyers are sedentary, unable to
leave metro cars while awaiting their stops. They usually have a little extra change on them. And they are able to empathize with the
struggle to make ends meet, for they are themselves the working
poor.

The train stops and a young boy steps onto the car and quickly
announces and displays his merchandise: Doublemint gum, 2
pesos. He then walks the aisle to service buyers. Subsequent hawkers sell harmonicas for 5 pesos, ink markers for 10 pesos, and a map
of Mexico City for 10 pesos, as well as pens, phone directories, document protectors, small photo albums, mini desk lamps, and
chocolate.

A man hands out pamphlets describing his predicament, a dis-
ability that prevents him from working. An old woman begs for
money.

Some metro entrepreneurs find more creative ways to earn a living. A young boy playing an accordion meanders past me while a
four- or five-year-old girl follows, extending a hat for offerings. A
blind man with an amplifier strapped to his chest serenades us

while his Walkman plays tinny background music of artificial per-
cussion, electronic drums, and rhythms. He is a kind of working
man's lounge singer on the tiresome daily commute.

Though reluctant at first, I gradually buy from these peddlers,
more abundantly as my time in Mexico City passes. This is the
social welfare system at work, I realize, informal as it is. Eventually,
I find that, in some frenzy of purchasing power, I want to buy from
every hard-working man, woman, and child that passes my way. So
for 10 pesos I buy a cheap, plastic beard trimmer that I know will
never work, pistachios for 5 pesos, tamarind candy, which I fiercely
dislike, and I stuff extra change into the hands of a begging mute
gentleman. I also pass out fruit to beggars. Later, while walking the
streets of Mexico City, I buy from more vendors. Near the Basilica
de Guadalupe, I pay the full asking price for a Mexican soccer jer-
sey for my brother. I don't bother bartering.

Maybe I am the kind of journeyman they're looking for as they
ply their goods, a guilty gringo who is used to so much more. As I
give, I find that my own tenderness toward them grows—adults
who should be enjoying the prime of their working lives, children
who should be in school.

A retired businessman, Humberto Sarmiento, who has worked
for almost every end of the production spectrum, from Texas
Instruments to regional Mexican companies, introduces me to
barely visible avenues and sidewalks surrounding a Mexico City
metro stop. Just three years ago, he says, these spaces were empty,
except for pedestrians and cars. Today, they are inundated with
peddlers who have built booths with awnings and have created an
uninterrupted market space.

Trying to pull out of deep indebtedness and attempting to stim-
ulate the domestic economy, Mexico has opened its fiscal borders
and liberalized its trade policies. Therefore, in Humberto's estimation, survival in today's economy requires connections—the more
international the better—and large sums of capital, both of which
are assets that most small and mid-level businesspeople in Mexico
are short on.

So, unable to compete with foreign companies, Mexican companies fold, and more and more urban workers labor informally alongside the formal business sector. In twenty years, from 1980 to 2000, the informal sector nearly doubled in Mexico, and it now comprises one-third of the urban workforce.[35]

Throughout Mexico City, in various marketplaces, hawkers belt out the monotone mantra, "un peso, un peso, un peso, un peso, un peso. . . . " They claim plots of sidewalk or street, put down a blanket to display their products: used or pirated CDs, hair barrettes, shirts, shoes, and purses, Spiderman toys, Gillette razors, Duracell batteries, Zippo lighters, toiletries, spools of cloth, magazines, candy, snacks, dolls . . . anything, new or used, manufactured or handcrafted, grown or slaughtered.

These sellers don't pay taxes. They're not registered with the government. Some may not be here selling their goods tomorrow. Others are part of well-organized vendor associations and will be here for years. Many of them pay a fee to a neighborhood boss or to the police who control their cement plot. For some, informal hawking has become their only means of earning an income.

These vendors, some of the least skilled of informal workers, are conspicuous throughout the global South. Though generally poor, they are entrepreneurs and innovative capitalists.

In Bangkok, food vendors line busy streets. Residents of informal settlements buy bags of fresh rice, chicken, fish, dragon fruit, and pineapple. Many poor people rely on the convenience of ready-to-eat, cooked food. It saves them time and money and, though many do still cook on small burners or charcoal-filled pots, they have no kitchen in their small homes.

Pedro, a vendor in Manila, sells cigarettes and candy at the perpetually clogged intersection of Domingo Santiago and Tuazon in Balic-Balic, in front of a 7-Eleven and a Jollibee fast-food restaurant. Like a waiter servicing diners, he palms a homemade, wooden box with compartments for several packs of Marlboros, the favored brand of most customers. He approaches rolled-down windows and quickly exchanges single cigarettes for 2 pesos. Pedro earns about 200 pesos a day, and his best customers are taxi and jeepney drivers.

"I make friends with the drivers," Pedro says. He used to paint homes, but five years ago his placement agency stopped giving him jobs.

A rather short, quiet man in a ball cap, shorts, T-shirt, and sandals, Pedro leaves his nearby home, just off of the railroad tracks, at seven in the morning to stand for ten hours between lanes of slow moving, exhaust-coughing jeepneys and other vehicles. He sells until noon and then again from the late afternoon to nine or ten at night. He doesn't work during the heat of the day, when it's raining, or if he's sick. Pedro must work seven days a week to support his wife and four children.

A police officer once coerced Pedro to pay bribes, threatened to end Pedro's Balic-Balic cigarette business. Over time and needing to maintain an income, Pedro says he contemplated other alternatives, going so far as to plan the murder of the officer. Unfortunately, the officer suddenly died, and one of the man's relatives accused Pedro of killing him. Authorities jailed Pedro in Manila's main prison.

"It's hard to be away from your family," he says. "If you don't have a family it's okay, but having a family it's very hard to be in jail." Then, after four years, the courts finally determined that the officer died of complications related to epilepsy, and Pedro went free.

In Manila and Mexico City and throughout the global South, skill and capital requirements vary across informal jobs and affect people's chances of finding work. In Nairobi, researchers found that repairing shoes, shoe shining, and cutting hair require little start-up capital and skills, but repairing vehicles, manufacturing furniture, and running a restaurant require more money and abilities.[36] In Bangkok, according to one study, income for semiskilled shopkeepers and brick haulers increases as they gain on-the-job experience. And education helps most informal workers, even unskilled vendors, to earn more money. Regardless of skill levels, informal workers must be organized, willing to work hard, and adept at recognizing opportunities.

Income levels vary as well. In fact, some informal workers earn more money than they would in the formal sector, and, as noted previously, they can easily access work that requires little skill and is flexible to their needs, but their jobs are less secure, lack training and benefits, and may require more hours of labor. Informal entrepreneurs pay high interest rates on informal loans and credit, have no insurance, and they must cope with limitations to the growth of their business, location, equipment, and buyers. Informal workers may have to pay bribes and depend on the whims of police or local leaders who prevent them from organizing. Their job locations may expose them to crime and environmental hazards such as industrial waste, without the benefit of labor regulation.

Housing and Other Sectors

Often, residents of informal settlements don't separate their work from their home. In Mathare 4A, the Nairobi settlement where Jane Matiba and her family live, secure housing can also mean secure employment. Home-based enterprises (HBEs) are key here. Residents manage stores, sublet rooms, and set up workshops in their homes. Without the need to commute using public transportation, HBE owners save money and have less impact on the environment. They also enable neighbors and other clients to spend their money within a settlement's economy. Similar to other residents, HBE owners cope with insecure land tenure, a lack of infrastructure, inadequate buildings, overcrowding, and eviction threats, but all of these problems simultaneously threaten both their businesses and their homes. It's therefore helpful to accommodate HBEs, in Mathare 4A and in other settlements, because for them secure land and housing simultaneously mean secure employment.[37]

Increasingly, the development and illegal subdividing of urban settlements is itself becoming a big business. Professional, organized syndicates gain control over settlements and then divide and sell plots for a profit. Generally, local politicians and officials, police officers, and military personnel have a hand in syndicates, either actively or as recipients of bribes, because in most places subdividing urban settlements is illegal. These developers only invest in initial services, such as roads or water pipes, and then sell buyers the "right to squat" while retaining legal title.[38] In Ilhuicamina, near Mexico City, the Antorchistas sold Juan Luis and Rosa the right to squat but then retained control and any future profits resulting from investments in their home or land. On a smaller scale, landlords may buy up several homes within a settlement and divide and rent them.

The informal housing market depends heavily on residents' sense of security. Without some assurance that demolition isn't imminent, people in poverty will not invest in their dilapidated homes. Potential home buyers in slums take into account a settlement's infrastructure, community organization, local politics, outright threats of eviction, and rumors about the landowner's plans for the settlement and his or her reputation. Settlements that are centrally located, easily accessible, in demand for other uses, and of high value may be at risk of eviction.[39] Some researchers say that in Manila, including Balic-Balic where the government is purportedly mulling over its plans to renovate the railway, the risk of eviction can lower the value of slum homes by up to 25 percent.[40]

When a society lacks the ability to administer an efficient system of property or home ownership, as observed in the last chapter, it is unable to fully capture the value of property in a market system. People have material goods and possessions, but without an adequate system for tracking legal property rights—such as a deed registry—they have no credit, no collateral, no ability to make these material things work harder as capital assets, the basic building blocks of capitalism. Informal, unregistered urban land and homes often go underutilized as assets.[41]

And yet housing in the informal sector may, in more secure settlements, still serve as an investment. Even if residents don't ever formally own their land or home, they may develop and improve their house and, unbeknownst to the real owner, sell it to other squatters for a profit. But improvements and construction are only possible when residents have access to extra up-front money to purchase materials or pay for labor.

Financing such a project can be difficult: of the world's 500 million poorest households, only 2 to 5 percent have access to formal or institutional credit.[42] Residents can generally borrow money informally and without collateral from neighborhood lenders, but such arrangements carry steep interest rates, and, if unpaid according to agreed-upon terms, borrowers can slip into cycles of indebtedness. Often people borrow from family members or friends or they pool resources, particularly during a crisis. Sometimes businesses will allow squatters they know to purchase goods on credit. In short, to make improvements in urban settlements, residents need an injection of extra money, and then they need an assurance of security in order to invest that money.

Unfortunately, many people in urban settlements spend a sizable portion of their income on gambling and games of chance hoping to get rich rather than saving for the future. In fact, while some informal residents are just as fiscally disciplined as their formal counterparts, many have never learned to save money. In Klong Toey, residents buy lottery tickets by the score. In Balic-Balic, they spend hours losing money while playing bingo and *jueteng*, an illegal numbers game.

In recent years, community or group savings-and-loan plans, in collaboration with sponsoring NGOs, have grown in popularity throughout the global South. These schemes depend on mutual trust and accountability as community members each contribute a sum of money on a daily, weekly, or monthly basis.

To pool resources in Kenya, one women's group required an initial contribution of 200 shillings and smaller ongoing payments. Forty-seven people, including only five men, became members, hoping to enjoy a share in the purchase of commercial plots of land, rental houses, corn mills, and other household items that members couldn't afford on their own. The group helped twenty of its members build houses.[43] Similarly, Raymund in Balic-Balic manages a rice-purchasing cooperative so that, by pooling resources, residents have more purchasing power.

A savings group in Valle de Chalco, organized by AMEXTRA, relies on a "solidarity scheme" in which five to twenty self-selected people agree to co-sign on loans. The scheme relies on participants' common stake in success as a form of human collateral. Because they are collectively responsible for loans, members naturally exclude irresponsible neighbors from joining. At weekly meetings, each member contributes 10 pesos toward loan payments.

Some individuals and families access loans directly from NGOs. In Lomas, Letty and Isaura turn loans into candy, snacks, flour, and soap to sell to neighbors. José borrows money to build his home for his family and parakeet.

Borrowers may also wish to begin a business in transportation by purchasing a bicycle, rickshaw, or minibus. In some cities, the vast majority of public transportation is informal. At one point in Lima, Peru, more than 90 percent of vehicles used for mass transit were operating informally.[44] Taxis or bicycles with sidecars frequent airports and bus stops to drive or pedal passengers to local destinations. Young men in Balic-Balic, when they build table-carts to glide residents along the tracks from one neighborhood to the next, are utilizing the few resources they have to create an efficient and useful means of transportation.

Access and Civil Society

Housing markets, transportation systems, investments, savings and borrowing schemes—these exist as vast informal sectors in developing nations, parallel to formal sectors. They represent alternatives to which poor and less privileged members of society must turn as means of survival when they lack the power and money necessary to access legal means.

Women in particular lack access. Many people view women as less worthy than men of earning an education, of learning to read and write or gain job skills. They have fewer job opportunities and receive less pay. In many regions of the world, cultural and legal dictates prevent women from inheriting land or owning property. Marriage and migration can remove them from family and supportive networks. Many fathers are absent—because of AIDS, war, alcoholism and drugs, or because they've left their families for mistresses or to begin new families elsewhere—and women must manage their households alone. But even when women provide their families with income and food, governments and others may not recognize them as household heads and instead defer to their husbands' wishes. Women experience violence, physical and sexual abuse, and malnutrition more often than men.

In Kenya, according to the World Bank, "If a woman has a small baby at the time of divorce, she is expected to care for it until it stops breastfeeding, and then she must return the child to the man. Sometimes a woman may decide to take her children, which is often not challenged because children are seen as a woman's only asset after divorce." One Kenyan woman describes her husbandless plight, "I don't have any house or any land or anything because I parted company with my husband and he does not want us."[45]

A Thai woman describes her struggles:

Right now I'm feeling overwhelmed. I'm working harder and cannot stop, otherwise we have no rice to eat. I sell the fish cakes here from early morning to six in the evening and then do housekeeping. It takes a lot of work to make even a small amount of money. I have a lot of work to do such as laundry, cleaning house, and finding food for our children. The youngest child is now sick so it's an additional responsibility.[46]

Meanwhile, more and more women are becoming the breadwinners in urban settlements.

For both men and women, gaining access to the privileges of the formal sector often means having the right connections. In Klong Toey, Aran knew this when he appealed to a politician to help his family secure their land and home. Residents in Klong Toey once appealed directly to the queen after a particularly devastating fire. She intervened and requested that the PAT spare the community from eviction. In addition, the presence of a nearby Buddhist *wat*, or temple, provides the settlement with a semblance of added security. Residents give donations to the temple monks; the monks offer prayers and teach Buddhist values, and, one researcher notes, "[E]victing a community that is supported by monks carries the same penalty as disobeying a wish from the King or Queen."[47]

Having good connections is particularly important when participation in democratic processes has little meaning, as in Balic-Balic, where residents trade their votes for much needed money, or in Ilhuicamina, where Juan Luis and Rosa must vote lockstep with the Antorchistas and their public gatherings are shams.

The most powerful means that poor people have to reform their society and access the formal sector is to work collectively, to organize. Many vendors, drivers, and other businesspeople participate in associations that represent them. Neighborhood networks come together to negotiate land rights, while groups of networks gather force to negotiate policies within an entire city or country.

Effective NGOs, community-based organizations, and neighborhood networks can influence local decision making. Throughout the world, civil society is having an increasingly vocal influence on laws and policies, and the same holds true for informal settlements. Commenting on Thailand, one researcher writes, "Slum dwellers who go to the residence of the prime minister to protest are assuming that they have an equal right to be heard, not just through their patrons, but as citizens. . . . Slum dwellers are beginning to believe that the government belongs to them and that they have a right to make demands of it."[48]

Simultaneously, social fragmentation in urban settlements may worsen because of economic strains, migration and transience, lawlessness, crime, and violence. Still, people's ability to organize, oppose or support lobbies and politicians, and keep officials and other people accountable gives them power.

Besides partnering with formal organizations, slum residents utilize a diverse arsenal of weapons to fight policies they consider unjust. They elect neighborhood leaders to represent them and network with other slum settlements to exchange strategies and come together for public protests. They nurture client-patron ties with particular government officials. They appeal to the media to publicize their efforts. They march and sign petitions. Many residents vote, but, as noted in Balic-Balic, simple, political promises or bribes can make voting a terribly undemocratic activity. By developing their settlements and demanding that the government recognize them and supply services, residents generally reinforce their sense of security. And in some cases they take legal action, though judicial success is rare.

Of course, corruption can render almost any means of resistance moot. In one Bangkok settlement, the government, in collusion with a banker seeking to redevelop the neighborhood, withdrew the settlement's small fire station. Within just a few months, multiple cases of arson occurred, a large portion of the settlement burned, and the city banned reconstruction. Regardless of democratic action by civil society, such an assertion of power can make residents' battles for justice seem virtually unwinnable.

The tactics that residents choose depend on the political and legal climate, the age of their settlement, and whether it's on private or public land, among other factors. Most often, successful compromises between settlement leaders, politicians, landowners, and bureaucrats involve discreet negotiations that tolerate an implicit undermining of a government's own laws. This mediation or "politics by stealth" lets officials save face with the public while responding to the demands of those whom the law is failing.[49] Officials will tacitly allow squatters to illegally remain on plots of land because it's more politically expedient than enforcing the law and causing more disturbance.

Control and power over settlements increasingly resides with nongovernment sources, including private businesses that influence politicians, city planning, and development, as well as the media and civil society that serve to amplify the cries for equality emanating from urban settlements. More and more, as governments in the South liberalize their economies, boundaries between business and government blur. Power over informal settlements may go well beyond local mayors and representatives.

Resourceful, but Still Dispossessed

"Isabel is the breadwinner," Myla says of her daughter. "I am a widow already. [Isabel] is the one taking care of the four children of my other [daughter] because her husband has left."

Myla, sixty-three, lives with and cares for her grandson and three granddaughters. She is thin, and her bangs hang just above her eyes. She wears small hoop earrings. A couple of years ago she and her grandchildren moved out of a house along the Balic-Balic railway tracks, near the Seares family, and into this more secure, more spacious home farther from the tracks. A plastic relief Hello Kitty and Disney cartoon characters—Pluto, Minnie, and Mickey—adorn the white walls of Myla's living room. She has two refrigerators, a twenty-inch television, VCR, and Nintendo video game system. Though they live on her earnings, Isabel lives almost 2,000 miles away.

Isabel works in Japan as a dancer and stripper. "After dancing they are forced to entertain the Japanese, but she didn't want to marry a Japanese because of their customs and tradition," Myla says, explaining that Isabel returned to Manila for a while after her boss told her to have sex with her clients, which Isabel hadn't realized was part of her job. About one-half of Filipina women trafficked to Japan have no real understanding of the kind of work they'll end up doing.[50]

To qualify to entertain in Japan, Isabel completed an elaborate and highly organized program, led by a promoter. After practicing with other aspiring girls for three years, she successfully completed a test. "Our folk dance here in the Philippines . . . the Japanese are very fond of it," says Myla. "[It is] part of the entertainment. They love Filipino dance, folk dance."

The promoter then determined that Isabel was ready and helped her obtain a visa, complete other paperwork, and find a job. Upon arriving in Japan, Isabel earned US$450 a month, though for the first month she received no money because her boss applied it toward her clothes, shoes, and other expenses.

Myla is proud of her daughter's work. In the eight years that Isabel has shuttled between Manila and Tokyo and other cities, she's earned more than one million pesos. "We are planning to buy a house and lot. . . . Maybe even in the provinces." Myla stumbles over her words while describing Isabel's success and begins to cry. "My daughter, she is good. She wants to bring up our standard of living, but I'm not in favor of [getting rich]. I'm just satisfied that we are eating three times a day."

Millions of women around the world present their bodies as one of the few assets they have to informally earn money. The majority of women knowingly enter these professions. Some women and children fall into prostitution naively, thinking they're being given work as waitresses or entertainers only to find they've been sold by traffickers or even relatives. And whether women in dire poverty have any true freedom in their choice to be prostitutes is debatable. Today, poverty and increased mobility and migration are feeding an ever-growing, international, informal market for sex.

I asked several tourists in the red-light districts of Bangkok, most of them from Europe or North America, whether they thought the women they visited wanted to be there, selling themselves. A twice-married Englishman named Chip drunkenly decried the torment of marriage. Bill, an Australian man with a wife and children, lambasted everything from institutionalized religion to U.S. foreign policy and his past relationships to justify his trysts in Bangkok while traveling on business. Virtually all of the men assured me that the women did want to work there. Besides, they reasoned, earning good money as an entertainer was better than struggling to survive in slums or in the countryside. Listening to Myla evince such pride in her daughter, one would think they were right.

I wonder, though, if these men would say the same thing about fire-eaters in Mexico City, who stand at busy intersections, a lighter in one hand, a rag-enshrouded stick in the other. Next to them is a can of fuel. These fire-eaters, blackened and grimy, bleary eyed and dazed, dip the stick in the can, shove it in their mouths, remove it, and light their breath into a fiery plea for help. They then solicit drivers for change. Arms extend from car windows and pay for the entertainment. Do these men choose to earn money in this way because they get a kick out of destroying themselves with poison and spectacle?

I also wonder about a shirtless man on the Mexico City metro who cries out to those around him for help, his chest and back pockmarked with hundreds of tiny slit-scars. The man displays a wadded T-shirt and places it on the ground. He then meticulously unfolds the shirt to its widest reaches to reveal a large pile of clear glass shards. Still bellowing to the crowd, he lays down on the glass, several times, first on his chest and then on his back. As he again gathers up the shards into his shirt and stands to collect money, glass fragments dangle from his body.

Are prostitutes in Bangkok any less brutalized than these bizarre entertainers? Would any of these men or women truly choose their given professions if they had other options?

Author and urban theorist Mike Davis powerfully dispels assumptions that working informally isn't such a bad option, that informal workers' optimistic entrepreneurialism will eventually win the day:

> The pundits of bootstrap capitalism, like the irrepressible Hernando de Soto, may see this enormous population of marginalized labourers, redundant civil servants and ex-peas-

ants as actually a frenzied beehive of ambitious entrepreneurs yearning for formal property rights and unregulated competitive space, but it makes more obvious sense to consider most informal workers as the "active" unemployed, who have no choice but to subsist by some means or starve. The world's estimated 100 million street kids are not likely—apologies to Señor de Soto—to start issuing IPOs or selling chewing-gum futures.[51]

While we should celebrate the ingenuity and diligence of squatters and informal workers and examine their tactics and, as appropriate, champion them, let's not doubt that Isabel and her mother and so many other people in the informal sector continue to live in poverty and would much rather enjoy dignifying work, economic security, and well-being. By definition, they remain excluded.

6

Cairo

Slum Living Conditions

"ALHAMDULLILAH. God has been good to me," says Ezzat Naim Guindy, age thirty. He used to trade in light fixtures and broken toys and guard garbage-laden donkey carts for his father. Now Ezzat is assistant to the director of public relations for a local nonprofit in Mokattam, a subsection of Manshiet Nasser, a massive informal settlement in southeast Cairo.[1]

Evicted from several other sites within the span of a decade, Ezzat's family and thousands of other people moved to Manshiet Nasser and then Mokattam in the mid-1960s and early 1970s when it was "a deserted, rocky, sandy hill with no access to roads, water, power, networks, or people," he says. "It was like a haunted mountain. A few scattered shacks dotted the landscape, but otherwise there were no human beings—just wolves and stray dogs."

Family and clan leaders decided to build homes at the base of a mountain on an abandoned quarry rather than next to nearby railroad tracks as the government had instructed. Closer to the "belly" of the limestone mountain, they reasoned, they'd be harder to evict. Arid and sandy, the settlement comprised what was then the extreme edge of Cairo, though today the city extends well past Mokattam. From the beginning, death rates among newborns and children were high, as was illiteracy. Disease and poverty were daily realities.

Collecting Garbage in Cairo

The oldest of six children, Ezzat walked two hours as a young boy to fetch water. Each morning, he also accompanied his father, Fawzi, on his garbage route. Fawzi had traded in tin, but in Mokattam he concentrated on electrical fittings from junked motors. He'd buy them from other garbage collectors according to weight, sort them at home according to market demand, and sell the parts and scraps to manufacturers. Ezzat helped gather and bag parts. Later, Fawzi turned to dealing in meat and used paper.

Initially, Fawzi refused to let his son attend school. He needed Ezzat for the business. So Fawzi's wife, Hasina, slipped Ezzat's birth certificate, a rare document in Mokattam, to a cousin, who used it to enroll in a nearby primary school. Still, at his mother's insistence, Ezzat eventually enrolled as well.

"My father could never resist my mother's tears!" he says. "He had to give in on condition that I keep up my chores with him after school. It was agreed."

In school, Ezzat learned arithmetic. "I began discovering that [my father] had been figuring deals incorrectly and that sometimes people would swindle him. My arithmetic made the family some money, and my father was glad he had given in. Later, he would postpone the money part of any business until I was around. He would weigh the merchandise, negotiate the terms, but tell business associates to wait until I got home to do the money bit!"

Garbage has always been Mokattam's most valuable material resource. At least 20,000 garbage collectors and sorters, *zabaleen* in Egyptian Arabic, now live here.[2] Mokattam's men, women, and children—as young as four and five years old—gather, sort, bundle, bag, compact, cut up, and burn, trade, or resell waste to earn an income and maintain local schools, clinics, and running water and other services. *Zabaleen* throughout Cairo collect up to one-third of the 10,000 tons of waste produced by Cairenes daily, recycling an incredible 80 to 85 percent of it and making the *zabaleen* some of the most efficient garbage managers in the world. More than 50,000 *zabaleen* in at least seven garbage settlements work and live in Cairo. Mokattam is the largest *zabaleen* settlement and has been called "the Silicon Valley of the garbage-scavenging world."[3]

Cairo's poor raise chickens, pigeons, geese, ducks, and occasionally goats or sheep. The *zabaleen*, most of whom are Coptic Christians, also raise pigs, using organic garbage as food. In fact, pigs were their entrée into the garbage business when they migrated from Upper Egypt in the 1930s and 1940s. Muslims, who comprise 90 percent of Cairo's population, believe pigs are unclean and leave them to the Copts.

But all of this—the sorting, the bagging, the raising of pigs—all of this occurs within and in front of people's homes in Mokattam. After men and older children return from a long morning collecting waste, women and children wade into the muck to sort soda bottles, by color, from orange peels, once-read newspapers from raggedy shirts, rotten plums from motor oil containers, chicken bones from the ubiquitous polyethylene bags.

Just as pervasive are flies and gaunt dogs, their noses low to the ground, rooting yet timid. A truck tire serves as a baby's playpen. Smoldering heaps of waste emit wisps of smoke. Barefooted children rifle through mountains of rubbish containing used syringes and glass. The carcasses of baby chickens, too clumsy to escape voracious, darting rats, decompose underfoot.

Filled plastic garbage bags and ten-foot, boulderlike canvas bags line the narrow streets and walkways that wind between Mokattam's brick buildings, which reach as high as seven stories. Residents set aside clean stories for personal living space and for relatives. Other floors hold garbage. The roofs are flat and have pigeon cages, water catchments, and unfinished columns with protruding rebar. On yet other floors pigs eat, sleep, and defecate. The grime of both the garbage and animals is everywhere. Narrow lanes, puddled and potholed, run crimson with pigs' blood.

Besides the desperate squeals of dying pigs, the babble of Mokattam sounds rather like the ocean. Churning machinery slices plastic into transportable, recyclable slivers in a syncopated rhythm like
the ebb and flow of crashing waves. Children laugh and pad along
the muddy ground, as if building sand castles together on a beach.
Donkey-tugboats bellow. But the smells of feces and garbage dis-
turb these seaside illusions, and the call to prayer emanating from
one of Cairo's five thousand mosques reminds residents of their
bustling, urban existence.

These are the living conditions in one of Cairo's informal settlements. As in Balic-Balic, Kibera, Lomas, and Klong Toey, the poor
of Mokattam face environmental dangers, conditions that threaten
their health, safety, and security, and expose them to disease, harsh
weather, pollution, and emotional trauma. While inadequate housing and land rights are the most prominent features of informal settlements, poor living conditions indelibly brand them as
communities of degradation, regardless of residents' innovation
and hope.

Ironically, in garbage-ridden Mokattam, unhygienic living conditions are also the people's sustenance. "Garbage" is relative. The
vast majority of Cairenes label empty medicine bottles, banana
peels, and frayed socks as waste. But for the *zabaleen*, plastic bottles
are valuable recyclables, peels are pig fodder, and old clothes
become woven rugs. Broken appliances are capital. Even pig
manure is an asset as fertilizer.

"They tell us that in the name of civilization we shouldn't be
doing this any more," says Bekhit, a fifty-four-year-old resident.
"But garbage is all that we know. Garbage has built our schools, our
small factories, everything else you see."[4]

In fact, spend enough time in Mokattam and the living conditions seem normal, even acceptable. Mothers and children sub-
merged in garbage for five and six hours a day simply become part
of the economic landscape. Men dragging donkeys that drag carts
that block traffic become a nuisance, but no more so than the stall
of rush-hour traffic or inclement weather. Even visually, women's

patterned caftans camouflage them against mounds of confused rubbish, making them imperceptible until they move. They become an ordinary part of familiar scenery.

Each night, shortly after midnight, the men and children of Mokattam set out in donkey carts and trucks on specific collection routes. The men scour buildings, floor by floor, filling baskets with waste. The children help empty the baskets into the cart or truck and stand guard.

"My two older sisters married garbage collectors, and my father decided to send my two brothers to school," says Samia Wadie Hanna of Mokattam. "I was the only one left to accompany him on the route and did so from the time I was five years old. We had the busiest route in Cairo. . . . If we did not make it out of the center of town in time, we would be jostled and abused by cars and buses."

Upon returning home, with children sitting twenty feet above the ground atop the day's haul, the collectors unharness the donkeys, lower the bed flap, and shovel the waste in front of and into their home. The women sort food scraps, paper, cardboard, tin, and glass, and, in more recent years, plastics with their bare hands or a board.

Samia used to help her father gather garbage from individual apartments, but one early morning she fell down a dark stairwell. Thereafter, he insisted she remain with the cart. When she was twelve, Samia hoped to finally enroll in school, but the very day her family was to apply for her admission, the one day she left her father alone on his route, someone stole their cart and donkey. So Samia's parents demanded that she continue working. Deeply disappointed, she nevertheless came to accept her role as *zabaleen*. "I . . . even learned to enjoy the few hours I spent with my father rolling into and out of Cairo. We would spend happy times together. He would teach me to count and do mental arithmetic sums."

After sorting plastic by type and color, the *zabaleen* wash it in boiling water and ammonia, slice containers in half, and then send the plastic through shredders before selling it to outside middlemen, who in turn sell it to manufacturers. They also bundle and sell paper and cardboard, smelt aluminum into stackable bars, and sell most glass to these same middlemen. They crush rags into cotton stuffing and weave sanitized rags into beautiful rugs with hand looms, under the direction of a local NGO. *Zabaleen* either burn the remaining garbage or dump it into an open desert pit just outside the city.

For the *zabaleen*, though, the real money is in pigs. Women carry organic slop to pig sties behind their homes, close to their living quarters. Some households corral their pigs up manured stairs and onto the roof.

In the early 1900s, the *wahiya*—literally the "people of the oasis"—collected and managed Cairo's waste by contracting with individual households. Then in the 1930s and 1940s a group of landless peasants from the El Badary district in Assiut in southern Egypt, forced from their homes by crop failures and joblessness, began purchasing organic waste from the *wahiya* to feed their pigs and then later began recycling materials.

Over time, the mostly Muslim *wahiya* became middlemen between households and these Coptic Christian *zabaleen*, maintaining collection rights and receiving monthly fees from households and recyclables from the *zabaleen*. The *zabaleen* have since suffered through multiple relocations as Cairo expands, but they continue to preserve familial ties through intermarriage and by living with extended families.

Although the *zabaleen* have raised pigs for years, large companies often own the animals. "It was always a garbage collector's goal to buy his own *zeriba* [pig sty] from the *mo'allim* [a man who helps migrants settle in the city] who set him up in the business," says Ezzat. "For then he could improve his income and not just have to endure the filthy living conditions of his home for someone else's benefit."

Romani, the oldest of six children, is a pig butcher. His family's home is midway up the limestone hill that is the southern border of Mokattam. They live along a steep road that leads to St. Sam'aan's, a Coptic monastery and group of churches on the hill that includes a cave sanctuary with seating for 20,000.

Though he's only twenty-three, Romani's tight, black curls are receding. He wears soot-colored pants and a blue, short-sleeve button-down shirt, untucked, and a steel watch on his left wrist. His beard, shaved low on his cheeks and running tight along his jaw line, is a symbol of grief, he says. Romani mourns the death of his grandfather. He lives with some friends but returned to be with his family a few days ago after hearing that his grandfather had passed away.

Blood crusts under Romani's fingernails, in the folds of his over-worked hands, streaked onto his pants and sandaled feet. His family keeps more than fifty pigs in a partially roofed, ground-level sty. From a hook on the wall of the sty hangs a pig's head and intestines drying in the heat, the same hook that his father uses to beat him, Romani says, motioning to scars on his arms, hands, and back.

Romani decides to butcher a pig. After sprinkling the pavement with wood shavings, he slices into a live pig's jugular with a ten-inch knife. The pig writhes violently for several moments, but it loses blood quickly and becomes slack. Romani then cleaves the pig's black, coarse skin from its body, and, with help from neighbors and other butchers, he hoists it onto a bar cemented into a wall that skirts the road. Remaining blood drains from the pig, onto the pavement. Nearby, mothers rest with their children in the shade of the wall.

Animals such as Romani's pigs provide only a small fraction of Egypt's food supply, and only about 3 percent of Egypt's land is suitable for agriculture, so the country is heavily dependent on imports for food, particularly wheat from the United States.[5] The poor have historically depended on food entitlements to survive, but market liberalization and austerity measures have decreased the government distribution of food. Only three items—bread, cooking oil, and sugar—remain partly subsidized.

Still, about one-third of households in Cairo's informal settlements raise animals, though the majority of them consume the animals only periodically.[6] The *zabaleen* sell most of their stock to pig traders and processors. These animals—sheep, chickens, pigeons, geese, and, in some newer, more spacious settlements, even horses and water buffalo—are also a means of investment and savings. The poorest households don't raise animals, though, because they lack startup money to buy animals and feed. Only a few households grow crops in peri-urban Cairo, mostly clover for livestock. Green space is rare here.

Manure is, of course, a concern in Mokattam. Fortunately, residents now compost dung outside the city, and farmers in the Nile Delta region use it as high-quality fertilizer. But in the mid-1970s, Samia recalls, people used dung cakes as fuel for baking. "Compost merchants had still not appeared on the scene, and every home had a little pile of manure sitting outside of its doorstep. . . . [T]here were really no streets at all. They were piles of manure separated by foot space for one foot at a time, and sometimes no space at all."

Samia also remembers the settlement's tin shacks, homes that residents could easily dismember if evicted. In 1975, only five Mokattam homes used permanent materials. During that same year, the settlement's lone Coptic church, also made of tin and wood, burned down. When Father Sam'aan, the church's priest, and other church leaders decided to rebuild on the hill overlooking the garbage village, they irreversibly altered the course of Mokattam.

Just six years later, permanent brick and stone comprised 80 percent of homes. The church had provided the settlement with greater legitimacy.[7] In addition, because the government relocated people to Mokattam from another settlement and as NGOs and state agencies have helped residents add services and improve infrastructure, residents' sense of security has grown, and they've invested in their homes, the majority of which now have reinforced concrete roofs, brick walls, and tile floors. Vertical construction has also provided people with more space. Most of them no longer cook, eat, sleep, and sort garbage in the same room, as they once did.

Mokattam has become, like Kibera and Klong Toey, a self-contained society, an independent city. Though facilities remain inadequate, residents have access to groceries, schools, and health clinics. As Mokattam gradually improves its buildings and infrastructure, more and more homes become businesses: barbershops, bakeries, pubs, machine shops, little stores selling toiletries, snacks, and cold drinks, and *shisha* cafés where men in caftans smoke hookahs and Cleopatra cigarettes and drink tea. Water spigots are within at least a few hundred feet of most homes, and electricity, necessary for the recycling machinery, is widely available.

Conditions are better in the lower sections of Manshiet Nasser, the settlement of 400,000 people that contains Mokattam, which is a more recently built district. Streets are wider. Cafés are more spacious. More homes have sewage lines and televisions. And residents in the other sections of Manshiet Nasser don't live in garbage.

In 1981 the World Bank and the Egyptian government began a project in Mokattam to improve the roads and infrastructure and provide electricity and water and sewage mains. Residents then linked illegal, self-help pipes to the major pipes, although these now frequently leak.

Various international donors, including Oxfam, Mother Teresa's Missionaries of Charity, and the Ford Foundation, followed with projects of their own. Residents invested more in their homes and businesses. The *zabaleen* eventually replaced many of their donkey carts with trucks and bought plastic granulators, compactors, cloth grinders, aluminum smelters, and tin processors, earning more income and developing better living conditions than in other Cairo garbage villages.

Televisions and cell phones are becoming more frequent in Mokattam. Tetanus is virtually nonexistent. Today, seven hundred families have collection businesses, and at least two hundred families own and operate recycling businesses, which are more profitable. Throughout Cairo, the garbage-collecting industry, worth an estimated US$22 million, provides anywhere from 40,000 to 75,000 people with income.[8]

Still, a glaring fact remains: the *zabaleen* continue to live in garbage.

Relocation and Privatization

Some public figures have repeatedly called for the relocation of the Mokattam *zabaleen*. The Cairo government, as part of a city beautification plan, proposed moving Mokattam's garbage operations more than eighteen miles outside of Cairo and into the Qattamiya desert. But the distance and lack of services would further burden the *zabaleen*, possibly beyond their ability to continue in the garbage business.

"It's impossible," said Mounir Nawar, vice president of the Mokattam Garbage Collectors' Association, which represents the *zabaleen*. "There's no water, no electricity yet, and no roads. The governor said he will do this for us. But the affair isn't so easy."[9]

Malaak Farag, twenty-eight, has collected garbage since his childhood and currently rents a truck to haul waste. He says he'd likely find other work. "It will be difficult to go there and back. My [truck] owner will refuse, or maybe he will take a lot of money."

Some speculate that, even if not officially relocated, the *zabaleen* would move with the garbage. Others predict that, if relocated, they would simply return to Cairo after finding the Qattamiya relocation a bust.

The Ministry of Housing, Utilities and Urban Communities proposes creating 70,000 housing units in Qattamiya and installing sanitation pipes, roads, phone lines, and green space and providing training and health care, libraries, schools, and other services, including loan programs. But urban relocation programs rarely work. The social upheaval, undesirable location, and distance from city amenities generally subvert program efforts. Almost assuredly residents don't receive adequate compensation for the buildings and neighborhoods they develop. And many residents simply sell off their new land and home for a quick profit. Besides, in Mokattam, government bureaucracy would likely cause *zabaleen* business to stagnate and fail to appreciate their technology and experience. And, as Malaak illustrates, people with home-based enterprises would suffer doubly, losing their homes and their income.

Until recently, Cairo had no centralized system to manage the 3.5 million tons of waste it produces each year, but the government is now privatizing garbage collection. "We cannot permit very deteriorating conditions to be within the peripheries of the city," said Abdel Rahim Shehata, then governor of Cairo, in reference to these changes. "[The *zabaleen*] are the ones targeted for improvement. We are trying to give them better houses, better health conditions, better education, better environment."[10]

The *zabaleen* have adapted to unsafe, unhygienic living conditions and converted inhumane work into an efficient, successful industry that has received international attention and awards. Understandably, the city wants to improve its polluted image and help the *zabaleen* enjoy better living conditions. But by simply wresting the garbage from them, many argue, the government ignores the *zabaleen's* experience and management skills and would disrupt their flow of income.

Residents of Mokattam aren't the first *zabaleen* to face these threats. "The garbage was on the streets; the children played in it," laments Magdi Hanayan, a fifty-year-old garbage sorter from Torah, a settlement in southern Cairo that recently lost its garbage-collection business to privatization and a desert dump. "But it was our business. It was part of our life."[11]

In early 2003, three multinational waste-management companies, two based in Spain and one in Italy, began collecting and managing much of Cairo's garbage. In addition to paying them US$50 million, the Egyptian government promised to provide the companies with land, tax breaks, and lower customs duties on imports. Although these companies recycle only a fraction of what the *zabaleen* process, government officials say the *zabaleen* lack the technology and systems necessary to keep the streets of Cairo clean. In addition to collecting garbage, these international companies clean the streets and build desert landfills, composts, and recycling centers.

"Unfortunately," says Willard Pearson, the USAID director in Egypt, "the existing system has not been able to keep up with the pace of growth in Cairo. . . . The demands of a modern society have here bumped up against a tradition of pre-modern society."[12]

These moves toward privatization in Cairo come on the heels of a garbage collection scheme in Alexandria, Egypt's second largest city, implemented by a French company, CGEA Onyx, a subsidiary of Vivendi. The secretary-general of the governorate of Alexandria celebrated Onyx's experience and available capital.

Some Alexandrian neighborhoods, instead of paying a fee to the *wahiya*, now pay for garbage collection as a percentage of their electricity bills, the much-criticized logic being that electricity consumption levels are indicators of living standards, which are in turn indicators of waste production. It also helps that the government's electricity services are fairly well organized, and conjoining these bills provides people with an incentive to pay fees because companies could cut residents' power.

Tarek Genena, president of EcoConServe Environmental Solutions, referring to Onyx's work in Alexandria, ungenerously conceded that, "It does not conflict with the company's strategy to employ some of the freelance waste collectors [the *zabaleen*]. They have experience in the matter, if you can call it that, and they would be trained to follow [Onyx's] routine." The Cairo Cleaning and Beautification Authority has encouraged companies to hire a few thousand *zabaleen*.

Such privatization, of course, parallels global trends to open markets, particularly in the global South, to foreign competition and ownership. But while the dangers of unmanaged garbage make the status quo indefensible, neither is it a given that outsourcing the work is Egypt's best option.

Along with most Cairenes, Laila Iskandar Kamel, founder of the Association for the Protection of the Environment (APE), which works in Mokattam, doesn't dispute the need to reform the city's collection system. But she takes a different approach than that of

Genena: "The *zabaleen* have taught us that garbage is a resource. You don't need a degree in waste management, [when] you see it every day."[13]

APE created Mokattam's manure composts and runs programs in paper recycling, rug weaving, and skills training. Conceding the inevitability of privatization, APE has also helped the government design new waste-management systems, encouraging the companies and government to negotiate solutions that separate garbage from *zabaleen* living quarters. The organization would like households throughout Cairo to separate their recyclables and organic scraps from other waste before giving their garbage to collectors and is in favor of relocating garbage operations outside the city but demands that privatization plans consider the abilities and needs of the *zabaleen*.

Kamel emphasizes that the *zabaleen* recycle more than 80 percent of the garbage they collect, at least four times what most major cities recycle. "Now the government is planning to landfill 80 percent. How smart is that?" she asks.[14]

Rizk Youssef, a lawyer and partner in a plastic granulating workshop in Mokattam agrees. "Before signing the contracts with the companies, the government should have studied the situation very well. It should have considered our needs."[15]

The multinationals have agreed to hire some *zabaleen*, give them uniforms, and standardize their equipment. But, says Adl, a garbage collector and sorter with eight children, the *zabaleen* are likely better off without them. "They want to pay me 5 Egyptian pounds per day. I make 10 pounds per day, and this is barely enough. How will I live?"[16]

Critics point out that the *zabaleen* manage garbage for US$2.00 to US$3.00 a ton, whereas the multinationals will cost the government as much as US$20 a ton.[17] And to pay the companies, Egypt is utilizing part of a $1.5 billion loan from the World Bank, increasing the nation's overall debt even as foreigners receive the bulk of the project's windfall and as thousands of Cairenes lose their jobs. Some suggest that the government could invest just a fraction of the US $50 million it is giving to these companies to provide *zabaleen* with health care, training, education, and improved collection and sorting systems.

Infitah: A Policy of Openness

This globalization of Cairo's garbage is an outcome of the nation's efforts to integrate into the world economy. In 1970, Anwar Sadat succeeded Gamal Abdul Nasser, Egypt's only president since the nation gained independence from Great Britain. Sadat initiated a policy of "openness" or *infitah*, setting a trajectory toward free-market liberalism and away from government control and provision. Structural adjustment programs, a result of financing with the International Monetary Fund, have since increased prices for basic commodities, cut public subsidies, and privatized industries, all integral facets of Egypt's economic liberalization.

Under Sadat, the housing sector grew, although arguably in the wrong direction. The government attempted to build some low-income homes but left most housing development to the private sector. Partly because of an injection of remittances from Egyptians working abroad during a regional oil boom, companies quickly created almost half a million units of new housing in the late 1970s and early 1980s even as land prices in Cairo shot up. But two-thirds of these structures lacked building permits, and by 1981 an estimated 80 percent of new homes developed informally.[18]

Because rigid planning and building regulations have made the costs of legal construction exorbitant and because officials virtually never enforce building regulations, evading the law is more profitable than conforming to building codes. Therefore, through bad governance, officials have encouraged illegal, unplanned development. Today, two-thirds of Cairenes live in informal settlements, although only a small portion of them comprise impoverished squatter communities such as Mokattam.

A large proportion of homes remain unaffordable to low-income people, causing residential vacancy rates to run as high as

15 percent.[19] Many residences, after years of neglect, are also unsafe. One quarter of Cairo's buildings are "about to collapse," according to the city's governor, and 40 percent fail to meet basic standards of hygiene.[20] Multiple building collapses have killed dozens of people during the last couple of decades, and a large earthquake in Cairo in 1992 killed thousands.

The government has created a series of master plans to redirect growth away from the urban core and agricultural lands along the Nile and into new satellite cities to the east and west, but they have had minimal success. Meanwhile, overpopulation adds more pressure. One of the densest cities in the world, greater Cairo has an average of 32,000 people per square kilometer.[21]

So while *infitah* has helped Egypt gain greater access to global trade, the government has whittled down food subsidies, and food security remains a real problem for many Egyptians. The privatization of garbage collection threatens the livelihood of thousands of people already living on the brink of abject poverty. And unwieldy bureaucracies and bad policies have led to a glut of cheap and even dangerous housing in Cairo, forcing the majority of residents to live in illegal structures.

This is the context within which the *zabaleen* of Mokattam negotiate a livelihood. While they know a de facto sense of security, they remain illegal and vulnerable and poor. As in other informal settlements throughout the global South, their living conditions lack the hygienic conditions and security known by other Cairenes and most people in rich nations.

Most Cairenes, of course, do not live like the *zabaleen*. Proud of their Muslim heritage, their ancient history, and the intellectual contributions of modern-day Egypt, Cairenes take their personal and familial honor quite seriously: close-quarter animal husbandry, garbage sorting, and poverty are subjects of shame for residents in this urban agglomeration known as the Mother of the World.

But the *zabaleen* remain proud as well. "I took over [a route serving] some houses in Shubra [a rich neighborhood] twenty years ago from my father when his father died," says Malaak Farag, as he sips thick, black coffee and rests after a day's work. "I'm satisfied with my work. I spend my time doing something useful for my family. I'm a professional, and the inhabitants of Shubra are respectable people, and they respect what I do."[22]

Ezzat Naim Guindy, who once traded in garbage and broken toys, now works for the nonprofit Association for the Protection of the Environment. He initially served on a rug-weaving project but has since represented the agency in foreign countries as assistant to the director for public relations, and he's learning to use computers. Through APE, he's helping other *zabaleen* learn new skills and recycling methods.

Samia Wadie Hanna grew up accompanying her father on garbage-collection routes. She has since worked her way into a training position with APE. She teaches other girls to weave special designs, and as a project officer she manages a warehouse, sales events, quality control, and the payroll. "I never dreamed that the day would come," Samia says, "when I would actually enter to eat and be waited on at a restaurant on the same street that had known me as a garbage-collector child, daughter of a garbage collector from Upper Egypt."

The *zabaleen* have applied their own local knowledge and learned to survive amidst disease, filth, and danger and to fill gaps left by deficient formal systems.

"We can't leave our jobs, not even for one day," says one Mokottam collector. "If we did, this city would rot."[23]

Unsustainable Cities

The living conditions of Mokattam are symptomatic of a disturbing reality: our world's cities are unsustainable. All cities expose people to toxic chemicals, auto emissions, and other pollutants. Cities consume alarming amounts of raw materials, products, and energy. They overburden freshwater aquifers and continually expand into fragile deserts, forests, and agricultural land, affecting both local and global environments.

Cities prosper for the benefit of some and to the detriment of others. They compete worldwide for industry and jobs, and they accommodate the needs of highly skilled, global professionals. As regions prosper, cities develop highways and shopping centers, and more people purchase their own cars.

As a city grows, so does its industrial and economic output, as well as its production of pollutants and use of raw materials and other natural resources, locally and through global networks. Over time, people do gain regular access to more efficient, cleaner, and cheaper fuels and dependable sources of potable water, but then they have less incentive to conserve. Land becomes unobtainable for the poor, who then must move to informal settlements where they experience insecurity and a lack of services. In the end, urban prosperity can actually result in environmental and social debasement, outcomes that economists call "negative externalities," particularly in the global South where living conditions often deteriorate for poor people, both rural and urban, even as economies grow.

As Cairo's urbanites prosper, they consume more and produce more garbage and unsalvageable waste. While in the short run the *zabaleen* and other garbage collectors benefit from sorting through rich people's garbage, the scarcity of resources, pollution, sickness, and social exclusion challenge the sustainability of Cairo's consumption and the capacity of its waste management system.

Cities in the global South in particular are failing to meet people's needs for health and security. They cannot continue to operate and grow as they currently do without compromising the resources and opportunities available for future generations, the very definition of being unsustainable.

These unintended, negative results of growth can pit economic advance, development, and prosperity against environmental concerns and well-being. To cope, individuals, cities, and nations negotiate a series of trade-offs within imperfect systems managed by imperfect people.

In Mokattam, for example, most homes have electricity. Residents enjoy relatively reliable water sources and permanent homes of brick and reinforced concrete. Originally relocated by the government and provided with some services, people believe they've earned a modest level of security. Through the collection and recycling of garbage they have a community-wide livelihood that provides them with income as well as a sense of place and usefulness. Mokattam has come a long way from the shacks of just a few decades ago. But to receive these benefits, people live in garbage. This is the trade-off they have made.

In Lomas de San Isidro on the margins of Mexico City, people buy water at exorbitant prices, temporary materials shelter them from the elements, and they live under the threat of eviction. Many residents travel trying distances to work each day. Yet they live on the outskirts of the dense, car-ridden center of Mexico City, more sparsely than the residents of Mokattam. They have their own plots of land with space to build, and they don't live in garbage.

In Cairo, some families choose to live in garbage in crowded neighborhoods rather than remain in rural poverty because they need access to education, health care, and other city services. In Mexico City, some residents who can't afford to pay rent choose to squat in Lomas, a potentially unsafe, former mine under threat of resettlement, but they are able to build their own homes in the manner they wish and to meet their own needs.

Likewise, people in informal settlements burn cheap fuel, such as dung, rice hull, corn stalks, and wood, for cooking and warmth, but get respiratory infections because of poor ventilation in tight living quarters. The concentration of people into settlements maximizes the use of valuable urban land and provides cheap labor that fuels the economy, but overcrowding fosters disease and conflict. These, too, are trade-offs.

In rich nations, residents choose to build homes in the wilds of nature to enjoy the privacy and aesthetics of wooded hillsides and grand vistas, yet such invasion can damage ecosystems and cause erosion and mudslides. Meanwhile, long-distance commuters spend endless hours driving, burning countless gallons of fuel. Loggers manage forest growth, provide jobs, create useful products, and strengthen the economy, but with similar negative results, including erosion, water pollution, and species degradation. With almost every gain comes a resultant loss.

In the case of Cairo, it makes sense for the government to deliver people from the misery of garbage, but civic leaders are also removing the livelihood of the *zabaleen* and rendering irrelevant their skills. Relocation schemes nobly attempt similar ends, but they destroy the social fabric and increase insecurity. Some argue that it makes sense for the government to contract with international companies who have the expertise, technology, and experience in waste management. Yet these companies salvage only one-quarter of what the *zabaleen* are able to recycle at many times the cost and thus increase environmental degradation.

Sustainable urban development will, when successful, provide people with necessary services without destroying the environment for future generations. Yet economic success generally leads to new consumption, new problems, and unsustainable development. And it's the poor who experience the brunt of the negative consequences of prosperity.

The United Nations Development Programme suggests using a concept of sustainable *human* development to pursue equitable economic growth that empowers people and preserves their capabilities and freedom to make choices while also regenerating the environment rather than exhausting it: "Human development is first and foremost about allowing people to lead the kind of life they choose—and providing them with the tools and opportunities to make those choices."[24]

While the *zabaleen* have witnessed strides in the development of Mokattam, surely they're not experiencing sustainable *human* development or living as they would choose. Living sustainably and in harmony with the environment requires money, knowledge, and technology. Or else it requires ingenuity to create and apply alternative models for living that somehow work against the inertia of the unsustainable status quo.

In the global South, poor people living on a steep slope on the outskirts of a city may cut down trees to burn or sell the wood, only to watch the hillside give way during a rainstorm, thrusting homes and entire settlements into the valley below. They may dump excrement and trash into a nearby canal hoping the water will carry away their waste yet still assume that flowing water is clean and use it for bathing. Governments may choose to provide informal settlements with electricity before sewerage because electricity is cheaper to install, even though a lack of adequate sewer services leaves thousands of people at risk of infection.

Privation is the primary reason the poor degrade the very environment on which they depend. People need resources, as well as know-how, to live sustainably, to bulldoze hillsides into safe, terraced homes and manage tree harvesting, to recycle, to manufacture and use goods efficiently and with little waste, and to put long-term environmental concerns before immediate needs to survive.

Nor do the rich have natural or immediate incentives to conserve. Our economic systems of accumulation and growth encourage consumption and the extraction of resources. Corporations fare better if they exploit resources quickly, regardless of environmental repercussions, and then encourage buyers to consume. As urbanites earn more income, they demand more space, more products, more cars, more individual independence, more personal comfort. These demands lead to more waste. Although the poor suffer the worst consequences of affluent consumption through water pollution and industrial and solid waste, air pollution affects all city residents.

It seems that only as cities and nations degrade their own living conditions to the point of threatening the very means of their prosperity do people enact and enforce ecologically sound policies. For example, dirty city streets, antiquated sewer systems, and air pollution degrade cities' living conditions and discourage tourists from visiting. Many cities, with their financial well-being at stake, respond by enacting laws to protect the environment in hopes that they'll attract these tourists and the money they spend.

When cities in developing countries are unable to meet people's economic needs or maintain a sound environment and healthy living conditions, they produce informal settlements that lack adequate water and other services, that suffer from pollution, overcrowding, disease, malnutrition, and safety hazards, that sequester large portions of society into enclaves of decline. Slum residents must compromise their own well-being to survive. According to one pair of researchers, "If an individual or household finds minimum standard accommodation too costly, they have to make certain sacrifices in the accommodation they choose to bring down the price to what they can afford. And they usually make sacrifices in environmental quality."[25]

These trade-offs have environmental repercussions at all levels, from the global to the local and even within households. Cities are the major culprits of global warming, acid rain, depletion of the ozone layer, and other global degradation. Generally, the larger a city and the richer its inhabitants, the more pressure that city puts on natural resources and the more pollution it creates. Thus the demands of large cities in the global South often alter entire regions and even dictate the use of rural land, sometimes preventing rural residents from meeting their own needs as they produce and harvest goods to service the needs of others. Uncontrolled urban expansion haphazardly consumes arable agricultural land in peri-urban areas. Egypt lost 10 percent of its most productive farmland to urban encroachment within just three decades.[26] This, along with population growth and low crop yields due to pollution, leads to food scarcity.

Unplanned sprawl usually segregates the poor to the city periphery and the least desirable districts and then sacrifices fields of green space for meadows of concrete. This leads to further erosion, pollution, and destruction of ecosystems. Rivers, lakes, shorelines, beaches, and fisheries quickly spoil. In one lake near Alexandria, Egypt, fish production dropped 80 percent because of industrial and domestic effluents in the water.[27]

At household levels, people suffer from the effects of toxins and pollutants in their water, air, soil, food, homes, and workplaces. In informal settlements that lack sewage systems, garbage removal, and water drainage, people have no means to deal with waste, so it often remains with them or within the neighborhood.

Without Services

Without electricity, residents of informal settlements burn coal, dung, kerosene, wood, and other available fuels for cooking and heating, further promoting deforestation and erosion on the periphery of cities. In close quarters, people inhale smoke and fumes, which cause respiratory diseases and other health problems that require medical attention, further draining household income. These fires can burn out of control and quickly wipe out hundreds of homes, especially when emergency vehicles cannot easily access neighborhoods. And without electricity, people have fewer sources of light, more waking hours in relative darkness, and fewer working hours.

Without solid-waste management, scavengers gather and sort through garbage and sell scraps and parts to manufacturers and, where possible, recyclers. People throw garbage into rivers, canals, streets, and on vacant land. They feed it to animals or they burn it, further polluting the air. Scavengers' mounds of waste attract rats, flies, cockroaches, and other disease-carrying pests. Waste clogs storm drains and sewer systems. It smells, is a fire hazard, and, as it decomposes, pollutes ground water. In our world's poorest cities, formal systems treat only about one-eighth of the garbage. In Manila, about 40 percent of solid waste reaches dump sites. At one point, an estimated fifty to one hundred tons of garbage ended up in Bangkok's rivers and canals each day.[28]

Without sewage systems, pathogens from excrement contaminate food and water and lead to various intestinal worms, including hookworm. Residents need sewage systems or latrines appropriate to their culture, local conditions, and available resources, yet the layout and density of settlements make creating such systems difficult and costly. Once in place, sewage systems can be expensive to maintain, and they may transport untreated waste away from homes and businesses only to deposit it directly into rivers, canals, or coastal waters.

Poisoned Water

Without sources of clean water, people revert to using water drawn from rivers full of industrial runoff, stagnant pools, or contaminated wells, and they risk waterborne diseases, including diarrhea, typhoid, hepatitis, and cholera. They cannot maintain personal hygiene and lack the means to wash themselves and their clothes, which leads to infections, skin diseases, scabies, lice, and fleas. In Kibera, men brew *chang'aa* with polluted water. In humid Klong Toey, naked children leap into cool, sewage-filled canals to cool off.

Population growth, urbanization, and industrialization all cause pollution and overuse of water resources. Agricultural run-off poisons water sources with fertilizers and biocides, and mining and other resource extraction fill rivers and lakes with heavy metals and topsoil. Water thick with lead, arsenic, mercury, and benzene can kill wildlife and humans alike.

Clean water is critical for health and well-being, and contaminated water is the source of most sicknesses in poor nations. At one point, patients suffering from waterborne diseases occupied 70 to 80 percent of hospital beds in the global South.[29] Without proper management of water resources, poverty cannot be eradicated.

But as cities grow, there's simply not enough clean water for everyone: global consumption of water has tripled in the last half century.[30] Mexico City draws so heavily from groundwater sources that some districts have sunk several feet. Groundwater use in Bangkok has exceeded more than twice the level considered safe for adequate aquifer recharge, causing the city to settle up to four inches each year.[31] Poor drainage systems and ever-encroaching concrete surfaces prevent groundwater infiltration and, along with erosion, cause flooding in Bangkok, Manila, and other cities.

Yet slum residents use less than half as much water as other people in their cities, and an even smaller proportion than people in rich cities, where water is easily available and cheap. In New York City, people use an average of 120 gallons of water a day for domestic purposes, including personal consumption, laundry, and so on. In Nairobi, people use just 4.5 gallons a day, presumably even less in Kibera and Mathare Valley. One study found that residents of high-income neighborhoods in Mexico City consume nine times the amount of water used by residents in low-income neighborhoods.[32]

In many urban settlements, residents travel great distances to retrieve water from wells, natural water sources, or communal taps that serve hundreds of people. They can spend several hours a day walking to these sources and waiting in queues, time they could spend earning more income. Samia in Mokattam recalls her childhood: "It seemed like we used to spend all of the daytime hours fetching water when we moved to Mokattam. It was always so far away." Ezzat Naim Guindy calls fetching water a "monumental, exhausting chore."

Some people choose to purchase water from vendors, paying twenty to thirty times the rate paid in rich neighborhoods for municipal water. In Lomas de San Isidro, residents may spend two days' wages for a week's worth of water. With increased development, water prices generally fall, but, as with other goods, people consume more.

When informal settlements do have water systems in place,

they're generally available only during specified times of the day or on certain days, sometimes for a just a few hours a week. Many residents with in-house water connections never actually receive water. Pipes may leak, burst, and be poorly maintained and therefore fail to deliver up to 40 to 60 percent of the water that leaves treatment plants.[33] In Manila, fixing many of the water mains requires shutting off the water systems of entire neighborhoods. Stoppages are listed in local newspapers days in advance to warn residents.

After use, much of the water in cities goes untreated. Only one-half of wastewater in Nairobi is treated, just 15 percent in Jakarta, Indonesia, and only 4 percent in Lima, Peru.[34] Within informal settlements, these figures are even lower. Standing water breeds infection and malaria-carrying mosquitoes, one of the leading causes of death in many regions of the global South.

Improved water services can have dramatic, positive effects on people's health and have even been shown to help residents improve their income levels. But to secure water, settlements need working, legal water mains and connections, means to treat used or polluted water, and disincentives to waste water.

Because agriculture accounts for the majority of all water use, farming can reduce the availability of water for urban residents even as the agricultural sector labors to meet urban demands for food and other goods. Therefore regions need efficient irrigation systems.

Deadly Air

In Cairo, air pollution causes between 10,000 to 25,000 deaths each year, and levels of lead and particulate matter in the air are among the highest in the world.[35] In a survey of Cairenes from various income levels, one-half of respondents complained of regular headaches, more than one-third had trouble going to sleep, and almost one-quarter had a serious disease, presumably, according to a study, because of pollution.[36]

Each autumn in recent years a black cloud has appeared over Cairo. Researchers cite various causes, including auto emissions, smoke from pottery and brick factories, and the burning of garbage and rice straw, although the overriding cause is thermal inversion, the generally seasonal phenomenon that occurs when a blanket of warm air traps cool air and pollutants within a region. In Cairo and Upper Egypt, thermal inversion occurs as autumn temperatures cool and desert winds stop blowing, trapping pollutants for up to six weeks. Thermal inversion occurs over Mexico City because mountains surround the valley agglomeration, which sits more than 7,000 feet above sea level. Here, too, the phenomenon intensifies the effects of pollution.

Auto emissions are a major pollutant in Mexico City and other large cities, including those in the global South, crammed with cars, trucks, vans, and buses. As some individuals prosper, one of the first things they purchase is a car, which represents mobility, urban affluence, and the power of private ownership. As cities explode with people, they generally explode with cars as well but then implode under the pressure of stifling pollution, traffic jams, noise pollution, and demands to build more roads on sparse and valuable urban land.

Rather than develop alternative methods for transportation, cities generally encourage dependence on cars by creating huge highways and parking garages, which in turn encourage sprawl. One report on the future of cities says, "[T]he car has produced a mobility revolution that has transformed cities worldwide, but it is now driving the city into a dead end, from which it cannot escape."[37]

The number of vehicles in Mexico City grew 30 percent in seven years, and the air pollution is so bad that the government has discouraged people from going outside during certain times of the day. In Bangkok, before the economic crisis in 1997, 300 new vehicles went on the streets each day. Cairo has more than two million automobiles. "The world has gone car-crazy," says *The Economist*, "and the measure of a metropolis is the size of its traffic jams."[38]

Other Pollutants

Living conditions in cities and informal settlements are also negatively impacted by hazardous industrial waste, which can be highly flammable and poisonous, carry bacteria and viruses, and cause cancer. Treating such waste is expensive. Most companies find it easier to dump it into bodies of water or, in the case of rich nations, export it to nations in the South where weak governments lack stringent guidelines on disposal. Storage and treatment facilities frequently border informal settlements.

Animal husbandry, as noted in Mokattam, also leads to food contamination, air and water pollution, and the spread of disease. Similarly, noise pollution from airplanes, construction, automobiles, and industry also affects people's living conditions. Informal industries that pollute cities include leather tanning, metalworking, and brick and tile making.[39]

Hazards and Disease

Most informal settlements develop on land that poses immediate dangers to residents, in low-lying districts that flood, on muddy hillsides, along busy streets, and next to factories, waste treatment plants, and airport runways. Several years ago, a section of the limestone hill overlooking Mokattam collapsed, killing forty people.

Tight living quarters increase the likelihood of household accidents because children have immediate access to poisons, open fires, and stoves. In Balic-Balic, Jam-Jam, the Seares's three-year-old son, spends hours of energetic play in a tiny home as trains buzz by his front door. Daily, the Seares risk household accidents and death as a result of their home's structure and location.

Poor housing conditions exacerbate the spread of disease and the contamination of food and water. Dirt floors and deteriorating roofs and walls expose people to intense sun and chilling rains, winds, and low temperatures, as well as to rats and other pests. Homes in informal settlements are often either dusty or, especially in flood-prone areas, damp. Food is unprotected. Poor ventilation and dense living conditions increase the spread of tuberculosis, influenza, mumps, and measles.

The poor cannot afford high-nutrient foods. When malnourished in these living conditions, they almost certainly become sick, which leads to greater poverty. Although urban residents generally live longer than their rural counterparts, the trend actually reverses in many informal settlements. Residents lack preventive, curative, and emergency health services, and if new to a settlement because of migration or relocation, they may have only their families to rely on when in crisis. In the garbage of Mokattam, residents suffer high rates of hepatitis, tuberculosis, emphysema, and infant mortality. Children frequently get lice, parasites, and infections.

Because of harsh and unsanitary living conditions, the poor are more vulnerable to disease than the rich. Among poor families in Manila, one in every five infants dies, whereas among the well-off, one in every thirteen infants dies. The poor are nine times more likely in Manila to have tuberculosis, twice as likely to suffer from diarrhea, and four times as likely to have typhoid.[40]

As noted in Kibera, Nairobi, the poor are also more likely to have HIV/AIDS. Throughout the global South, men migrate in search of work, which leads to the dissolution of families, promiscuity, and the spread of HIV. Prostitutes and their children are particularly vulnerable to infection. Intravenous drug use is prevalent in some districts, and many poor people remain ignorant of prevention methods. The poor also lack the means to treat opportunistic diseases associated with HIV/AIDS. Once infected, they lose their meager sources of income.

Exclusion

Segregated into cities' fringe areas, the urban poor live on the psychological and social margins of society as well.

Many urbanites view animal husbandry and other rural practices in Mokattam and other settlements as underclass activities. Raising animals can be a source of embarrassment to many in Egypt where appearances and dressing well are central to personal dignity and acceptance by others. In fact, one researcher discovered that Egyptians in poor neighborhoods consider clothing a more accurate indication of status than even housing. Thus, the *zabaleen* are looked down upon, says Laila Iskandar Kamel of the Association for the Protection of the Environment.

"The ignoble task that the garbage collectors [perform make] their physical appearance seem odious to Cairenes," she says. "A distinct feeling of being unwanted and unwelcome in the modern section of Cairo [adds] to the increased sense of isolation felt by garbage collectors."[41] In Cairo, rich and poor alike blame the poor for pollution, which causes bad living conditions: pollution is dirt, the poor are dirty, therefore the poor are the cause of pollution, so the thinking goes.[42]

In order to survive poverty, the *zabaleen* have learned to submit themselves to the work of garbage sorting. "The *zabaleen* system is a good system, with human beings loyal to the garbage business," says the director of the Cairo office of Egypt's Environmental Affairs Agency. "They accept socially and psychologically to work with the garbage. And that is not easy to find."[43]

One expert on the Middle East tracked the living conditions of poor Egyptian households and found that the poor lack information, diverse media, and various activities that wealthy people take for granted, though the poor take particular solace in watching television, a window into life outside of poor settlements. "More significantly, [televisions] provide relief and enjoyment which were previously lacking," she says. "Now everyone shares in the enjoyment TV introduces into a life of urban poverty, where cinema visits are at best rare and memorable life experiences and holidays, vacations and even birthday celebrations are empty words only."[44]

Being poor is boring. Not that the urban poor are in want of things to do. Rather, they work and cook and clean and care for children, but then have few genuine diversions or opportunities for leisure.

Indeed, particularly within households, "continued stimulus overload" can cause mental stress. One study found that in Bangkok, "[H]ousehold crowding as a chronic stressor is detrimental to psychological well-being. . . . [B]eing in [a more] crowded household contributes to psychological distress, unhappiness and irritability, and can even lead a person to think about suicide."[45] Urbanites may cope with overstimulation by physically or emotionally withdrawing from others. Or they segment relationships, allowing them to remain superficial or impersonal.

People in informal settlements do enjoy personal relationships and networks. In older neighborhoods especially, they have very intimate ties and are well integrated into their surroundings. But the challenges of urban poverty can rend even the closest ties and lead to a general breakdown of society. Some people will turn to crime to survive, gain status, or pay for drug and alcohol addictions. Sometimes entire neighborhoods become known, accurately or not, as havens for crime and destructiveness, further stigmatizing residents.

Furthermore, migration and displacement can break cultural and social ties, leaving people demoralized and unsupported. Poor roads and a lack of services make exhausting and frustrating work of everyday activities such as washing clothes and cooking food. Poor people may see wealthy people—next door, on city streets, on television, in advertisements—as a constant reminder of their lower status and lack of resources. Living in informal settlements on the periphery, in fear of demolition, and in close proximity to wealthy neighborhoods fosters bitterness and dissension. Often ethnic conflict compounds people's resentment. The mental toll of living in informal settlements is high, and it leads to alcoholism and drug addiction, bloodshed, hopelessness, and broken families.

Under such conditions, men in informal settlements may become lackadaisical and angry and turn to alcohol. Without work, they feel useless and inadequate, so they withdraw from their homes. They may gather together in bars and cafés or they may take out their frustrations on their wives, beating them and then seeking comfort from other women. Women often work for wages even while trying to care for children and manage their marriages and households.

But moments of hope and dignity do occur, especially when these men manage to successfully provide for their families. Observing families in poor neighborhoods of Cairo, one researcher says, "When a man comes home with a washing machine for his wife and daughter, the consequences for family loyalty and family coherence are immeasurable. Women and children feel more cared for, the husband feels more appreciated. The flat is no more a monument to his failings. . . . He now shares in making it into a home."[46]

Hope for Sustainable Cities

Urban settlements and cities in the global South actually have great potential for meeting people's needs efficiently and equitably. In reality, cities are strategically concentrated to enable people to share land and resources, to save energy, and to promote trade and culture. Concentration can foster social and political cohesion, well-organized transportation, and the development of new technologies, media, and communications. It's easier to deliver services to people when they live together than when they're dispersed throughout the countryside. Dense populations also preserve open spaces for agriculture and wilderness.

In short, dense cities are, potentially, excellent models for sustainable living. The problem is that highly concentrated cities generally fail to provide residents with quality living conditions and instead consume more resources than they renew.

Sustainable cities will effectively mobilize resources and empower people to consume and waste less, to labor for the betterment of society, and to live equitably with sufficient goods and services. Sustainable cities will utilize the environment and its resources but conserve them for future use as well. They will have policies that encourage efficiency and punish waste. Residents of sustainable cities will have clean water, sanitation, quality transportation, and renewable sources of energy. People will thrive in freedom and security without having to make trade-offs that degrade the environment or their own living conditions and health.[47]

Sustainable cities will properly manage waste so that people don't have to live in garbage with rats and pigs and filth.

What sustainable cities will not do is produce more Mokattams.

7

Conclusion

Knowing the Dispossessed

JOANNE AND SAMMY SEARES live in the Balic-Balic railway community with their three children, Gellie, Iren, and Jam-Jam. A couple of times each hour a train bursts past their home, just a few feet from their front door.

Letty sells soap and snacks in Lomas de San Isidro. She prays that her husband, Leonardo, will get a job soon, that he won't have to migrate to the United States to find work.

Ezzat enjoys his work with the Association for the Protection of the Environment in Mokattam. He is learning new skills and helping people. But most importantly, he no longer gathers and trades garbage for a living.

There is no other family in the world like the Seares family. Letty is the only woman with her specific past and experiences. No matter where you go, you'll not find another Ezzat.

As I wrote in the introduction, the primary goal of this book is to introduce you, the reader, to these individuals living in informal settlements in the global South. Through the stories of Letty and Ezzat and others, I hope that you've learned more about life in urban poverty and that your concern for these men, women, and children has grown. My hope is that because of them, you'll care more about the big picture, that the blight of urban settlements is a massive and growing problem: one in every six people in the world today lives in an urban slum.

Frankly, I'm also interested in moving you to respond.

I don't have any theories of city planning or programmatic solutions to prescribe. Plenty of families and agencies and networks are doing incredible work to battle urban poverty in the South. They're the experts. Instead, I'm interested in how individual readers, having encountered a few of our world's one billion slum residents, will respond.

If you reside in a developed nation and you truly wish to help the people you've read about, you must first personalize their suffering, take it on as your own. You must also reflect on how your own actions—your purchases, attitudes, and lifestyle—may, in fact, fuel their suffering. Only then can you act effectively to help the poorest of the poor in urban slums.

Cultivating Compassion

Kenyan environmentalist and human rights activist Wangari Maathai won the Nobel Peace Prize in 2004. Several years ago she founded the Green Belt Movement, a grassroots nongovernmental organization that aims to conserve the environment and develop communities, primarily by teaching people to plant and tend trees. Commenting on the failure of international development efforts to lift Africa out of poverty, she made the following statements as part of a speech at a women's conference. I quote her at length because her words ring true not only for Africa but for regions throughout the world suffering under poverty and injustice:

> [Africa] continues to be marginalized politically and economically and even socially. There is lack of genuine support, cooperation and equal partnership from the rich international community. . . . But as if to justify relief and financial aid, people from the rich countries are more willing to go to Africa to implement relief services like feeding emaciated infants, discover Africans dying of horrible diseases like AIDS

and Ebola, be peacekeepers in war-torn countries and send horrifying images of tragedies for television.

Hardly any of the friends of Africa are willing to tackle the political and economic decisions being made in their own countries and which are partly responsible for the same horrible images brought to their living rooms by television. Relevant questions are deliberately avoided and those who ask them fall out of favor and become political targets. And therefore, those who are responsible for tragedies in Africa escape blame which is laid at the feet of the victims.

And Africa continues to be portrayed in a very degrading and dehumanizing way. As if when others elsewhere look worse off than [our]selves, it feels better and luckier. Perhaps it is playing on human nature: when Africa is projected as negatively as possible, it makes others elsewhere feel better and overlook the economic and political policies of their own countries, many of which are responsible for the situations they see on television.[1]

While we need to pursue economic development aggressively and empower residents in informal settlements, we personally do little sustainable good unless we escape the safe insulation of television and other media and the occasional feel-good acts of charity that do more to ensure our own personal comfort than create real transformation.

Maathai warns that instead of identifying with suffering people, we keep them at a distance. We pity them. Even when we travel to be with people in need, we still, in a sense, lob relief efforts from afar, over walls that cordon us into identities defining us as "us" and them as "them."

Whether we feed emaciated infants, as Maathai says, or simply write a check to support an agency's work, if we wish to act for the good of people living in urban poverty we must accept their suffering as our own on an intimate level, allow "them" to be "us." Only then will we understand their needs and perspectives, only then will we act beyond self-interest and remain dedicated to the fight.

But we're not as compassionate as we think we are. As Henri Nouwen and his co-authors point out in *Compassion*, suffering is unattractive, difficult, and painful, not something we're naturally attracted to, and yet real compassion enjoins us to identify with others' suffering as much as possible. It "asks us to go where it hurts, to enter into places of pain, to share in brokenness, fear, confusion, and anguish. . . . Compassion requires us to be weak with the weak, vulnerable with the vulnerable, and powerless with the powerless."[2]

Suffering, as much as our cultures of comfort claim otherwise, is part of life. Merely to pursue ease and abundance and avoid understanding others' pain (or even our own) is to refuse to engage with the world. The poor are in touch with this suffering. They understand loss and weakness. They understand how the world works. If we truly want to have compassion for people in poverty, we'll seek to understand suffering. As Nouwen and others put it, "Compassion means full immersion in the condition of being human."

Deep, genuine compassion, though, doesn't come naturally to us. Following the December 2004 Indian Ocean tsunami that killed hundreds of thousands of people and destroyed the homes and livelihoods of millions of others, one commentator wrote,

> So why haven't I given to the tsunami funds? Because I haven't been sufficiently moved to. Why not? . . . The short answer is that the south Asians are too distant and too foreign. The way human beings are made, we give up most of our interpersonal emotions to our families and friends. What little is left we spread among people, or causes, with whom we feel some natural sympathy. . . . I have no connection with them, no handle on which to hang my sympathy. . . . These folk in south Asia, though: They are people-in-the-abstract, not people-I-have-anything-to-do-with. . . . [I]t's just that the warmth of my feelings for these poor people doesn't rise to the level of reaching for my checkbook.

On the surface, these sentiments seem almost heartless, and yet the author puts his finger on some truth: We don't naturally respond to suffering unless it invades our own personal circles, whether they're physical, emotional, or even monetary. We mourn more dramatically, for example, when someone dear to us dies than when tragedy strikes an entire populace. This is normal. He adds, "People who look like us, behave like us, and speak our language, are easier for us to engage with in the abstract than people from other groups."[3]

Differences among peoples and cultures are real. Distance and ignorance of one another keep us apart. Even after reading this book, you may be wondering how you'll ever truly identify with the experiences of people living in informal settlements.

Consciously or not, we identify and differentiate ourselves and others through a variety of means: a passport, culinary tastes, ethnic heritage, language, religion, style of dress, the amount of melanin in our skin. Our own identity becomes a point of reference that defines who we are and how we relate to the rest of the world. It also helps define who we are not.

I am an English speaker, an American who grew up under the tutelage of a particular canon of literature, particular versions of American and world history, a specific political heritage. I am not a resident of the global South, living in urban poverty, pining for stable work and decent health care for my children.[4]

Once during a meeting, Warren Buffet, believed to be the second wealthiest man in the world and considered by some to be the greatest stock market investor of our time, challenged a roomful of people to think about the following scenario: Imagine a lottery in which every person on earth receives a ticket. These six billion or so tickets assign the following circumstances, which individuals must enjoy or endure for the rest of their lives: place of birth, sex, race, type of ruling government, parents' names, income levels, and occupations, IQ, health risks, weight, height, eye color, hair color, and so on. He then spoke about the small probability in such a lottery of being born into privilege and said that people should be grateful and not take favorable circumstances for granted.

Buffet then asked each of his listeners to imagine he or she was selected to be the one person to create the world's systems—the governments, the militaries, laws, job markets, and social programs. The catch was that they had to design these systems *before* they looked at their lottery ticket. Buffet then questioned whether people's systems would change if they'd been born into drastically different circumstances.[5]

Buffet basically encourages his listeners to recognize the privileged ingredients that comprise their identities. He then asks them to momentarily set aside these identities so they can better empathize with others. Similarly, we must question how we identify ourselves, the ingredients we're born with as well as the ones we choose, and then set aside these identities to better embrace others.

The tsunami commentator is correct in that we relate best to people similar to ourselves. But he fails to get beyond "the warmth" of his feelings because he only empathizes according to his own self-interest. This commentator refuses to play the Buffet lottery. How can we base our attachments and sympathies—our very identities—on our own self-interest and then reasonably expect our world to flow with generosity and love? Must we wait until we've been "sufficiently moved" to do something about suffering in informal settlements?

True compassion demands that we step back from our own deeply ingrained identities and negotiate new identities that accommodate others and their suffering. I'm advocating that we each go beyond the confines of social custom, race, nationalism, even family, to embrace a wider, though more painful, identity and then sacrifice as we would for those dearest to us, and sacrifice as we might to save our own necks. We must each suspend our inward-looking identities and accommodate a wider worldview, one that embraces others who are so very different from ourselves, who endure pain that we can hardly fathom.

In the Gospel of Matthew Jesus questions a crowd, "Who is my mother and who are my brothers?" (Matthew 12:46-50, NRSV). He goes on to give a divine perspective on who our brothers, sisters, and mothers are in reality. He does not define familial relationships by bloodlines but rather by those who do the will of God. One obvious conclusion is that God does not identify humans as we identify ourselves. We should take note.

As we mold and remold our sense of self, we'll cultivate real compassion for people in need. This requires diligent effort, and we must in a sense sacrifice our current, comfortable worldviews, even our theologies. If we live with views of ourselves and God that ignore the severe suffering of others or that don't account for the blight of urban slums, then our views are inadequate, short-sighted. Our worldviews and identities will crumble when we finally do encounter personal affliction.

My first visit to a Nairobi slum changed me—my view of the world, my view of myself, even my conception of God—irrevocably. I'm not sure how long I'd survive if Kibera or Mokattam or Balic-Balic were my lottery ticket.

Revamping our identities and faith to align ourselves with others, particularly those who suffer, can be an enormous sacrifice of comfort and privilege. As several settlement residents pointed out to me, the suffering of people in slums is nothing short of evil: the disease, the addiction to gambling and alcohol, the flippant endangering and murder of children, the daily loss of dignity and hope. However one chooses to describe it, the struggle is spiritual at its core.

Jesus also says, "If anyone would come after me, he must deny himself and take up his cross and follow me. For whoever wants to save his life will lose it, but whoever loses his life for me will find it. What good will it be for a man if he gains the whole world, yet forfeits his soul? Or what can a man give in exchange for his soul?" (Matthew 16:24-28, NRSV). Jesus' words assure us that there's a way to lay down our lives, to bear the cross of compassion.

As Thomas Merton, a Trappist monk, writer, and activist, puts it, "We must contain all divided worlds in ourselves and transcend them in Christ."[6] In compassion we embrace a fragmented world of suffering. In Christ, we discover a compassion that rises above this suffering.

I admit that cultivating compassion takes time, a lifetime, really.

And yet we're so limited in our time and our abilities and resources. Not everyone has the privilege of visiting informal settlements, meeting residents, hearing firsthand of their hopes and ideas. The important thing, though, is that we begin and remain on this journey of compassion. Identifying with the poor, in our own town or city and in other countries, is always a work in progress. Somewhere along the way, though, in our overly mechanized, distracted existence, we may discover our own impoverishment and need as well. Only then will we encounter the poor.

Lifestyle Choices

In a rapidly globalizing world, arguments contending that our actions have no effect on others, even people thousands of miles away, grow flimsy. As Maathai recognizes, our political and economic decisions are partly responsible for others' suffering. Like the butterfly effect of chaos theory, the notion that something as simple as the flap of a butterfly's wings can, through a complex series of subsequent events, affect the climate continents away, our actions affect people living in poverty in the global South, many of whom live in informal settlements.

Does the fact that our actions affect these people make us responsible for their suffering? Not necessarily. But once we realize that, in fact, our actions can and do affect them, we become culpable when we choose to do nothing. As privileged people with exponentially more material goods than the urban poor in the South, we must reevaluate how our decisions about individual and corporate resources affect others. This book has looked at a few legacies of colonialism and the effects of some current trade policies on the South. These are complicated issues. I encourage you to learn more.

We can't expect to be part of fair economic systems until we first take responsibility for our own financial practices. Become aware of whom your money supports through your spending habits and where your money goes before making too much noise over global economics. Tracing the effects of our economic decisions requires diligent research and engagement with others who understand trade, poverty, and issues of social justice. But in today's digital world of information exchange and instant media, ignorance is no excuse.

For example, stop and consider where your coffee, your blue jeans, your vegetables, and CDs come from and which companies profit from your purchases. Choose to support businesses that treat their workers well, that have sustainable impacts on the environment. If you invest money in companies or mutual funds, research them thoroughly to ensure that they're committed to equitable business practices.

A diverse array of foods and other goods are now available as fair-trade items, including couscous, chocolate, olive oil, and honey, as well as musical instruments, puppets, pencils, batiks, and greeting cards, just to name a few. Fair trade enables you to direct a larger portion of your money directly to workers and artisans in developing nations. Patronize businesses that support fair trade and drink fair-trade tea and coffee so that farmers in poor countries can directly benefit. The list of resources at the end of this book includes a few agencies and sources to help you learn more about spending your money equitably.

Then act to transform your society. At your workplace, encourage your co-workers and management to utilize fairly traded goods. Join a campaign to challenge your national leaders to support truly fair trade and debt forgiveness in the global South.

This book also examines the unsustainability of our cities. We must learn to question our insatiable consumerism and seek to live as sustainably as possible, for our current demands for goods cannot continue indefinitely. Through our consumption, we risk the well-being of future generations and provoke growing consumerism in poor countries as they develop.

Evaluate your own practices, your eating habits, your use of energy, your personal consumerism. Are you conscious of the specific waste and pollution that result from your consumption and the manufacturing of the items you buy? Could you walk or ride a bike or the bus more often than you do rather than drive a car? Does the food you eat require thousands of miles of transportation and fuel costs and rely on the heavy use of unsafe pesticides and fertilizers? Purchase organic, locally grown foods. With each purchase you make, ask yourself whether you truly *need* an item and whether you could meet your felt need in some alternative way, by, for example, borrowing the item from a friend or neighbor or purchasing the item with someone else so that you can share it. By living together, in community, we can consume less.

Finally, consider how you view material goods in the first place. Do you see them as a personal right? Something you've earned? Do you feel you or your children truly need to have *the best available* goods? I encourage you to escape the race to out-purchase your neighbors. Enable someone else to have adequate resources to survive before you demand *the best*.

In short, I'm suggesting that you seek to live as simply as possible. This requires sacrifice, for living simply can actually be inconvenient and expensive. Consuming conscientiously takes time. And it's usually countercultural and difficult to consistently seek simplicity. One author describes the attempt to live simply in our schizophrenic, technology-inundated world of consumption as a process of "holy frustration."[7] Nevertheless, we must humbly begin with our own lifestyles before we reprove our society for its self-engorgement.

As Warren Buffet suggests, consider how you might design our world's systems if you didn't already know your lottery ticket: Would your spending and consumption—your financial support for our world's current systems—be different if you weren't insulated from the negative impacts of your spending and consumption?

This is a terribly inadequate list of ideas and suggestions. Again, I encourage you to explore the list of resources and then examine your own spheres of influence—your purchases and lifestyle, the policies of your government, the actions of companies you support—and discover more ways to impact your world justly and sustainably.

Serving the Urban Poor

I'm on a lifelong journey to identify with people suffering injustice. And I wish to understand, more and more, how my decisions, my government and local organizations, and my spending habits and personal consumption affect others, for good or ill. My convictions have led me to the following concrete actions: I regularly read magazines, books, and other media dedicated to issues of social justice. I write letters to my congressmen. My wife and I attend a church where we're minorities so that, when they're suffering or experiencing hardship, we can cultivate compassion for people so very different from us. We choose to live in an economically and racially diverse neighborhood. In these contexts, we're learning to befriend people from different races, socio-economic classes, and educational backgrounds, to give to and receive from them. On a similar note, we ensure that our daughter has friends with backgrounds different from her own.

We nurture relationships with people in the global South by regularly writing Sammy and Joanne Seares in Balic-Balic, Manila, and by financially supporting a child living in a slum community and an African university student who is working for justice. We also have regular contact with friends and agencies working among the urban poor. As professional communicators, we've committed to using our skills to fight oppression, and we travel to developing countries on occasion to meet people and gather information. We own one car and try to walk or use the bus as often as possible. We purchase used clothing, and we receive vegetables from a local, community-run farm. If our income increases, we give a higher percentage of it away rather than simply increasing our consumption. Whenever possible, we participate in peace marches.

I share all this not because we've somehow achieved a consistently fair and equitable lifestyle. In fact, I'm too embarrassed to reveal our failings, the ways in which many of our choices still feed others' suffering and the unsustainable status quo. And it's undoubtedly obvious by now that all of our efforts—in service, in spending and consumption, in identifying with the poor—as compassion filled and well intentioned as they may be, constitute imperfect struggles. I share this list of what we try to do based on my conviction that concerns about injustice and urban poverty must translate into concrete action. And dealing with such global problems can be overwhelming; it's helpful to begin with specific, tangible examples of how we might respond.

I challenge you to act practically, to pray, to give your money and other resources toward eradicating suffering in urban slums. Read more and inform yourself of the debates and politics surrounding these issues. Advocate and campaign for justice. Support agencies active in informal settlements. Consider personally serving alongside the urban poor.

Below are some suggestions for further action. This is by no means an exhaustive list.

Learn. The resources at the end provide a short list of books and other sources to help you learn more about informal settlements and related issues. Use these to begin a study of urban poverty, and then delve deeper into specific issues that move you or relate to you. Many of these organizations assisted in the creation of this book. Visit their websites or contact them to learn more about their work. I've also provided a few items to guide you in examining your lifestyle and interior life.

Pray. The more I've learned about the suffering of others, the more I've begun to roll up my sleeves and begin the hard work of helping them. My faith has become fiercely practical, and I'm fervent in my anger over the evil that people have to endure. Honestly, though, the more I've learned, the less I've prayed. But I trust that this is merely one stage in my faith journey and in my lifetime response to injustice, that I'll receive the added faith I need to maintain hope and continue to trust that a good and loving God overcomes such suffering. I will pray for the people I know in urban slums. I encourage you to do the same.

Financial support. You can also contact the organizations I've listed below to donate money or other resources and possibly to volunteer in some capacity. With these and other organizations, you can use your money to support efforts that empower poor people rather than enable them to become dependent on handouts. And don't doubt that you have resources to give, regardless of how strapped you may feel compared to people around you. Be generous until it hurts. To attempt to justify hoarding our money, either as individuals or as nations, churches, or businesses, is to justify others' suffering. And when it comes to supporting work among the urban poor, money donated from rich nations, managed properly, goes further in poor nations than it does back home.

In Tegucigalpa, Honduras, I once met a woman named Angela who made corn tortillas each morning by hand and sold them out of her home, one lempira for four tortillas, or, at that time, the equivalent of about six cents. I gladly purchased twenty-four tortillas and gave Angela some extra lempiras. The tortillas were tastier than anything you'd find in most grocery stores in rich nations. It quickly struck me that if six cents netted me four tortillas, a mere US$10 could purchase more than 650 tortillas, and I realized that my money certainly worked harder there in Tegucigalpa than it did in the States. Now, I still like to convert mentally the spending habits and income of people in rich countries into the currency of Angela tortillas (AT). A $1.50 cup of coffee, at an exchange rate of 1:66, costs, say, 100 AT. A new compact disc is worth about 1,200 AT, enough to compensate Angela for several weeks of labor. A new CD player costs anywhere from 6,000 AT to 25,000 AT, a Hummer H2 about 3.6 million AT. A tortilla maker in the States earns around 1.8 million AT a year, though she performs the very same tasks as Angela.

Though I believe her family had additional sources of income, tortilla currency illustrates how difficult it is for people like Angela—and the cities and countries that they live in—to compete in international job and commodity markets. Tortilla currency helps me keep perspective on how much more my money can do in the hands of people in Mathare Valley and Klong Toey and other settlements.

A final note regarding money: Simple living shouldn't just lead to a larger savings account or more investments. Rather, simple living can free up your money—as well as your time and energy—to make it available to people in need. As a friend recently described it, simple living allows us to "facilitate greater generosity." I know some individuals who live conscientiously and are therefore able to give one-quarter, one-half, and even more of their income toward fighting urban poverty and other injustice. But they're not just giving it away. They're still wisely and thoughtfully investing money, but the dividends are greater than monetary.

Go. Then of course there's the response that likely comes to mind for many readers, the commitment to go and serve cross-culturally in informal settlements. The previous chapters feature a few people who have trained, taken risks, and made great personal sacrifices to serve crossculturally in these difficult contexts, people such as Aaron and Emma Smith in Balic-Balic (though of course Emma grew up in the community and in that sense isn't serving crossculturally). Both of them are college educated and capable. Yet they've forgone the comforts of living in the United States and instead choose to live in Balic-Balic, alongside people in poverty, amidst violence, drugs, and pollution. We need many, many more people like Aaron and Emma to leave the comfort of home to work in urban slums.

On a similar note, many people go to informal settlements on short-term introductory or volunteer trips, which enable them to serve, learn more firsthand, and develop personal relationships with residents. Meeting people in the flesh can quickly thrust us into a deeper experience of compassion. Such trips are serious investments of time and money, not to be taken lightly or viewed as adventures in foreign lands. Traveling with a group or agency to serve among the urban poor can be a wonderful, life-altering experience. But don't go unless you're ready to invest yourself in the local people you visit, as well as people back home upon your return who need to hear about the people and problems you've witnessed. Go with a willingness to at least consider some kind of long-term commitment to support a program monetarily or by helping them in some other way. Travel simply, as a pupil eager to learn, not as a tourist.

Equip. We need more people to dedicate themselves to equipping and resourcing local people working in informal settlements such as Pastor Imbumi Makuku in Kibera, Laila Iskandar Kamel in Mokattam, and Pastor Danny in Balic-Balic. Global travel not only allows people from rich nations to visit more easily and work in informal settlements, it also enables us to partner more with indigenous agencies and individuals. We have the resources and knowledge to provide them with training, money, appropriate technology, and other materials so that they can serve, often more effectively than we or other foreigners might.

Build relationships. Whether it's by sponsoring a child in an urban slum and getting to know her family or traveling to serve in an informal settlement or coming alongside people that work in these places, personally investing yourself into relationships is key to sustaining your interest and passion. Reach across class, race, and other lines to relate to people in urban poverty and receive their input and learn about their experiences. Beware, though, that these relationships may be costly to you personally, for as you invest yourself in others and get to know them, your compassion for them will grow and their losses and disappointments may intimately become your own.

Work locally. While the depth of needs in the global South demands that we assist people beyond our own borders, we should simultaneously work alongside people facing injustice in our own context. Find ways to serve the poor locally. Spend time with people who share a common concern for justice. Together, organize projects or campaigns. Seek to impact your own immediate spheres of influence.

These are just a few of the ways you can change your lifestyle and serve the urban poor and others in need. Otherwise, be creative and consider your own interests and abilities: build relationships with student groups who can match you with a student in the global South whom you can support; sponsor a child through monthly donations and write him or her letters regularly (see resources); serve through your local church; form a group to pray and discuss issues of social justice; write letters or call local and regional leaders to encourage them to address issues of injustice in your area and at national and international levels. But, foremost, express solidarity with the urban poor through your lifestyle choices, and educate loved ones and friends about the suffering that we, by our own actions, can add to or mitigate.

Lose Your Life

Don't doubt that an individual can make a difference. I've just listed several people who are serving the urban poor, including Pastor Makuku and the others. Wangari Maathai established the Green Belt Movement in Kenya in 1977, and the agency has since helped plant more than thirty million trees, one at a time, to empower communities to improve their environment and better utilize natural resources. Laila Iskandar Kamel tells of a New Yorker who purchased several bundles of rugs made out of rags by people in Mokattam, sold them out of her apartment, and then donated money back to development efforts in the garbage village. And there's a good reason that people in almost every corner of the globe purchase Coca-Cola and other products: billions of *individuals* consume them.

Mother Teresa, from her ministry in a Kolkata (Calcutta) slum, said,

I do not agree with the big way of doing things. To us what matters is the individual. To get to love the person we must come in close contact with him. If we wait till we get the numbers, then we will be lost in the numbers. And we will never be able to show that love and respect for the person. I believe in person to person; every person is Christ for me, and since there is only one Jesus, that person is only one person in the world for me at that moment.[8]

So find some way to serve the urban poor and find others to join you. But don't expect success overnight, and don't expect to change every system or situation. At current rates, within a decade of this writing we'll have more than twenty cities in the world with more than ten million inhabitants, most of them in poor nations. By the 2030s, the number of people living in informal settlements could double to about two billion, and we've yet to find some programmatic panacea for urban blight. To identify with and serve alongside the poor for the long haul while facing such staggering problems requires measured persistence and endurance. It also requires a strength that we don't possess.

In light of such challenges, Mother Teresa's words are again helpful. "If the work is looked at just by our own eyes and only from our own way, naturally, we ourselves can do nothing. But in Christ we can do all things. That's why this work has become possible, because we are convinced that it is he, he who is working with us and through us in the poor and for the poor."[9]

Cultivate compassion. Align your lifestyle with your convictions. Serve. Trust that, in Jesus' words, by losing your life you'll gain true life.

Notes

1. Introductions Are in Order

1. Robert McAfee Brown, *Theology in a New Key* (Philadelphia: Westminster Press, 1978), 61, cited in Suzanne C. Toton, *World Hunger: The Responsibility of Christian Education* (Maryknoll, N.Y.: Orbis Books, 1982), 155.

2. Shubhangi R. Parkar, Johnson Fernandes, and Mitchell G. Weiss, "Contextualizing Mental Health: Gendered Experiences in a Mumbai Slum," *Anthropology & Medicine* 10, no. 3 (2003): 291-308.

2. Manila

1. Elisia S. Adem, *Urban Poverty: The Case of the Railway Squatters* (Manila: Social Research Center, University of Santo Tomas, 1992), 45; see also Lynda B. Valencia, "Railways: A Priority Project of the Government," August 7, 2003, Philippines Social and Environmental News, www.bayanihan.org.

2. Adem, *Urban Poverty*, 42.

3. Stella P. Go, "Recent Trends in Migration Movements and Policies: The Movement of Filipino Professionals and Managers," in *Migration and the Labour Market in Asia: Recent Trends and Policies, International Migration*, The Japan Institute of Labour, and the Organisation for Economic Cooperation and Development (Paris: OECD Publications, 2002), 350.

4. Currency conversions for the Filipino peso in this chapter, unless otherwise identified, are 56 pesos to US$1.00 (October 2004).

5. Stanley Karnow, *In Our Image: America's Empire in the Philippines* (New York: Ballantine Books, 1989), 205-6.

6. United Nations Statistics Division, Social Indicators, New York, http://unstats.un.org/unsd/demographic/products/socind/illiteracy.htm (last accessed July 2005).

7. Rasna Warah, "Mathare Killings: Why Low Income Settlements Are Ticking Time Bombs," *The East African*, June 9, 2003 (accessed online through LexisNexis Academic Universe).

8. Ted Anana and Denis Murphy, "Evictions and Fear of Evictions in the Philippines," *Environment and Urbanization* 6, no. 1 (April 1994): 40-49.

9. Republic of the Philippines, Congress of the Philippines, Fifth Regular Ses-

sion, Republic Act No. 7279, Urban Development and Housing Act of 1992, Article VII, Section 28, July 22, 1992; this section also draws from an unpublished paper by Aaron Smith, "Biblical Ethics of Squatter Demolition."

10. United Nations Human Settlements Programme (UN-HABITAT), *The Challenge of Slums: Global Report on Human Settlements 2003* (London: Earthscan, 2003), 270. Figures on city populations in the global South vary widely. For the sake of consistency, I use United Nations data when possible. Many of these figures are quite conservative compared to other sources.

11. Joyce Mulama, "Rights: Doubts Grow on U.N.'s Goal of 'Cities Without Slums,'" Global Information Network, October 9, 2003, 1 (accessed online through LexisNexis Academic Universe).

12. City of Manila, www.cityofmanila.com.ph/population.htm for 1918 Manila statistics; Winnie V. Mitullah and Kivutha Kibwana, "Tale of Two Cities: Policy, Law and Illegal Settlement in Kenya," in *Illegal Cities: Law and Urban Change in Developing Countries,* ed. Edésio Fernandes and Ann Varley (New York: Zed Books, 1998), 199, for Nairobi statistics for 1901 and 1962; Alan Gilbert and Ann Varley, "From Renting to Self-Help Ownership? Residential Tenure in Urban Mexico Since 1940," in *Housing and Land in Urban Mexico,* ed. Alan Gilbert (San Diego: Center for U.S.-Mexican Studies, University of San Diego, 1989), 20, for Mexico City statistics for 1910 and 1940; Michael Smithies, *Old Bangkok* (New York: Oxford University Press, 1986), 50, for the 1883 Bangkok statistics; Desmond Stewart, *Cairo* (London: Phoenix House, 1965), 12, for the 1882 Cairo statistics; for all other statistics, see United Nations Population Division of the Department of Economic and Social Affairs, *World Urbanization Prospects, The 2001 Revision* (New York: United Nations, 2002).

13. UN-HABITAT, *The Challenge of Slums,* xxv.

14. Ibid., xxv, 13.

15. Ibid., 26.

16. Angus Maddison, *The World Economy: A Millennium Perspective* (Paris: OECD Publications, 2001), 126.

17. Society for International Development (SID), *Pulling Apart: Fact and Figures on Inequality in Kenya* (Nairobi: SID, 2004), xiii.

18. U.N. Development Programme, *Human Development Report, Cultural Liberty in Today's World,* 2004, 188. Although the United States ranks eighth on the United Nation's Human Development Index (HDI), a measure of development based on life expectancy, education, and national income, America has by far the greatest disparity between the rich and the poor among the top twenty nations on the index.

19. UN-HABITAT, *The Challenge of Slums,* 53.

20. Benjamin Barber, *Jihad vs. McWorld* (New York: Times Books, 1996), 237.

21. Babar Mumtaz, "Why Cities Need Slums," *Habitat Debate* 7, no. 3 (September 2001) http://www.unhabitat.org/hd/hdv7n3/20.htm.

22. Sheila Coronel, Yvonne Chua, Luz Rimban, and Booma Cruz, *The Rule-makers: How the Wealthy and Well-Born Dominate Congress* (Manila: Philippine Centre for Investigative Journalism, 2004).

23. World Bank, Poverty Reduction and Economic Management Sector Unit, East Asia and Pacific Regional Office, *Philippines—Growth with Equity: The Remaining Agenda, A World Bank Social and Structural Review*, Report No. 20066-PH (May 3, 2000), 43.

24. Karnow, *In Our Image*, 198, 209.

25. Asian Development Bank, "Economic Trends and Prospects in Developing Asia: Southeast Asia," *Asian Development Outlook 2002* (2002), 20-81; Asian Development Bank, *Poverty in the Philippines: Income, Assets, and Access* (January 2005), xiii; Gavin Shatkin, "Obstacles to Empowerment: Local Politics and Civil Society in Metropolitan Manila, the Philippines," *Urban Studies 37*, no. 12 (2000): 2357-75.

26. Shatkin, "Obstacles to Empowerment," 2365.

27. Saskia Sassen, *The Global City: New York, London, Tokyo* (Princeton, N.J.: Princeton University Press, 2001).

28. Abby Tan, "No Expenses Spared in Philippines Model City: A New Hong Kong?" *Christian Science Monitor* 88, no. 223 (October 11, 1996), 6.

29. Portions of this section first appeared as an article entitled "Immersion in Manila" (www.servantpartners.org) and as "For Yours Is the Kingdom of God," *PRISM* (September/October 2005).

3. Nairobi

1. Portions of this section first appeared in October 2002 as "Partnering to Transform the Slums of Nairobi" (www.servantpartners.org).

2. U.N. Integrated Regional Information Networks (IRIN), "Focus on Clashes in Kibera Slum," December 13, 2001 (http://www.irinnews.org/); Declan Walsh, "In Foreign Parts: Kenya's Literary Renaissance Gives a Voice to Urban Living," *The Independent* (United Kingdom), October 11, 2003 (http://independent.co.uk/c/?ec=500); John Mbaria, "Kibera and the Politics of Dispossession," *East African*, Monday, July 15, 2002 (accessed online through LexisNexis Academic Universe).

3. Andrew Harding, "Nairobi Slum Life: An Evening in Kibera," British Broadcasting Company (BBC), October 8, 2002, http://news.bbc.co.uk/1/hi/world/africa/2297259.stm.

4. Andrew Harding, "Nairobi Slum Life: Into Kibera," British Broadcasting Company (BBC), October 4, 2002, http://news.bbc.co.uk/1/hi/world/africa/2297237.stm.

5. Currency conversions for the Kenyan shilling in this chapter not otherwise referenced are at the rate of 79 shillings to US$1.00 (August 2002).

6. Madeleen Wegelin-Schuringa and Teresia Kodo, "Tenancy and Sanitation Provision in Informal Settlements in Nairobi: Revisiting the Public Latrine Option," *Environment and Urbanization* 9, no. 2 (October 1997): 181-90.

7. Danna Harman, "Kenya's Slums: New Political Battleground," *Christian Science Monitor* (December 10, 2001), 6.

8. This history of Kibera relies heavily upon David Clark, "Kibera: Social Dynamics of a Low Income Neighbourhood in Nairobi," Makerere University, Kampala, Uganda, April 1972; Timothy Parsons, "Kibera Is Our Blood: The Sudanese Military Legacy in Nairobi's Kibera Location, 1902-1968," *International Journal of African Historical Studies* 30, no. 1 (1997): 87-122; Mbaria, "Kibera and the Politics of Dispossession"; and personal interview with Imbumi Makuku, July 2002.

9. U.N. Integrated Regional Information Networks (IRIN), "Focus on Clashes in Kibera Slum"; United Nations Human Settlements Programme (UN-HABITAT), *The Challenge of Slums: Global Report on Human Settlements 2003* (London: Earthscan, 2003), 219.

10. Winnie V. Mitullah and Kivutha Kibwana, "A Tale of Two Cities: Policy, Law and Illegal Settlements in Kenya," in *Illegal Cities: Law and Urban Change in Developing Countries,* ed. Edésio Fernandes and Ann Varley (New York: Zed Books, 1998), 193, 196.

11. Yodon Thonden, "Juvenile Injustice: Police Abuse and Detention of Street Children in Kenya," from the Human Rights Watch Children's Rights Project, June 1997, www.hrw.org/reports/1997/kenya.

12. Carolyn Martin Shaw, *Colonial Inscription: Race, Sex, and Class in Kenya* (Minneapolis: University of Minnesota Press, 1995), 10.

13. "Expert Calls for New Roads, Transport Policy," *East African Standard,* May 12, 2003 (accessed online through LexisNexis Academic Universe).

14. David Etherton, *Mathare Valley: A Case Study of Uncontrolled Settlement in Nairobi* (Nairobi: Housing Research & Development Unit, University of Nairobi, 1971), 3 (accessed online through LexisNexis Academic Universe).

15. Parsons, "Kibera Is Our Blood," 103.

16. Judith Achieng, "Development—Kenya: Slum to Benefit from Euro Changeover," Global Information Network, New York, January 4, 2002, 1.

17. United Nations Programme on HIV/AIDS, *UNAIDS 2004 Report on the Global AIDS Epidemic* (Geneva, June 2004), 191.

18. Mitullah and Kibwana, "A Tale of Two Cities," 199; Clark, "Kibera: Social Dynamics of a Low Income Neighbourhood in Nairobi," 8.

19. Mbaria, "Kibera and the Politics of Dispossession."

20. Joyce Mulama, "Rights: Doubts Grow on U.N.'s Goal of 'Cities Without Slums,'" Global Information Network, Inter Press Service, New York, October 9, 2003, 1 (accessed online through LexisNexis Academic Universe).

21. Human Rights Watch, *Human Rights Watch World Report 2003* (New York: Human Rights Watch, 2003), 41-46 (http://hrw.org/wr2k3/pdf/introduction.pdf).

22. U.N. Integrated Regional Information Networks (IRIN), "Focus on Clashes in Kibera Slum."

23. "The View from the Slums: Kenya's Rulers Keep the Poor Poor, But Still Win Elections," *The Economist* (June 29, 2002), 44.

24. Harding, "Nairobi Slum Life: An Evening in Kibera."

25. Etherton, *Mathare Valley*, 9.

26. Davan Maharaj, "Kenya's Women Wage War on Moonshine to Get Their Men Back," *Los Angeles Times*, Saturday, March 30, 2002, final edition, A17.

27. Lana Wong, ed., *Shootback: Photos by Kids from the Nairobi Slums* (London: Booth-Clibborn, 1999), epilogue.

28. Philip Ngunjiri, "Kenya's Urban Youth Take to the Internet," November 2000 (www.africana.com/articles/daily/index_20001126.asp).

29. United Nations Food and Agriculture Organization, Statistical Databases (FAOSTAT), http://faostat.fao.org (last accessed July 2005); The Tea Board of Kenya, "Kenya Tea Exports Year 2003," www.teaboard.or.ke/statistics.asp; Chris Mburu, "Country to Grant Tea Factories Export Processing Zones Status," *East African*, October 13, 2003 (accessed online through LexisNexis Academic Universe).

30. "Tea Development Agency Puts Its Money on New Tea Trial in an Effort to Improve Prices," *Nation* (Kenya), November 11, 2003 (accessed online through LexisNexis Academic Universe).

31. Reed Kramer, "Kenya Is Safe and a Gateway to Africa, Kibaki Tells Business Group," AllAfrica Global Media, October 8, 2003, www.allafrica.com.

32. Isaac Esipisu, "Why Adding Value to Tea Exports Is Necessary," *Nation* (Kenya), December 16, 2003 (accessed online through LexisNexis Academic Universe).

33. James K. Nyoro, *Agriculture and Rural Growth in Kenya* (Nairobi: Tegemeo Institute, Egerton University, 2002), 17; "Farmers Subsidy Fund Gets Nod," *East African Standard*, October 23, 2003 (accessed online through LexisNexis Academic Universe).

34. Specialty Coffee Association of America, 1999 Market Report, www.coffeeresearch.org/market/use.htm.

35. Patrick Majute, "Kenyans Take to Coffee," Associated Press, December 26, 2002, business section, B3.

36. Mike Davis, "Planet of Slums, Urban Involution and the Informal Proletariat," *New Left Review* 26 (March/April 2004): 5-34.

37. World Bank, World Development Indicators database, 2003, http://www.worldbank.org/data/wdi2005/index.html; Rick Lazio, "Some Trade Barriers Won't Fall," *New York Times*, August 9, 2003, editorial section, A11.

38. "The Stark Reality of Globalization," *Nation* (Nairobi), Saturday, August 23, 2003 (accessed online through LexisNexis Academic Universe).

39. Gumisai Mutume, "Mounting Opposition to Northern Farm Subsidies," *Africa Recovery* 17, no. 1 (May 2003): 18.

40. "The Long Reach of King Cotton," *New York Times*, August 5, 2003, editorial section, A14.

41. Office of the United States Trade Representative, *2005 Comprehensive Report on U.S. Trade and Investment Policy toward Sub-Saharan Africa and Implementation of the African Growth and Opportunity Act* (May 2005), p. 9.

42. Marc Lacey, "U.S. Trade Law Gives Africa Hope and Hard Jobs," *New York Times*, November 14, 2003, A1.

43. Peter Hall and Ulrich Pfeiffer, "Background Report on the World Report on the Urban Future 21" (London: Urban Future 21, July 2000), 24.

44. "'Aid' Leads to Bankruptcy in Malawi, Mozambique & Kenya," *The Chronicle Newspaper*, AllAfrica, Inc., December 22, 2003 (http://www.afrol.com/articles/10712).

45. "Dirt Out, Cash In," *The Economist*, November 29, 2003, 44.

46. Robin Hodess, ed., with Jessie Banfield and Toby Wolfe, *Global Corruption Report 2001* (Berlin: Transparency International, 2001), 236; "Scandals Then and Now," *The Economist*, July 10, 2004, 42; "The View from the Slums," *The Economist*, June 29, 2002, 44.

47. Elisia S. Adem, *Urban Poverty: The Case of the Railway Squatters* (Manila: Social Research Center, University of Santo Tomas, 1992), 137.

4. Mexico City

1. Alan Gilbert and Ann Varley, "From Renting to Self-Help Ownership? Residential Tenure in Urban Mexico since 1940," in *Housing and Land in Urban Mexico*, ed. Alan Gilbert (San Diego: Center for U.S.-Mexican Studies, University of California, 1989), 13-37.

2. Gareth A. Jones, "Between a Rock and a Hard Place: Institutional Reform and the Performance of Land Privatization in Peri-urban Mexico," in *Current Land Policy in Latin America: Regulating Land Tenure under Neo-liberalism*, ed. Annelies Zoomers and Gemma v.d. Haar (Amsterdam: Koninklijk Instituut, 2000), 201.

3. Unless otherwise indicated, currency conversions for the Mexican peso in this chapter are 9 pesos to US$1.00 (April 2002).

4. Abel A. Alves, *Nature & Bodies, Land & Labor: Mexico's Colonial Legacy* (Meadville, Penn.: Allegheny College, 1991), 40.

5. Ibid., 3.

6. Peter Ward, "Political Mediation and Illegal Settlement in Mexico City," in *Housing and Land in Urban Mexico,* ed. Gilbert, 135-52.

7. Jones, "Between a Rock and a Hard Place," 209.

8. Kevin Sullivan, "26 Killed in Mexico; Land Dispute Blamed," *Washington Post,* June 3, 2002, A10.

9. British Broadcasting Company (BBC), "Mexican Farmers Strip in Protest," June 5, 2003, http://news.bbc.co.uk/2/hi/americas/2966496.stm.

10. Jose Noel D. Olano, "Land Conflict Resolution: Case Studies in the Philippines," in *Land Reform: Land Settlements and Cooperatives,* Food and Agriculture Organization of the United Nations, no. 2 (2002), 84-97.

11. J. W. Harbeson, "Land Reform and Politics in Kenya, 1954-70," *Journal of Modern African Studies* 9, no. 2 (1971): 231-51, cited in Tom M. Konyimbih, "Major Issues of Smallholder Land Policy: Past Trends and Current Practices in Kenya," *Land Reform: Land Settlements and Cooperatives,* Food and Agriculture Organization of the United Nations, no. 2 (2001), 49.

12. Geoffrey Payne, ed., *Land, Rights and Innovation: Improving Tenure Security for the Urban Poor* (London: ITDG Publishing, 2002); Ellen M. Bassett and Harvey M. Jacobs, "Community-based Tenure Reform in Urban Africa: The Community Land Trust Experiment in Voi, Kenya," *Land Use Policy* 14, no. 3 (1997): 215-29.

13. Payne, ed., *Land, Rights and Innovation,* xx.

14. S. Rowton Simpson, *Land Law and Registration* (Cambridge: Cambridge University Press, 1976) 1, cited in Peter Dale, "Land Tenure Issues in Economic Development," *Urban Studies* 34, no. 10 (October 1997): 1621-33.

15. Clarissa Augustinus, "Land in an Urbanizing World—A Contentious and Complex Web of Widely Varying Rules Around the World," *Habitat Debate,* December 2003, 4.

16. This section relies on Mika-Petteri Törhönen, *Land Tenure Confused: Past, Present and Future of Land Management in Zanzibar* (Helsinki: Helsinki University of Technology, Department of Surveying, Institute of Real Estate Studies, 1998), and Dale, "Land Tenure Issues in Economic Development."

17. Danna Harman, "Life Skills for Young Orphans," *Christian Science Monitor,* October 2, 2001, 1.

18. Törhönen, *Land Tenure Confused,* 6.

19. Anna Lowenhaupt Tsing, *Friction: An Ethnography of Global Connection* (Princeton, N.J.: Princeton University Press, 2005), 172.

20. Augustinus, "Land in an Urbanizing World," 4.

21. Klaus Deininger et al., "Land Policy to Facilitate Growth and Poverty Reduction," *Land Reform: Land Settlement and Cooperatives,* United Nations Food and Agriculture Organization, no. 3 (2003), 14.

22. Hernando de Soto, *The Mystery of Capital: Why Capitalism Triumphs in the West and Fails Everywhere Else* (New York: Basic Books, 2000), 124-30.

23. Ibid., 157.

24. Geoffrey Payne, "Urban Land Tenure Policy Options: Titles or Rights?" paper presented at the World Bank Urban Forum, Westfields, Virginia, April 3-5, 2000.

25. United Nations Human Settlements Programme (UN-HABITAT), *Urban Land for All* (Nairobi, 2004), 16.

26. See Payne, "Urban Land Tenure Policy Options," and Payne, *Land, Rights and Innovation.*

27. UN-HABITAT, *Urban Land for All*, 15.

28. Payne, "Urban Land Tenure Policy Options," and Törhönen, *Land Tenure Confused.*

29. Elisabeth Malkin, "La Muerte Comes for a Poverty Program," *Business Week*, July 3, 1995, 22.

30. Ibid.

31. Marco Morell, "Ecological Collapse and Poverty in Mexico City," *Swiss Review of World Affairs* 8 (August 2, 1996): 4-6.

32. See Norman C. Habel, *The Land Is Mine: Six Biblical Land Ideologies* (Minneapolis: Fortress Press, 1995); and Walter Brueggemann, *The Land* (Philadelphia: Fortress Press, 1977).

5. Bangkok

1. Louise Brown, *Sex Slaves: The Trafficking of Women in Asia* (London: Virago Press, 2000), 55-56.

2. Yardfon Booranapim and Lynn Mainwaring, "Risk and Reward in the Thai Sex Industry," *International Journal of Social Economics* 29, no. 10 (2002): 766-80.

3. Fr. Joseph H. Maier, "Klong Toey Slum, Little Girl Lost," *Bangkok Post*, October 22, 2000 (accessed online through LexisNexis Academic Universe).

4. Joanne Burke, *Women of Thailand* (New York: Women Make Movies, 1997), color videotape.

5. "Klong Toey Activist Hails 'War on Drugs,'" *Nation* (Thailand), December 4, 2003 (accessed online through LexisNexis Academic Universe).

6. Burke, *Women of Thailand.*

7. Mike Davis, "Planet of Slums, Urban Involution and the Informal Proletariat," *New Left Review*, no. 26 (March/April 2004): 5-34.

8. Keith Hart, "Informal Income Opportunities and Urban Government in Ghana," *Journal of Modern African Studies* 11 (1973): 61-89.

9. P. W. Daniels, "Urban Challenges: The Formal and Informal Economies in Mega-cities," *Cities* 21, no. 6 (2004): 501–11.

10. Philip Amis, "Regulating the Informal Sector: Voice and Bad Governance," in *Urban Governance, Voice and Poverty in the Developing World*, ed. Nick Devas (London: Earthscan, 2004), 145-63.

11. Graham Alder, "Tackling Poverty in Nairobi's Informal Settlements: Developing an Institutional Strategy," *Environment and Urbanization* 7, no. 2 (October 1995): 85-107.

12. Dominik Enste and Friedrich Schneider, "Hiding in the Shadows: The Growth of the Underground Economy," Economic Issues no. 30, International Monetary Fund, Geneva (2002) (http://www.imf.org/external/pubs/ft/issues/issues30/).

13. Erhard Berner, "Informal Developers, Patrons, and the State: Institutions and Regulatory Mechanisms in Popular Housing," paper presented at a European Science Foundation/Network-Association of European Researchers on Urbanization in the South (ESF/N-AERUS) workshop, "Coping with Informality and Illegality in Human Settlements in Developing Cities," Leuven, Belgium, May 23-26, 2000; Amis, "Regulating the Informal Sector," 148-49.

14. Berner, "Informal Developers, Patrons, and the State," 4.

15. A version of this section first appeared in Mark Kramer, "Dispossessed: Living without Place or Power," *PRISM* 10, no. 2 (March/April 2003): 8-12.

16. Bryan Tinlin, "Urban Poor and Public Policies in Thailand: An Assessment of the State's Implementation of Slum Relocation and Upgrading in Klong Toey District, Bangkok," discussion paper no. 52 (Toronto: York University Department of Geography, 1999), 25-30.

17. James Ockey, *Making Democracy: Leadership, Class, Gender and Political Participation in Thailand* (Honolulu: University of Hawaii Press, 2004), 125.

18. Srawooth Paitoonpong, *Consultations with the Poor, National Synthesis Report: Thailand*, (preliminary draft), World Bank (August 1999), 4; Sakchai Kirinpanu and Yap Kioe Sheng, "Once Only the Sky Was the Limit: Bangkok's Housing Boom and the Financial Crisis in Thailand," *Housing Studies* 15, no. 1 (2000): 11-27.

19. Radhika Savant Mohit, "A Level Playing Field: Security of Tenure and the Urban Poor in Bangkok, Thailand," in *Land, Rights & Innovation: Improving Tenure Security for the Urban Poor*, ed. Geoffrey Payne (London: ITDG Publishing, 2002), 281; see also Shahed Anwer Khan, "Attributes of Informal Settlements Affecting Their Vulnerability to Eviction, a Study of Bangkok," *Environment and Urbanization* 6, no. 1 (April 1994): 25-39.

20. Urban Community Development Office (UCDO), "Housing Loans: Supporting Poor People's Own Shelter Strategies," *UCDO Update* (Bangkok), no. 2 (October 2000), 24-25.

21. Anil B. Deolalikar, "Poverty, Growth, and Inequality in Thailand," Economics and Research Department Working Paper Series No. 8, Asian Development Bank (April 2002), 4.

22. Paitoonpong, *Consultations with the Poor*, 4.

23. Noppawan Piaseu, Basia Belza, and Bettina Shell-Duncan, "Less Money Less Food: Voices from Women in Urban Poor Families in Thailand," *Health Care for Women International* 25, no. 7 (August 2004): 604–19.

24. Deepa Narayan, ed., *Voices of the Poor: Can Anyone Hear Us?* (New York: Oxford University Press for the World Bank, 2000), 79.

25. Urban Community Development Office (UCDO), "What the Economic Crisis Has Meant for Thailand's Urban Poor Communities," *UCDO Update* (Bangkok), no. 2 (October 2000), 2.

26. Narayan, *Voices of the Poor*, 81.

27. Enste and Schneider, "Hiding in the Shadows"; Elisia S. Adem, *Urban Poverty: The Case of the Railway Squatters* (Manila: Social Research Center, University of Santo Tomas, 1992), 51; Amis, "Regulating the Informal Sector," 147; interview with Bertha Angelica Albores Ramirez, Director of Social Communications at the Valle de Chalco City Hall, State of Mexico, April 11, 2002.

28. Davis, "Planet of Slums, Urban Involution and the Informal Proletariat," 15; United Nations Economic Commission for Europe (UNECE), *Land Administration Guidelines, with Special Reference to Countries in Transition* (New York: United Nations, 1996).

29. Hernando de Soto, *The Mystery of Capital: Why Capitalism Triumphs in the West and Fails Everywhere Else* (New York: Basic Books, 2000), 20.

30. Amis "Regulating the Informal Sector," 145.

31. Dorothy Munyakho, "Poverty and Ill-Health Go Hand in Hand," *World Health* 45, no. 6 (November-December 1992): 6-7.

32. Berner, "Informal Developers, Patrons, and the State," 3; Vito Tanzi, "The Underground Economy: The Causes and Consequences of This Worldwide Phenomenon," *Finance & Development* 20, no. 4 (December 1983): 10-13; also cited in David L. Lindauer, "Parallel, Fragmented, or Black? Defining Market Structure in Developing Economies," *World Development* 17, no. 12 (1989): 1871-80; Enste and Schneider, "Hiding in the Shadows."

33. Pinelopi Koujianou Goldberg and Nina Pavcnik, "The Response of the Informal Sector to Trade Liberalization," *Journal of Development Economics* 72, no. 2 (2003): 463-96; Enste and Schneider, "Hiding in the Shadows."

34. Berner, "Informal Developers, Patrons, and the State," 12-13; Daniels "Urban Challenges," 509.

35. Francisco Alba, "Mexico: A Crucial Crossroads," The Migration Policy Institute (March 2004) www.migrationinformation.org/Profiles/display.cfm?ID=211.

36. W. J. House, "Nairobi's Informal Sector: Dynamic Entrepreneurs or Surplus Labor?" *Economic Development and Cultural Change* 32, no. 2 (January 1984): 277-302.

37. Petronella W. Kigochie, "Squatter Rehabilitation Projects That Support

Home-Based Enterprises Create Jobs and Housing: The Case of Mathare 4A, Nairobi," *Cities* 18, no. 4 (2001): 223–33.

38. Geoffrey Payne, *Urban Land Tenure and Property Rights in Developing Countries: A Review* (London: Intermediate Technology, 1997), 7.

39. Emiel A. Wegelin and Chantana Chanond, "Home Improvement, Housing Finance and Security of Tenure in Bangkok Slums," in *Land for Housing the Poor*, ed. Shlomo Angel (Singapore: Select Books, 1983), 79; Mohit, "A Level Playing Field," 278.

40. Joseph Friedman, Emmanuel Jimenez, and Stephen K. Mayo, "The Demand for Tenure Security in Development Countries," *Journal of Development Economics* 29, no. 2 (September 1988), 185-98.

41. de Soto, *The Mystery of Capital*, 40-67.

42. United Nations Development Programme, *Human Development Report 1997: Human Development to Eradicate Poverty* (Oxford: Oxford University Press, 1997), 62.

43. Narayan, *Voices of the Poor*, 122.

44. Hernando de Soto, *The Other Path, The Invisible Revolution in the Third World* (New York: Harper & Row, 1989), 93.

45. Narayan, *Voices of the Poor*, 155, 157.

46. Piaseu, Belza, and Shell-Duncan, "Less Money Less Food," 610.

47. Tinlin, "Urban Poor and Public Policies in Thailand," 57-58.

48. Ockey, *Making Democracy*, 148.

49. Amis, "Regulating the Informal Sector," 161.

50. Brown, *Sex Slaves*, 91.

51. Davis, "Planet of Slums, Urban Involution and the Informal Proletariat," 25.

6. Cairo

1. Ezzat's and Samia Wadie Hanna's stories are based on profiles in Laila R. Iskandar Kamel, *Mokattam Garbage Village, Cairo, Egypt* (Cairo: Stallion Graphics, 1994), 100-110.

2. Wael Salah Fahmi, *Urban Sustainability and Poverty Alleviation Initiatives of Garbage Collectors Community: A Stakeholder Analysis of the Muqattam 'Zabaleen' Settlement in Cairo*, paper presented at the European Network for Housing Research (ENHR): Growth and Regeneration Conference, July 2-6, 2004, Cambridge, United Kingdom, 4; some sources say 30,000: Dena Rashed, "Trashed Lives," *Al-Ahram Weekly*, no. 624 (February 6-12, 2003), weekly.ahram.org.eg/2003/624/fe1.htm.

3. Paul Salopek, "Cairo's Pickers about to Be Dumped," *Chicago Tribune*, March 2, 2003, Sunday final edition, A8.

4. Ibid.

5. Jörg Gertel and Said Samir, "Cairo: Urban Agriculture and Visions for a 'Modern City,'" in *Growing Cities, Growing Food: Urban Agriculture on the Policy Agenda,* ed. Nico Bakker et al. (Feldafing, Germany: Food & Agriculture Development Centre, 2000), 209-34.

6. Ibid.

7. Fahmi, *Urban Sustainability and Poverty Alleviation Initiatives,* 7.

8. Mark Huband, "The Dirty Business of Keeping Egypt's Capital Clean," *Financial Times* (London), July 17, 1999, International section, 5; Fahmi, *Urban Sustainability and Poverty Alleviation Initiatives,* 4.

9. Elizabeth Bryant, "In Cairo, Zabaleen Lead Attack on Trash," *St. Petersburg Times* (Florida), March 5, 1999, South Pinellas edition, National section, 1A.

10. Ibid.

11. Howard Schneider, "Cairo Trashes an Ancient Profession," Washington Post Foreign Service, Middle East Journal, September 11, 2000, 17A.

12. Jon Sawyer, "Garbage Collectors Fear Livelihood Is Threatened," *St. Louis Post-Dispatch*, September 15, 2002, Newswatch section, 1B.

13. Interview with Laila Iskandar Kamel, July 9, 2002.

14. Salopek, "Cairo's Pickers about to Be Dumped."

15. Sarah Gauch, "Egypt Dumps 'Garbage People,'" *Christian Science Monitor*, January 6, 2003, World section, 7.

16. Ibid.

17. Emad Mekay, "Egypt: Mubarak and World Bank Trash the Garbage Pickers," IPS-Inter Press Service, March 4, 2003 (accessed online through LexisNexis Academic Universe).

18. André Raymond, *Cairo*, trans. Willard Wood (Cambridge: Harvard University Press, 2000), 349; David Sims, "What Is Secure Tenure in Urban Egypt?" in *Land, Rights and Innovation: Improving Tenure Security for the Urban Poor,* ed. Geoffrey Payne (London: ITDG Publishing, 2002), 79.

19. Keith Sutton and Wael Fahmi, "Cairo's Urban Growth and Strategic Master Plans in the Light of Egypt's 1996 Population Census Results," *Cities* 18, no. 3 (2001): 135-49.

20. Azza Khattab, "And We All Fall Down," *Egypt Today*, May 2002, 74-79.

21. Gertel and Samir, "Cairo: Urban Agriculture and Visions for a 'Modern City,'" 209.

22. Huband, "The Dirty Business of Keeping Egypt's Capital Clean."

23. Sawyer, "Garbage Collectors Fear Livelihood Is Threatened."

24. United Nations Development Programme (UNDP), *Human Development Report 2004: Cultural Liberty in Today's Diverse World* (New York: United Nations, 2004), v.

25. Jorge E. Hardoy and David Satterthwaite, *Squatter Citizen: Life in the Urban Third World* (London: Earthscan Publications, 1989), 157.

26. Ibid., 208.

27. Ibid., 210.

28. United Nations Human Settlements Programme (UN-HABITAT), *The Challenge of Slums: Global Report on Human Settlements 2003* (London: Earthscan, 2003), 114; UN-HABITAT, "Global Urban Indicators Database: Version 2," Nairobi (2002); Kirk Smith and Yok-Shui Lee, "Urbanization and the Environmental Risk Transition," in *Third World Cities: Problems, Policies, and Prospects,* ed. John Kasarda and Allan Parnell (Newbury Park, Calif.: Sage Publications, 1993), 176.

29. P. Wurzel, "Water Supply and Health in the Humid Tropics," paper read at the International Colloquium on the Development of Hydrologic and Water Management Strategies in the Humid Tropics, July 15-22, 1989, Townsville, Australia, as cited in Smith and Lee, "Urbanization and the Environmental Risk Transition," 168.

30. Clifton Coles, *The Futurist*, January/February 2003, as cited in Laura Coulter, "Righting Water Wrongs," *PRISM* (May/June 2005): 8-14.

31. Smith and Lee, "Urbanization and the Environmental Risk Transition," 172.

32. UN-HABITAT, "Global Urban Indicators Database: Version 2"; Hardoy and Satterthwaite, *Squatter Citizen*, 151.

33. Smith and Lee, "Urbanization and the Environmental Risk Transition," 172.

34. UN-HABITAT, "Global Urban Indicators Database: Version 2."

35. Cam McGrath, "Progress in Campaign to Snuff Out Smog Cloud," Inter Press Service, December 30, 2001 (accessed online through LexisNexis Academic Universe).

36. Nicholas S. Hopkins and Sohair R. Mehanna, "Living with Pollution in Egypt," *Environmentalist* 23, no. 1 (March 2003): 17-28.

37. Peter Hall and Ulrich Pfeiffer, "Background Report on the World Report on the Urban Future 21" (London: Urban Future 21, July 2000), 29.

38. Marc Levinson, *The Economist*, vol. 348, issue 8084, (September 5, 1998), C3; "Black Clouds Over Cairo," Financial Times Information Global News Wire, October 31, 2003 (accessed online through LexisNexis Academic Universe).

39. Allen Blackman, "Informal Sector Pollution Control: What Policy Options Do We Have?," *World Development*, 28, no. 12 (2000) 2067-82.

40. Diana Silimperi, "Health and the Environment in Urban Poor Areas: Avoiding a Crisis through Prevention," Capsule Report Number 1 (Arlington, Va.: Environmental Health Project, March 1996), 2.

41. Kamel, *Mokattam Garbage Village, Cairo, Egypt*, 4.

42. Hopkins and Mehanna, "Living with Pollution in Egypt," 27.

43. Bryant, "In Cairo, Zabaleen Lead Attack on Trash."

44. Unni Wikan, "Living Conditions among Cairo's Poor—A View from Below," *Middle East Journal* 39, no. 1 (Winter 1985): 7-26.

45. Theodore D. Fuller et al., "Chronic Stress and Psychological Well-Being: Evidence from Thailand on Household Crowding," *Social Science and Medicine* 42, no. 2 (1996): 265-80.

46. Wikan, "Living Conditions among Cairo's Poor," 13.

47. Janice E. Perlman, "Innovative Solutions Create Urban Sustainability," *Urban Environmental Solutions* 5, no. 1 (March 2000); online version, http://usinfo.state.gov/journals/itgic/0300/ijge/gj-04a.htm.

7. Conclusion

1. Wangari Maathai, "Bottlenecks of Development in Africa," speech presented to the 4th U.N. World Women's Conference (Beijing, China, August 30-September 15, 1995).

2. Henri Nouwen, Donald P. McNeill, and Douglas A. Morrison, *Compassion: A Reflection on the Christian Life* (New York: Doubleday, 1983), 4.

3. John Derbyshire, "We and They, The World and I," *National Review Online*, January 12, 2005, www.nationalreview.com/derbyshire/derbyshire200409010849.asp.

4. Portions of this section adapted from Mark Kramer, "Losing Identity That It Might Be Found," *Social Justice Review* 90, nos. 9-10 (September-October 1999): 148-50.

5. See http://darrenjohnson.blogspot.com (last accessed July 2005). The lottery scenario actually originates with John Rawls, *A Theory of Justice* (Cambridge, Mass.: Belknap Press of Harvard University Press, 1971).

6. Thomas Merton, *Conjectures of a Guilty Bystander* (Garden City, N.Y.: Doubleday, 1965), 21.

7. Doris Janzen Longacre, *Living More with Less* (Scottdale, Pa.: Herald Press, 1980), 9.

8. Malcom Muggeridge, *Something Beautiful for God: The Classic Account of Mother Teresa's Journey into Compassion* (San Francisco: Harper & Row, 1986), 118.

9. Ibid., 107.

Resources for Learning and Action

Below are just a few of the resources available to help you learn more about informal settlements, as well as a few items on simple living and fighting injustice. Chapter endnotes also cite many useful books, articles, and sources.

Organizations

AMEXTRA (Asociación Mexicana de Transformación Rural y Urbana, A.C., Mexican Association for Rural and Urban Transformation), Mexico City, www.amextra.org. Pursues holistic transformation among farmers, indigenous peoples, women, and children in both rural and urban areas.

APE (Association for the Protection of the Environment), Mokattam, Cairo, www.ape.org.eg. Serves garbage-collector communities in Cairo.

Balic-Balic Christian Church (BBCC), Balic-Balic, Manila, Pastor Danny Francisco, Danny_Francisco83@yahoo.com. Railway-community church empowering the urban poor.

Catholic Charities, Alexandria, Virginia, www.catholiccharities usa.org. Social services in the U.S. including advocacy and training.

Catholic Network of Volunteer Service (CNVS), Takoma Park, Maryland, www.cnvs.org. Coordinating agency that connects volunteers to service opportunities in the U.S. and around the world; their Response Directory enables you to match your interests and skills with specific programs.

Catholic Relief Services (CRS), Baltimore, Maryland, www.catholic relief.org. U.S. Catholic relief and development agency working in more than 90 countries.

Global Urban Trek, Madison, Wisconsin, www.urbana.org/feat. trek.home.cfm. Series of short-term trips that challenge college students to serve among the poor in urban slums.

Life in Abundance (LIA) International, Addis Ababa, Ethiopia, www.liaint.org. Holistic programs for church-based community development in several countries in Africa. Royalties from the sale of this book go to support the ministry of LIA International.

Maryknoll, Maryknoll, New York, www.maryknoll.org. Maryknoll priests, brothers, sisters, and lay missioners serve the poor and oppressed in cities featured in this book and around the world.

MYSA (Mathare Youth Sports Association), Mathare Valley, Nairobi, www.mysakenya.org. Leadership development, sports programs, community development, and self-help projects for youth.

Servant Partners, Pasadena, California, www.servantpartners.org. Holistic-church planting among the world's urban poor.

UN-HABITAT (United Nations Human Settlements Program), Nairobi, www.unhabitat.org. Promotes sustainable cities and villages to provide adequate shelter for all.

Fair Trade

Ten Thousand Villages, www.villages.ca. Markets handcrafts from people in the Third World.

The International Fair Trade Association, www.ifat.org. A global association of fair-trade organizations, selling everything from fairtrade coffee and tea to chocolate, batiks, and gift cards.

Child-Sponsorship Programs

Write either of these agencies to request sponsorship opportunities in specific regions or countries:

Compassion International, Colorado Springs, Colorado, www.compassion.com. Advocates for children and matches them with individual donors.

World Vision, Federal Way, Washington, www.worldvision.org. Sponsor an individual boy or girl, a child suffering the impact of HIV/AIDS, or a family.

Bibliography: Informal Settlements

Bessenecker, Scott, ed. *Quest for Hope in the Slum Community.* Waynesboro, Ga.: Authentic Media, 2005.

Fernandes, Edésio, and Ann Varley, eds. *Illegal Cities: Law and Urban Change in Developing Countries.* New York: Zed Books, 1998.

Grigg, Viv. *Companion to the Poor: Christ in the Urban Slums.* Waynesboro, Ga.: Authentic Media, 2004.

Gugler, Josef, ed. *The Urban Transformation of the Developing World.* Oxford: Oxford University Press, 1996.

Hardoy, Jorge E., and David Satterthwaite. *Squatter Citizen: Life in the Urban Third World.* London: Earthscan, 1989.

Mitlin, Diana, and David Satterthwaite, eds. *Empowering Squatter Citizens: Local Government, Civil Society and Urban Poverty Reduction.* London: Earthscan, 2004.

Narayan, Deepa, ed. *Voices of the Poor: Can Anyone Hear Us?* New York: Oxford University Press for the World Bank, 2000.

Neuwirth, Robert. *Shadow Cities.* New York: Routledge, 2005.

Payne, Geoffrey, ed. *Land, Rights and Innovation: Improving Tenure Security for the Urban Poor.* London: ITDG, 2002.

de Soto, Hernando. *The Mystery of Capital: Why Capitalism Tri-*

umphs in the West and Fails Everywhere Else. New York: Basic
Books, 2000.

———. *The Other Path: The Invisible Revolution in the Third World*.
New York: Harper & Row Publishers, 1989.

United Nations Human Settlements Programme (UN-HABITAT).
*The Challenge of Slums: Global Report on Human Settlements
2003*. London: Earthscan, 2003.

Wong, Lana. *Shootback*. London: Booth-Clibborn, 2000.

Bibliography: Personal Response

Alternatives for Simple Living, www.SimpleLiving.org.

Foster, Richard J. *Freedom of Simplicity*. San Francisco: Harper &
Row, 1981.

Gordon, Graham, *What If You Got Involved? Taking a Stand against
Social Injustice*. Cumbria, U.K.: Paternoster Press, 2003.

Longacre, Doris Janzen. *Living More with Less*. Scottdale, Pa.:
Herald Press, 1980.

Muggeridge, Malcom. *Something Beautiful for God: The Classic
Account of Mother Teresa's Journey into Compassion*. San Francisco: Harper & Row, 1986.

Nouwen, Henri, Donald P. McNeill, and Douglas A. Morrison.
Compassion: A Reflection on the Christian Life. New York:
Doubleday, 1983.

Perrotta, Louise, and Gina Fontana (photographer). *All You Really
Need to Know about Prayer You Can Learn from the Poor*. Ann
Arbor, Mich.: Servant Publications, 1996.

Volf, Miroslav. *Exclusion and Embrace*. Nashville, Tenn.: Abingdon,
1996.

Films/Video

de Graaf, John, and Vivia Boe, producers. *Affluenza* (Oley, Pa.: Bull-
frog Films, 1997) 56 mins. On consumption and affluence, see
also www.pbs.org/affluenza for further resources.

Joffé, Roland, director. *City of Joy* (Columbia Tristar, 1992) 132 mins. An American doctor visits a Kolkata slum. Rated PG-13. See also the book by the same title by Dominique Lapierre (Garden City, N.Y.: Doubleday, 1985).

Meirelles, Fernando, and Kátia Lund, directors. *City of God* (Miramax Films, Portuguese, 2002) 130 mins. A visually impressive film that traces the life of young gang members in a Rio de Janeiro *favela*. Note: this movie is brutally violent and rated R.

Stevenson, Andrew, and Joanna Schwartz, directors. *Earth Report v: Land Rites* (London : TVE, 2001) www.tve.org, 27 mins. Documentary survey of urban land tenure issues around the world.

Periodicals

One of the best ways to learn about foreign countries or cities is to read their local newspapers, many of which are now available online, such as Kenya's *Daily Nation* (www.nationmedia.com) and *The Standard* (www.eastandard.net). See also www.allafrica.com.

Habitat Debate, published by the United Nations Human Settlements Programme, Nairobi, Kenya, www.unhabitat.org/hd.

PRISM Magazine, published by Evangelicals for Social Action, www.esa-online.org.

Of Related Interest

No Room at the Table
Earth's Most Vulnerable Children
Donald Dunson
ISBN 1-57075-491-8

Moving stories of at-risk children around the world and how to help them

Donald Dunson tells the stories of our children—from New Orleans to the Sudan. Each chapter profiles three or four individuals as it probes an issue affecting the world's children, including hunger and poverty, war, sexual exploitation, homelessness and the universal need for love.

"The moving stories told by Father Dunson are certain to inspire compassionate action and greater solidarity. Faith requires no less of a response. Christians are called to create a table at which all the poor, suffering, exploited and vulnerable children of the world have a place."
—*Most Reverend Anthony M. Pilla*
Bishop of Cleveland

Please support your local bookstore or call 1-800-258-5838.
For a free catalog, please write us at
Orbis Books, Box 308
Maryknoll, NY 10545-0308
or visit our website at www.orbisbooks.com

Thank you for reading *Dispossesed: Life in Our World's Urban Slums*
We hope you profited from it.